Global Migration and Social Change

Series Editor: **Nando Sigona**,
University of Birmingham, UK

The *Global Migration and Social Change* series showcases original research that looks at the nexus between migration, citizenship and social change.

Forthcoming in the series

*Migration, Crisis and Temporality at the Zimbabwe-South Africa Border:
Governing Immobilities*
Kudakwashe Vanyoro

Out now in the series

*Mediated Emotions of Migration:
Reclaiming Affect for Agency*
Sukhmani Khorana

*The EU Migrant Generation in Asia:
Middle-Class Aspirations in Asian Global Cities*
Helena Hof

*Migration, Health, and Inequalities:
Critical Activist Research across Ecuadorean Borders*
Roberta Villalón

*Navigating the European Migration Regime:
Male Migrants, Interrupted Journeys and Precarious Lives*
Anna Wyss

Find out more at
bristoluniversitypress.co.uk/global-migration-and-social-change

Global Migration and Social Change

Series Editor: **Nando Sigona**,
University of Birmingham, UK

International advisory board

Leah Bassel, University of Roehampton, UK
Avtar Brah, Birkbeck, University of London, UK
Sergio Carrera, CEPS, Belgium
Elaine Chase, University College London, UK
Alessio D'Angelo, Middlesex University, UK
Alan Gamlen, Monash University, Australia
Andrew Geddes, European University Institute, Italy
Roberto G. Gonzales, Harvard University, US
Elżbieta Goździak, Georgetown University, US
Jonathan Xavier Inda, University of Illinois, US
David Ingleby, University of Amsterdam, Netherlands
Anna Lindley, SOAS University of London, UK
Cecilia Menjívar, University of California, US
Peter Nyers, McMaster University, Canada
Jenny Phillimore, University of Birmingham, UK
Ben Rogaly, University of Sussex, UK
Paul Spoonley, Massey University, New Zealand
Susanne Wessendorf, London School of Economics, UK
Amanda Wise, Macquarie University, Australia
Elisabetta Zontini, University of Nottingham, UK

Find out more at
bristoluniversitypress.co.uk/global-migration-and-social-change

SOCIAL NETWORKS AND MIGRATION

Relocations, Relationships and Resources

Louise Ryan

First published in Great Britain in 2024 by

Bristol University Press
University of Bristol
1-9 Old Park Hill
Bristol
BS2 8BB
UK
t: +44 (0)117 374 6645
e: bup-info@bristol.ac.uk

Details of international sales and distribution partners are available at bristoluniversitypress.co.uk

© Bristol University Press 2024

British Library Cataloguing in Publication Data
A catalogue record for this book is available from the British Library

ISBN 978-1-5292-1354-6 hardcover
ISBN 978-1-5292-1355-3 paperback
ISBN 978-1-5292-1356-0 ePub
ISBN 978-1-5292-1357-7 ePdf

The right of Louise Ryan to be identified as author of this work has been asserted by her in accordance with the Copyright, Designs and Patents Act 1988.

All rights reserved: no part of this publication may be reproduced, stored in a retrieval system, or transmitted in any form or by any means, electronic, mechanical, photocopying, recording, or otherwise without the prior permission of Bristol University Press.

Every reasonable effort has been made to obtain permission to reproduce copyrighted material. If, however, anyone knows of an oversight, please contact the publisher.

The statements and opinions contained within this publication are solely those of the author and not of the University of Bristol or Bristol University Press. The University of Bristol and Bristol University Press disclaim responsibility for any injury to persons or property resulting from any material published in this publication.

Bristol University Press works to counter discrimination on grounds of gender, race, disability, age and sexuality.

Cover design: Andrew Corbett
Front cover image: Stocksy/The Laundry Room

Bristol University Press uses environmentally responsible print partners.

Printed in Great Britain by CPI Group (UK) Ltd, Croydon, CR0 4YY

Contents

List of Figures		vi
About the Author		vii
Acknowledgements		viii
1	Introduction: Embarking on a Book about Networks	1
2	Conceptualising Migrant Networks: Advancing the Field of Qualitative Social Network Analysis	14
3	Researching Migration and Networks: Empirical and Methodological Innovations	37
4	Social Networks and Stories of Arrival	59
5	Employment, Deskilling and Reskilling: Revisiting Strong and Weak Ties	81
6	Evolving Networks in Place over Time: A Life Course Lens	104
7	Transnational Ties: Narrating Relationality, Resources and Dynamics over Time	128
8	Conclusion: Thoughts and Future Directions	152
Appendix		166
Notes		170
References		173
Index		197

List of Figures

3.1	Adrianna's sociogram	57
6.1	Irène's sociogram	107
7.1	Agnieszka's sociogram	130

About the Author

Louise Ryan is Senior Professor of Sociology and Director of the Global Diversities and Inequalities Research Centre at London Metropolitan University. A graduate of University College Cork, she has been researching migration for over two decades and during that time has written several books and numerous highly cited articles in leading international journals. Her books on migration include: *Gendering Migration* (with Wendy Webster, 2008), *Migrant Capital* (with Umut Erel and Alessio D'Angelo, 2015) and *Revisiting Migrant Networks* (with Elif Keskiner and Michael Eve, 2022). The latter book was awarded the International Migration, Integration and Social Cohesion (IMISCOE) prize. Louise's contribution to migration research was recognised with a Fellowship of the Academy of Social Sciences in 2015. Her work has been supported by grants from various funding bodies including the Economic and Social Research Council, European Framework 7 and Horizon 2020 programmes. She is Chair of the British Sociological Association.

Acknowledgements

Unsurprisingly, while writing a book about networks, I am mindful of how my own personal and professional networks supported this project.

I am very grateful to colleagues and friends who provided feedback on drafts of individual chapters of this book: Basak Bilecen, Elif Keskiner, Umut Erel, Alessio D'Angelo, Isobel Ni Riain, Michael Eve and Janine Dahinden.

Some of the data presented in this book arise from projects undertaken with colleagues and I am grateful for their agreement to draw upon that data here. Details of all the projects are presented in the Appendix.

Much of the original research underpinning this book was undertaken at Middlesex University, the idea for the book was formed during a Professorial Fellowship at the University of Sheffield and the final manuscript was written during my new post at London Metropolitan University. I am grateful to colleagues at all three universities who encouraged and supported this book in different ways.

I want to thank Maynooth University Social Sciences Institute for the Visiting Fellowship (2021–2) that enabled me to create the time and space to put the finishing touches to the manuscript. A special thanks to colleagues at the Institute for feedback at two seminars relating to draft chapters.

I also want to extend my thanks to the anonymous reviewer who provided such detailed, helpful and encouraging feedback on the manuscript, and to staff at Bristol University Press for all their work, especially Shannon and Anna.

The poem by Máirtín Ó Direáin is cited by kind permission of Cló Iar-Chonnacht. The extract from the song 'Cricklewood' is quoted with the permission of John B. Keane's family. I am grateful to Billy Keane and to Grainne McPolin for brokering the introduction (networks in action).

I am exceedingly grateful to all the participants from my many research studies who agreed to take part and gave so generously of their time, especially those who kindly allowed me to recontact them over many years. Social research simply would not be possible without the willing cooperation of our participants.

ACKNOWLEDGEMENTS

Most of the analysis for this book was undertaken during the various national lockdowns in 2020–1. I wish to extend my heartfelt thanks to my husband, Donatus, son, Finnian, and sister, Isobel, for all their support and encouragement and for putting up with me while I invested so much time on this book project.

1

Introduction: Embarking on a Book about Networks

> Networks are important to the routine operations of households, crucial to the management of crises, and sometimes instrumental in helping respondents change their situations. Many provide havens: a sense of belonging and being helped. Many provide bandages; routine emotional-aid and small services that help the respondents cope with the stresses and strains of their situations. A sizable minority provide safety nets that lessen the effects of acute crises and chronic difficulties. Several provide social capital to change situations (houses, jobs, spouses) or to change the world (local school board politics, banning unsafe food additives, stopping cruelty to animals).
>
> (Wellman and Wortley, 1990: 583)

Key statement of intent

As highlighted in the opening quote, networks are multifaceted and wide ranging, providing access to varied resources (Wellman and Wortley, 1990). Indeed, in recent decades, there has been a marked increase in social network research, across a number of fields (Conway, 2014; Healy, 2015; Maltseva and Batageli, 2019; Tubaro et al, 2021). Hence, it has been argued that, as a disciplinary project, social network research has grown from a 'peripheral position' or 'niche' specialised subfield 'into a central project within contemporary sociology' (Healy, 2015: 176). Migration researchers have also increasingly embraced social network analysis (SNA) (Dahinden, 2016; Bilecen et al, 2018; Lubbers et al, 2021; Keskiner et al, 2022).

Nonetheless, it has been noted that the notion of 'a network' is often defined differently by scholars (Knox et al, 2006; Ryan and Dahinden, 2021). As the influential social network scholar Barry Wellman observed, 'many analysts and practitioners' have misused network analysis as a 'mixed bag of terms and techniques'. While some 'hardened it into a method', others 'softened it into a metaphor' (1997: 20). By using the concept of networks metaphorically, Wellman argues, researchers risk 'treating all units as if they had the same resources, all ties as if they were symmetrical, and the contents of all ties as if they were equivalent' (1997: 20). This book, focusing on the specific field of migration studies, takes up the challenge of going beyond the metaphor in social network research.

Social networks have been a key focus of my research for almost 20 years. Reflecting on why I became so interested in networks, I realise I have always been fascinated by relationality. Growing up in Ireland, I remember listening to my mother, grandmother and aunts chatting about distant relatives and being enthralled by these family ties over generations as I tried to make sense of a tangled web of distant cousins, including the more exotic ones in the US whom I never met. At school, I was always curious about friendship formations: why some people became friends with others, why some students appeared to be popular with lots of connections, while others seemed socially isolated. This interest in friendship groups may also explain (at least in part) my obsession with US comedy series crafted around dense friendship ties like *Friends* and *The Big Bang Theory*. Indeed, these shows are very aware of the friendship formulae as a key aspect of their success. In one intriguing episode of *The Big Bang Theory*, theoretical physicist Sheldon tries to develop an algorithm to explain the optimal friendship network in the aptly titled *Stu the Cockatoo is New at the Zoo*.[1]

The 'eureka' moment for me came in 2011 when I was interviewing Chantal, a research participant in a study of highly skilled migrants in London's financial sector. Occasionally, when engaged in a research encounter, a participant says something that resonates with the researcher on a deeply personal level, sparking a train of thought that was utterly unanticipated. Chantal, after a career break to have children, had recently returned to university as a mature student. Explaining her choice of research topic, she cited Crick's gossip test: choose your research topic based on the subject you would spontaneously start to gossip about with friends.[2] Although I had never before heard this phrase, it instantly struck a chord with me and, in that moment, I realised that was precisely what I had been doing. My personal curiosity about interpersonal relationships had spawned my research interest in social networks.

Since the early 2000s, I have been exploring migrants' relationality and considered, firstly, how new friendships are formed in new places, as well as how pre-existing, transnational relationships are negotiated over time. Hence, I have analysed the obstacles but also the opportunities navigated by migrants in forging and maintaining various kinds of social *relationships* (Ryan, 2004; 2007a). Secondly, I have sought to understand the practical, informational, social and emotional support that migrants access through these particular social ties. In so doing, I have focused not simply on potentially available (latent) resources but on *realisable resources*, to understand what is willingly shared among specific social ties (Ryan et al, 2008).

Thirdly, drawing on Bourdieu (1986) and Granovetter (1983), I explored the *relative location* of actors within a social hierarchy (Ryan, 2011a). In this way, I have shown that the value of a particular connection may depend not so much on ethnic identity, but rather on whether the social tie is 'horizontal', occupying a similar social position, or 'vertical', occupying a higher social position than the focal migrant participant (Ryan, 2016). Moreover, going beyond the weak tie thesis (Granovetter, 1973), I have questioned the meaning and significance of tie 'weakness'. My research shows that social ties require a particular level of trust, mutuality and shared interest in order to impart valuable resources such as job-related information (Ryan, 2016; 2022). Furthermore, focusing on spatio-temporal dynamics, I am interested in how social relationships evolve and change over time (Erel and Ryan, 2019). Using longitudinal qualitative research techniques, and a life course perspective, I have shown how ties can change and evolve so that some strengthen, while others weaken and fade (Ryan and D'Angelo, 2018). Hence, beyond a weak tie versus strong tie dichotomy, I have proposed a continuum of dynamic relationships that evolve and change over time (Ryan, 2022).

Throughout my career, I am lucky to have worked with some great colleagues, who generously shared their expertise. Thus, my work on SNA has benefited from the advice and feedback of many people, several of whom I have co-authored with, and whose work I cite throughout this book. In particular, my thinking on SNA has greatly benefited from collaborations with scholars such as Janine Dahinden, Basak Bilecen and Miranda Lubbers. Moreover, I have gained valuable insights through shared writing projects with Michael Eve, Paola Tubaro, Antonio Cassili and Elif Keskiner. Some of my conceptual and empirical approaches to researching networks have emerged through my long-term working relationships with Alessio D'Angelo (Tubaro, Ryan and D'Angelo, 2016; Ryan and D'Angelo, 2018; D'Angelo and Ryan, 2021), Jon Mulholland (Ryan and Mulholland, 2014b, c; Ryan and Mulholland, 2015) and Umut Erel (Ryan, Erel and D'Angelo, 2015; Erel and Ryan, 2019). Thus, rather like network analysis itself, I cannot claim to have developed my thinking in isolation; on the contrary, my views have evolved over time due to my position in a network of inspiring scholars.

Throughout my work, I have drawn primarily on qualitative methods, including visual methods, informed by classical social network scholarship. In this way, my work, alongside some key collaborations with colleagues, has been advancing the field of qualitative SNA (Ryan and Dahinden, 2021). As explained in more detail in Chapter 2, I am interested in the role of interpretation and meaning making not only in how networks are perceived but also how they are presented in research encounters (D'Angelo and Ryan, 2021). Hence, in recent years, my work has explored how network stories are generated, co-constructed and crafted in interactions between researchers and participants (Ryan, 2021).

This book builds on and takes forward that endeavour and so aims to advance qualitative SNA in migration research in three key ways: epistemologically, methodologically and empirically.

Epistemologically, my work advances understandings of networks beyond a simple metaphor at one end of the spectrum and a hard measurable fact at the other (Wellman, 1997). Instead, inspired by theorists such as Krackhardt, White and Mische as well as narrative analysts such as Somers and Plummer, this book presents my framework of 'telling network stories'. In so doing, I analyse relational meanings, emotions and tensions, as well as intersubjectivity and how relationality gets filtered through processes of perception and self-presentation in research encounters. Thus, I aim to understand networks as dynamic discursive devices.

Methodologically, this book presents the techniques underpinning my framework of telling network stories by using rich in-depth interviews, including longitudinal research with participants reinterviewed over time, in combination with sociograms to visualise networks of relationships. These methods seek to understand how participants describe and make sense of social ties in words and pictures. Using analytical frameworks informed by narrative analysis (Somers, 1994; Plummer, 2002), I examine how network stories are shaped by wider contextual factors including sociocultural framing but also the co-production aspects of the research design and encounter between participant and researcher. In this way, as explained in Chapters 2 and 3, my book seeks to significantly advance the field of qualitative SNA.

Empirically, this book offers new insights by bringing together, for the first time, data generated over almost 20 years of researching migration to London. I bring into conversation interviews with migrants from different historical periods from the 1940s to the 2010s, diverse countries of origin and varied immigration routes and, drawing upon an intersectional lens, I consider how their network stories are framed by complex, multi-layered and dynamic identities over time. In presenting this large corpus of qualitative data from my different migration studies, this book suggests how existing data sets can be amalgamated and reanalysed to offer new insights. In the next section, I briefly summarise the different research projects that form the empirical material for this book.

Research career

This book draws together, for the first time, qualitative data generated over numerous projects spanning almost 20 years.

I started to undertake empirical research with migrants in London in 2000 during a post-doctoral fellowship at what was then the University of North London. I benefited enormously from the mentorship of Professor Mary Hickman, who has become a good friend over the years. At that time, I had no particular interest in analysing social networks. Focusing on oral history interviews with Irish women who had migrated in the first half of the 20th century, my main interests were the experiences of migration, gender and employment patterns, and negotiations of ethnicity during a time of anti-Irish hostility in Britain (Ryan, 2003). However, networks quickly emerged as a key theme of the data. While most of the women left rural Ireland and made the arduous journey to London alone, their migration stories, reflecting high levels of Irish female migration throughout the 20th century, described predominantly female networks of sisters, aunts, cousins and friends who had already made the journey ahead of them (see Chapter 4). From then on, I became fascinated by the role of networks not only in enabling and encouraging migration but also in processes of adjusting to destination contexts. Moreover, ongoing connections with home, via transnational networks, also emerged as an important theme, as most of the women had sent home regular remittances to support ageing parents and younger siblings in Ireland, as further analysed in Chapter 7.

In 2004, I was lucky enough to secure a three-year research fellowship at Middlesex University, where I eventually was made a permanent member of staff, and so began my long association with the Social Policy Research Centre and colleagues such as Rosemary Sales, Mary Tilki, Eleonore Kofman, Jon Mulholland and Alessio D'Angelo. While working in that busy research centre, I undertook a dizzying array of research projects, far too many to mention here. However, the bulk of the data presented in this book arises from that extraordinarily fruitful period of my career. My studies with Irish nurses from the post-war period, recently arrived Polish migrants, highly skilled French migrants in the City of London, highly qualified Irish migrants during the global financial recession, Muslim women and so on were all carried out during 12 years at the Social Policy Research Centre.[3]

I would like to say that my research projects were always driven by a clear rationale and coherent career vision. But, in reality, many of those projects emerged almost in a happenchance or serendipitous way. One obvious example is how I stumbled into researching Polish migration. Having spent several years researching Irish migrants, following EU enlargement in 2004, my colleagues Rosemary Sales and Mary Tilki and I became curious about the sudden and largely unanticipated arrival of large numbers of Polish migrants. In fact, I was inspired by a chance remark by a Cork friend, living in South London, who was having a new kitchen installed. Noting that all the workmen were recently arrived Eastern European migrants, he joked 'the Poles are the new Irish'. I was immediately intrigued and keen to investigate.

Indeed Rosemary, Mary and I initially planned to do a comparison study of Poles and Irish. But, in the end, we decided to focus only on Poles, a decision that was to open up a whole new world of Polish research for me.

I well remember my first forays into Polish migration research circles. I felt somewhat apprehensive as a non-Pole and with no prior connections with Poland. I was encouraged by positive responses I received from established researchers in the field, especially Michal Garapich and Anne White, who made me feel welcome and have continued to be supportive over the years. During my many trips to Poland, I also found a warm welcome from leading academics such as Pawel Kaczmarczyk and, in particular, Izabela Grabowska, Weronika Kloc-Nowak and Aleksandra Grzymała-Kazłowska, who have become friends and with whom I continue to collaborate.

Research is often shaped by dynamic sociopolitical contexts. Following the London bombings on 7 July 2005, there was renewed attention on London's Muslim communities. From 2008 to 2010, I was invited to participate in an exciting new venture with the London Borough of Barnet. Through the Barnet Muslim Engagement Partnership, I had the opportunity to work with diverse Muslim organisations across the borough. Through this initiative, I was able to conduct several studies with Muslim women. The experiences of those women are threaded throughout this book, especially in Chapters 5, 6 and 7.

Conversations with Jon Mulholland led to a new research project focusing on highly skilled migrants in the financial sector. From 2008, the impact of the economic crisis sparked new concerns about how London, especially as a global financial centre, would adapt. As migration scholars, we wondered how migrants in London would respond to the economic recession. As an under-researched group, Jon suggested to look at the French. A significant focus of that project was the role of networks, especially within the financial sector both locally in London but also globally. A fascinating observation arising from that study was the differentiated experiences of networking. While business networking was actively supported and facilitated across the sector, the difficulties of accessing friendship networks raised new and often unexpected challenges for our participants. Our analysis of these data led us to coin the concept of 'embedding' (Ryan and Mulholland, 2015), which was later elaborated as 'differentiated embedding' (Ryan, 2018; Mulholland and Ryan, 2022) to understand complex, multidimensional and dynamic processes of belonging and attachments to particular people and places over time. This topic will be discussed at length in Chapters 4 and 5 of the book. It was during that study that Jon and I experimented for the first time with using sociograms to map social networks graphically. Developing visualisation techniques was to become a key feature of my network research in subsequent years, as discussed in more detail in Chapter 3.

The global financial recession also sparked other waves of migration. After many years in which Irish migration to Britain had been in decline, the recession and the associated collapse of the so-called Celtic Tiger economy in Ireland led to a new surge of migration. Having begun my migration research with a focus on historical Irish migration, in 2013, working in partnership with the 'Irish in Britain' organisation, I conducted a study with recently arrived, highly qualified young people from Ireland. I was curious to understand how these young professionals might differ from previous waves of Irish migrants. In researching their social networks, I was powerfully struck by the impact of new technologies. These young people were embracing all sorts of social media to maintain long-distance ties to family in Ireland but also their scattered friendship networks across the world. Their experiences were in sharp contrast to earlier waves of migrants who relied on letters and long, arduous journeys by ferry and bus to maintain transnational connections. However, as discussed in Chapter 7, the role of new technology cannot be simply assumed and its impact on long-distance networks is not necessarily straightforward.

After 12 years at Middlesex University, in 2016 I embarked upon a new career opportunity. Moving to the University of Sheffield, I took up a three-year Professorial Fellowship. This was a marvellous opportunity to focus on new research collaborations. In 2017 I was part of a team of colleagues, led by Sue Yeandle, who won a large Economic and Social Research Council (ESRC) grant, 'Sustainable Care', to research ageing and care. I co-led a work package, with Majella Kilkey, along with Magdolna Lőrinc and Obert Tawodzera, focusing on migrants and experiences of ageing across two sites – London and Yorkshire. Having started my migration research career with older participants, it was wonderful to return to working with older people for that new study. The project enabled me to bring together my interest in older Irish migrants with Polish migration, focusing on post-war migration from Poland. Moreover, the study also included a group with whom I had not previously worked but in whom I am very interested – post-war migrants from across the Caribbean.[4] The experiences of migrants from the Caribbean who arrived in London in the 1950s brings powerful insights into experiences of racism but also the value of social networks in helping migrants navigate unfamiliar and sometimes hostile environments, as discussed in Chapters 5 and 6.

It is not the aim of this book to present a general history of migration; neither do I seek to review the specific history of Irish or Polish or Caribbean migration to London. That research has been conducted in great detail by other eminent scholars. For example, for a detailed analysis of Irish migration to Britain see books by Hickman (1995), MacRaild (1999), Delaney (2000), Walter (2001), Gray (2004) and Trew (2016), among others. Polish migration to Britain has been discussed in books by Sword (1996), Burrell (2006), Zubrzycki (2013) and White (2017), among others. There are many books on the history of Caribbean migration to Britain – a selected few include James and Harris (1993), Byron (1994), Chamberlain (2002), Webster (2005) and Olwig (2007).

In 2020 a new opportunity arose when I was offered the post of Senior Professor and Director of the Global Diversities and Inequalities Research Centre, at London Metropolitan University. Returning to a university where I had started my research career, exactly 20 years earlier, is quite surreal. Moreover, undertaking this career move while writing a book spanning my research trajectory seems even more surreal.

Embarking on a book

Over the years I have written dozens of articles about migration. I have edited three books on migration with my friends and colleagues Wendy Webster, Alessio D'Angelo, Umut Erel, Elif Keskiner and Michael Eve. But I had never before written a monograph based on my migration research.

It would have been easy to rely on my published work to identify particular themes and stories. Over the last two decades, I had published several articles on each of the individual studies mentioned previously. But I soon realised that to rely on my previous analysis and findings would limit the opportunities for new insights and themes to emerge from the combined data set. After all, each data set had been analysed as a stand-alone body of data guided by a particular set of literature and research questions. Analysing the combined data sets, as a whole, would present new opportunities to work across the enlarged corpus of diverse data.

Making the decision to reread and reanalyse all the transcripts was exciting but also overwhelming. Here, the UK national lockdown of spring 2020 provided an unexpected opportunity (as explained in more depth in Chapter 3). Working from home, with all travel suspended, conferences cancelled and gyms, cinemas and restaurants closed, I had no excuse but to begin work on the transcripts. Rereading transcripts after ten or 15 years proved rewarding and enlightening; I saw new themes – I looked at them differently now as my knowledge and understanding had changed over the years.

Immersing myself in these migration stories provoked many emotions in me. As a migrant myself, it is perhaps not surprising that I should be drawn to research migration. Nonetheless, there have been many occasions when this topic felt too 'close to the bone'. There have been moments when migrants' stories touched me deeply and provoked soul searching about my own migration experiences (Nowicka and Ryan, 2015). Of course, in the context of interviews, I resisted the temptation to share my immediate personal reactions, instead engaging in the emotional labour of masking my feelings (Ryan, 2008a). In Chapter 3, I discuss reflexivity and my own dynamic positionalities in the interview encounters, but for now, by way of setting the scene, I would like to share one example.

In 2013, as part of a study of Irish highly qualified migrants, I met Catriona, a young woman who, like me, came from Cork in southern Ireland. The interview took place in the beautiful Royal Festival Hall cafe on the banks of the River Thames in central London. As Catriona shared her story, I found myself empathising with many of her experiences, in particular when she began to reflect upon her changing relationship to Ireland and considering the likelihood of ever returning to live there permanently. Suddenly Catriona started to recite a poem she had learned at school. As she began to say the words, I was transported back to the classroom of my youth, where I too had learned the Gaelic language poem *Stoite* (meaning uprooted) by Máirtín Ó Direáin. Reflecting on his own migration from the rural west of Ireland, Ó Direáin contrasts the lives of his ancestors, rooted in the local landscape, with his own uprooting to an alien city:

> Dúinn is éigean
> Cónaí a dhéanamh
> In árais ó dhaoine
> A leagfadh cíos
> Ar an mbraon anuas

> ([we] Must hole up, In private rentals, Where the landlord, Would charge money, For the damp on the walls.)[5]

Following through the theme of uprooting, Catriona reflected on whether it was possible to ever return and re-root in the place of origin. She stated that when you migrate

> 'you've got to untie a bit of yourself and therefore you can never go back 'cos you can never remake that same tie. You're a different person and therefore you can never go back and it just resonates more and more with the years, the sense of you're no longer the same, so you can never go back because it's just not the same situation you left'. (Catriona, Ireland, 2000s[6])

Her statement made me think about the extent of my own continued embedding in Cork, as well as aspects of my gradual uprooting or dis-embedding (Ryan and Mulholland, 2015) over time, and the possibilities of return after two decades of migration. Observations made by participants, not only Irish participants but migrants from many different countries, such as Chantal cited earlier, often triggered personal reflections for me. Rereading all the transcripts for the purposes of writing this book brought me back to those initial reactions but also, with the passage of time, evoked new reflections, especially about different life course stages.

I have always been mindful of the enduring role of propinquity despite advances in new technology (Ryan, 2007a); physical co-presence remains crucial for hands-on care, especially for sick or elderly relatives (Von Koppenfels, Mulholland and Ryan, 2015). The COVID-19 global pandemic reminded us all of the contingency of mobility as travel restrictions were imposed by many governments around the world. I was unable to visit Ireland or see my parents in person for 18 months. Thus, while the pandemic gave me time to write this book, it also underscored for me the salience of geographical distance, especially for migrants who were prohibited from travelling across national borders (Kloc-Nowak and Ryan, 2022). This experience also highlighted the different ways in which care responsibilities within transnational networks are experienced and managed by people 'here' and 'there'. While I was in London, unable to travel, my sister in Cork took on the key caring role for my parents throughout the protracted period of the pandemic. Hence, my participants' stories, my own personal biography and wider geopolitical events all impinged in particular ways on the development of this book.

In line with my qualitative approach to network stories, this book offers a number of 'thick descriptions' (as explained in Chapters 2 and 3) to present some of my data in meaningful, engaging and digestible ways. The first of these is Kathleen's story, which is presented here to illustrate a number of the themes that will be explored in later chapters throughout the book.

Kathleen's story

Kathleen, who left the west of Ireland in 1949, was interviewed in 2005 as part of the study on migrant nurses. Kathleen narrated her migration journey through stories of relationality: "my sister Nora came the year before me". Indeed, Nora's migration had been encouraged by a female cousin who was already working in London. Although Kathleen also wanted to go to London, her eldest sister opposed the plan: "My [eldest] sister didn't want me to leave, to go away … She asked me to stay and she would get me a job". This job was cleaning and childminding for a local farmer. Thus, within Kathleen's close network of female ties there was disagreement about whether or not she should migrate. Even kinship ties do not always operate in unison. Having stuck the local job for a year, Kathleen recalled: "I thought there must be more to life than this". While thinking what to do next, a newspaper advertisement caught her eye:

> '[T]his advert in the *Connacht Tribune*, a woman would be in [local] hotel, such and such a date. I wrote to her and she gave me an appointment ... the National Health Service had just started looking for people, mainly women, and there was a good bit of work going at the time.' (Kathleen, Ireland, 1940s)

Established in 1948, the British National Health Service (NHS) actively recruited student nurses from overseas including Ireland. As Kathleen recounted, this recruitment targeted even small Irish towns. Kathleen was interviewed and shortly afterwards "got a letter saying I was successful and that I would have an interview again and a medical at a hotel in Dublin. Dublin was out of this world to me; I had never been to Dublin in my life".

It is noteworthy that although she had never been to a city like Dublin, Kathleen seemed to have no qualms about heading to London. That was a common feature among my Irish interviewees from that period, and suggests the strength of the culture of migration and the role of social networks in making London seem easily attainable (Ryan, 2004; 2008b). Due to former colonial ties, Irish citizens could travel to Britain without a visa but it is apparent that other mechanisms of controls and checks were in place:

> 'the medical went on I think for two days in Dublin cos they had x-rays and then they had to wait for the results ... They were very strict on hygiene, "de-lousing" they called it ... You had a bath and then they made sure of your clothes, they went through every stitch. I often wondered, you know, "what the hell did they think we were?" But we had to put up with it if we wanted to go ... I felt a bit humiliated but I thought I had to just get on with it to get to London'. (Kathleen)

The extent of these medical tests needs to be understood within the historical context of deep-rooted associations between migrants and disease (Kraut, 1995; Crawford, 1997). In British public health discourses, migrants, including the Irish, were often linked with the spread of foreign diseases among the British population (Darwen et al, 2020). Thus, border crossings were checked to prevent the importation of infections. Having passed these stringent and humiliating medical tests, Kathleen boarded the boat for Britain and began her nurse training in London. We will hear more about Kathleen's story in later chapters.

This short extract shows the interplay between direct recruitment into a job and a network of strong kinship ties. Kathleen had a job and guaranteed accommodation in the nurses home, so she did not rely on networks for practical support. Nonetheless, her sister and cousin in London played influential, if indirect, roles, and served as role models for Kathleen, making migration to London seem not only possible but also attractive. Although her motivations were largely economic, there was also a sense of adventure: "it was quite an adventure, you were young and you were healthy and you just took life as it came".

The structure of the book

This book now unfolds over seven chapters. Chapter 2 presents my conceptual framework of 'telling network stories' and how it has grown out of 20 years of my migration research. Chapter 3 describes the research methods used in the book and my decisions about how to present such a large corpus of qualitative data through a series of thick descriptions. Taken together, Chapters 2 and 3 present my contribution to advancing the field of qualitative SNA, in migration research, epistemologically, methodologically and empirically.

Chapters 4, 5, 6 and 7 present the rich stories of migrants drawn from my various research projects. The chapters are organised thematically and bring into conversation, for the first time, stories of different migrants in London, from across varied waves of migration from the 1940s through to the 2010s.

Chapter 4 begins with stories of arrival and explores the role of networks in my participants' migration processes. I show how networks of strong ties to relatives and friends may shape migration decision making, but other factors may also be influential in migration trajectories. Thus, as illustrated by Kathleen's story, adopting the framework of network stories reveals the confluence of diverse actors and contextual factors, including immigration regimes and recruitment practices.

Chapter 5 then focuses especially on the field of employment and how my participants accessed jobs and navigated sometimes hostile work places. In so doing, I analyse social ties along a continuum of dynamic strong and weak ties and consider how networks may play both direct and indirect roles across different labour market sectors ranging from health care, construction and education to banking.

Chapter 6 explores dynamic social ties over time and how participants forged new relationships in new places. This chapter analyses factors that may enable friendship formations but also the obstacles that migrants may encounter, including racism and anti-immigrant sentiment, in accessing networks and embedding in local sociality and neighbourhoods in London.

Chapter 7 addresses transnational networks and explores how long-distance relationships are negotiated over time, including through the ageing process, with implications for caregiving and care receiving. Moreover, rather than looking at long-distance ties in isolation, by drawing on network stories, this chapter considers how local ties in London may intersect with long-distance ties in ways that inform decisions about returning back to the origin country, especially in retirement.

Obviously, there is a certain linearity to how the chapters are organised. Drawing on a life course perspective (Elder, 1994), I am interested in understanding how social relationships evolve and change over time. Thus, I consider both biographical time but also wider sociohistorical time. However, that is not to suggest a simple linear notion of time. Indeed, the network stories in this book present complex narratives, rather than a linear structure, and hence reveal the sometimes circular, messy, uneven nature of migrants' experiences.

Chapter 8 concludes by summarising the overall contributions of this book, especially towards advancing the field of qualitative SNA in migration research. Moreover, looking to the unfolding challenges of Brexit, the pandemic, climate emergency, wars and political instability, the book suggests new avenues for network research within and beyond migration studies.

2

Conceptualising Migrant Networks: Advancing the Field of Qualitative Social Network Analysis

> social networks were often used either metaphorically or only describing dyadic relations ... the absence of SNA in migration studies left relatively unexplored how these networks are composed and structured, how they evolve over time, which resources are exchanged through such networks, and how they are embedded in larger structures, so that links with migration processes and outcomes were often assumed rather than empirically investigated.
>
> (Bilecen, Gamper and Lubbers, 2018: 2)

Introduction

Scholars have long been interested in social networks in enabling and supporting chain migration (Tilly and Brown, 1967; Hugo, 1982; Massey and España, 1987; Boyd, 1989). A migrant network has been defined as 'a web of social ties that links potential migrants in sending communities to people and institutions in receiving areas' and in so doing 'dramatically lower costs of international movement', giving 'powerful momentum' to the migration process (Massey and España, 1987: 733).

By the late 1980s, a 'growing body of research existed regarding the role of social networks in the etiology, composition, direction and persistence of migration flows, and in the settlement and integration of migrant populations in receiving societies' (Boyd, 1989: 639). In the following decades, this body of work continued to grow, with particular attention on networks as sources of migrants' capital, facilitating migration and settlement but also in the maintenance of transnational lives (Gurak and Caces, 1992; Portes, 1998; Castles and Miller, 2003; Jordan and Duvell 2003; Faist and Ozveren, 2004).

Nonetheless, as noted in the opening quote of this chapter, there were also increasing criticisms about the loose ways in which the concept of 'network' was applied within migration research (Wierzbicki, 2004; Ryan, 2007a), often resulting in a metaphorical use of networks (for a discussion see Bilecen et al, 2018; Ryan and Dahinden, 2021). Moreover, there was growing concern that the relationship between networks and capital was being assumed rather than properly examined and analysed (Portes, 2000; Anthias, 2007; Erel, 2010; Ryan, Erel and D'Angelo, 2015; Keskiner, Eve and Ryan, 2022). Furthermore, the tendency within migration studies to simply take for granted ethnic networks has been increasingly challenged (Wimmer, 2004; Schiller, Çağlar and Guldbrandsen, 2006; Eve, 2010; Dahinden, 2016). As Eve argued, ethnic ties cannot be simply assumed as natural, but should stimulate enquiry into their roots so that we can develop a 'sociological explanation of particularities and an account of how they emerge from preceding ties' (Eve, 2010: 1245). It was also apparent that more work was needed on network changes over time (Lubbers et al, 2010; Ryan and D'Angelo, 2018). Far from being static, migrants' social relationships ebb and flow both temporally and spatially (Erel and Ryan, 2019).

To offer more precise analysis of the formation, dynamism, relationality and flow of resources, migration scholars have been encouraged to draw upon the well-stocked toolbox of SNA (Boyd, 1989; Ryan, 2007a; Ryan et al, 2015; Bilecen et al, 2018; Keskiner et al, 2022). Beyond merely describing webs of ties, SNA pays attention to antecedents and consequences. In other words, rather than taking networks for granted, SNA explores how particular ties came about and evolved (antecedents) and examines what networks do and what the outcomes of specific relationships are (consequences) (see Borgatti and Ofem, 2010). In analysing migrant networks, this book pays attention to both the antecedents and consequences of particular social ties within and between particular places.

In recent years there have been many examples of how concepts and methods informed by SNA can enrich migration research (for example, Bilecen and Sienkiewicz, 2015; Molina et al, 2015; Dahinden, 2016; Ryan and D'Angelo, 2018; Wissink and Mazzucato, 2018; Kindler, 2021; Lubbers et al, 2021; Sommer and Gamper, 2021). Many of these and other sources will be drawn upon throughout this book; therefore, it is not my intention here to provide a comprehensive review of that growing corpus of literature. Instead, this chapter sets out my conceptual framework that informs the analysis throughout the book. While my methodological contribution to qualitative SNA is discussed in more detail in Chapter 3, the key focus of this chapter is my recent epistemological work around networks as dynamic discursive devices. In so doing, I highlight my contribution at the nexus of migration research and SNA in four particular ways.

Picking up some of the persistent challenges within migrant social network research, this chapter explores, firstly, what is gained by going beyond the merely metaphorical use of networks and applying network analysis. Drawing on classical network theorists, I explain my approach to analysing relationality between particular social ties, situated within specific structural contexts and the associated consequences for actor agency.

Secondly, although migration scholars have been encouraged to embrace SNA, that is not to imply a purely quantitative approach to network analysis. SNA has been criticised for prioritising methodological innovations over conceptualisations (Scott, 1988; Knox et al, 2006; Azarian, 2010). However, my work is especially interested in relationality and the meaning of interpersonal connections. Therefore, inspired by theorists such as Krackhardt, White and Mische as well as narrative analysts such as Somers and Plummer, this chapter presents my framework of 'storytelling' to understand networks as sites of meaning making, interpretation and presentation of self.

Migrant networks are often assumed to be sources of valuable resources (practical, informational, social and emotional); however, these cannot be taken for granted. Hence, a third contribution of this chapter is to consider the consequences of migrants' social ties in terms of access to particular kinds of resources. In so doing, I discuss notions of 'bonding' and 'bridging social capital', as well 'weak ties', and reflect upon how these have been ethnicised in much migration research. By critically interrogating these social ties and the capital seemingly inherent within them, and drawing upon the framework of network stories, I offer more nuanced understanding of the opportunities and obstacles that migrants encounter in generating resources from diverse connections.

Fourthly, it might be argued that network analysis offers a snapshot of relationality and is of limited use in understanding change over time (for a discussion see Lubbers et al, 2021; Mazzucato, 2021). In this chapter, addressing the challenge of understanding temporal dynamics in network analysis, I turn to the life course framework (Elder, 1994) to explore how interpersonal relationships are situated within the intersections of biographical and historical time. Locating migrant networks within temporal and spatial dynamics, I argue that network stories can enable an understanding of tie antecedents, that is, how new ties are formed in new places and how pre-existing, long-distance ties may be sustained or fade over time.

But first, we begin by briefly considering Maryam's story.

Maryam's story

Originally from Somalia, Maryam arrived in London from a Kenyan refugee camp in 1999. Those who move through refugee routes may wish to avoid telling their stories through dominant discourses of victimhood (Bernhard, 2020; Speed et al, 2021). In our interview, Maryam chose to say little about her experiences in the refugee camp and instead framed her narrative through the active agency of building a new life in London. Her narrative recounted the obstacles she needed to overcome. Transferring her cultural capital from Somalia to London proved challenging:

> 'You know, it is funny when I first went to the job centre, I told them I used to be a secretary back home. I was trained in typing and shorthand, but not in computers – we didn't have computers back then. They told me I cannot get a job here so I should go and be a cleaner. I said "what, how?" You know, Louise, when people don't know where you come from or what you had back home, they don't respect you. I used to have everything, but you can lose everything. So now this woman is telling me to be a cleaner and I said "no, excuse me, I am a fully trained secretary"'. (Maryam, Somalia, 1990s)

Before the Somali civil war, Maryam's family had been affluent; however, upon arrival in London, her cultural capital was not validated and she faced downward mobility. Being told to become a cleaner was an affront to her sense of identity and self-worth. Without economic capital, Maryam described how she became stuck in a "benefit trap": "I needed benefits. I don't like claiming benefit. But you know when you live in temporary accommodation the rent is £325 per week, so if you get a job how will you afford to pay that rent every week. So you are in a benefit trap".

Nonetheless, Maryam was determined not to be beaten by the system: "If you sit down and think you are a victim then you will go nowhere". Networks play a key role in Maryam's narrative. Without economic resources, and unable to convert her cultural capital, she put energy into mobilising social capital (Erel, 2010). Her first move was to begin volunteering in a charity shop as a way of meeting people and making local connections.

In attempting to build a social network from scratch, Maryam also turned to a friend: "So I contacted one of my friends, a Kenyan girl, she is a Christian, and I asked her if she could help me. She said okay". Together, the two friends set up a women's support group. It is noteworthy that Maryam should mention her friend was Christian. Utilising her interpersonal and communication skills, including her English language proficiency, Maryam forged a wide network of connections within London's voluntary sector. Indeed, Maryam built many horizontal and vertical ties across ethnic and religious lines to access relevant know-how and resources: "people have different skills and I think I am blessed, you know, my friends call me 'social capital'. I make friends with people very easily. I chat to everyone". The fact that Maryam emphasised her social skills and told her story in terms of 'social capital' reveals much about the presentation of her networked self (D'Angelo and Ryan, 2021). Her experience in London's vibrant voluntary sector, in the early 2000s, meant not only that the concept of social capital was familiar to her but also that she valued it as an empowering resource. As discussed further in Chapter 6, Maryam mobilised her connections with key stakeholders in order to tackle racist abuse against Somali families on a North London housing estate. In this way, she acted as a broker spanning a structural gap (Burt, 2009) between migrant families and local officials. However, Maryam's activism also drew criticism from some quarters, including from some Muslim women: "One woman said to me that I should not do inter-faith dialogue, that I should not sit down with priests or rabbis. She said I was not a good Muslim ... I went home and cried".

It is noteworthy that not all network ties are positive; some ties may have negative effects. As a Muslim woman, a refugee and a Black African, Maryam was confronted by expectations and stereotypes about how she should behave, including from co-ethnics (Endelstein and Ryan, 2013). Issues of identity, ethnicity, religion, gender and class all intersect to shape social experiences (Phoenix and Pattynama, 2006), but also strategies for action within particular sociostructural contexts.

In ten years, from arriving in 1999 to when we first met around 2009, Maryam became a well-known activist for women's rights and anti-racism. Having met her at several community events, I followed her activities with interest. Throughout her work, Maryam used her immense energy and networking skills to challenge social inequality: "My journey was not easy but I am a strong woman. All this discrimination and racism, you know people try to brush that away, but it will never finish. It is deep".

Maryam's story raises many themes that will be further highlighted in this chapter and later, throughout this book.

Looking beyond the metaphor: adopting a network lens to understand relationality

Within migration research, the term 'network' is often used in vague and generalised ways to include a variety of different relationships including family, friends, neighbours, workmates, co-ethnics, co-religious and so on (see Boyd, 1989). The resources assumed to be flowing through these ties also vary enormously, for example, jobs, accommodation, emotional support, as well as remittances back to the origin countries (Massey and España, 1987). But using the metaphor of network to describe all such ties risks simplifying and conflating a range of diverse and dynamic relationships. The use of 'network' as a metaphor risks 'treating all units as if they had the same resources, all ties as if they were symmetrical, and the contents of all ties as if they were equivalent' (Wellman, 1997: 20). Thus, rather than simply being self-explanatory, it is necessary for researchers to consider and clarify what they mean by 'network' and also how this concept is applied in research contexts (Scott, 1988; Knox et al, 2006).

In this book, I aim to go beyond the metaphor by offering more nuanced understanding of how relationships are perceived and presented and what this says about meaning making and flows of resources within webs of interpersonal connections. As a migration researcher, I have long been interested in the potential of SNA as a well-stocked toolbox that can help to explore, theorise and understand migrants' webs of relationships and the resources therein (Ryan, 2007a; Ryan et al, 2008). This potential has been noted by others over the years, most notably in a special issue of the journal *Social Networks* in 2018 which brought together a number of migration researchers who have been pioneering in their use of SNA, and in which I had the pleasure to contribute (Ryan and D'Angelo, 2018). As cited in the opening quote to this chapter, the special issue editors (Bilecen, Gamper and Lubbers, 2018) extolled the potential of applying SNA to migration studies. In my own work, going beyond vague metaphors and attempting to gain deeper insights into diverse relationships between social actors, I have found it useful to turn to classic social network research.

SNA can be traced back to the 1930s and the work of Moreno, who used the term sociometry to graphically map social relationships between groups of people (Freeman, 2000). Initially researching the friendship networks of girls in an American high school, Moreno's core argument was that someone's position in a network of relationships can have real consequences for them, such as influencing attitudes and behaviour.

In the 1950s, social anthropologists began to use the concept of 'network' to explain community structures and relationships (Barnes, 1969; Mitchell, 1969). One of the most influential early studies of networks was Elisabeth Bott's (1957) research on conjugal roles among married couples in London. Although she did not set out to research networks, Bott was soon struck by the varied ways in which relationships with kin, friends and neighbours seemed to impact on couples' everyday lives. She observed considerable variability in the connectedness of interpersonal networks. While some couples had disconnected ties (that is, ties to people who did not know each other), dispersed over wide geographical areas, other couples had tight, close-knit, highly connected, local ties. But rather than merely describing networks, Bott was interested in how these webs of relationships might influence the attitudes and behaviour of couples. For Bott, networks operated at a sort of meso level between individual actors and wider social structures. In this way, wider societal expectations, for example about gender roles, were filtered through the advice and influence of extended kin, friends, work colleagues and neighbours in ways that may reinforce or challenge specific patterns of behaviour. Thus, rather than assuming that gendered divisions of labour were simply a product of social determinism or individual choice, Bott identified the mediating role of interpersonal networks.

Bott's analysis has proven influential and underlines a key appeal of a social network perspective: by overcoming 'methodological individualism' (Wellman, 1979), while at the same time avoiding structural determinism (Knox et al, 2006: 124). Within migration studies, this feature of network analysis has been especially helpful. As Monica Boyd noted in her seminal paper, a key advantage of a networks perspective is avoiding an under-socialised view on the one hand, where all migration is apparently motivated by individual choices, and on the other hand, an over-socialised view, whereby structural factors determine international movement. 'Social relations both transmit and shape the effect of social and economic structures on individuals, families and households' (1989: 642). Echoing Bott's earlier observation, Boyd concludes that networks 'mediate between individual actors and larger structural forces' (1989: 661).

As network research grew, especially in the US, associated with Harvard University and the work of Harrison White, there was increasing interest in the more technical aspects, such as measuring network size, to understand structure and density (see Scott, 1988). One of the most influential researchers to emerge from that group was Barry Wellman. In his famous study of East Yorkers, in a suburb of Toronto, Wellman used the network perspective to challenge the 'lost community' thesis associated with urban living. In fact, his work is helpful in questioning the 'bowling alone' thesis, suggesting the atomisation of social life and fragmentation of society (Putnam, 2000).

Far from being atomised, most people in Wellman's study had numerous, differentiated ties in their networks. Furthermore, by applying a network lens, Wellman was able to show that rather than a traditional, spatially bounded sense of community, ties were often geographically dispersed and specialised across a range of varied relationships to diverse actors including kin, friends and co-workers. Nonetheless, neighbours also featured in the networks of East Yorkers and most participants valued having good relationships with neighbours even if those were not intimate friendships. Thus, rather than a geographically bounded community in the classic sense, Wellman and colleagues instead proposed a 'personal network' type of community: 'socially diverse, spatially dispersed, and sparsely knit' (Wellman and Wortley, 1990: 559). Although Wellman was not studying migrants, his notion of a spatially dispersed network has clear relevance for understanding migrants' relationality.

As is apparent throughout the discussion so far, the fundamental concept of SNA is relationality (Borgatti and Ofem, 2010: 19). But this is not only about studying relationality per se, but also, as demonstrated by researchers like Bott and Wellman, understanding the consequences of particular relationships. Thus, as Nick Crossley notes, we cannot separate networks from discussions of relationality and vice versa: 'the social world is a network of interactions and ties, of numerous types and on various scales, between actors who are themselves formed in those interactions. Actors are always in-relation to one another ... their actions are always interactions' (2015: 68).

However, beyond human actors, some network scholars, following Latour and Actor Network Theory, suggest that networks also include non-human actors such as pets and objects (Herz and Altissimo, 2021). However, I share Crossley's approach and focus only on human actors. Moreover, it could be argued that organisational actors – such as trade unions or formal associations – should also be included within networks (Herz and Altissimo, 2021). While the main focus of my work is on interpersonal webs of relationships, of course it is necessary to understand these as situated within wider structural contexts where state actors shape possible actions, for example through immigration regimes, as discussed in later chapters.

Furthermore, when analysing interpersonal relationships, one is not assuming reciprocity, cordiality and mutual support. In discussing complex relationality within networks, one is reminded of Simmel's observation that relationships can be 'pregnant with the contradictory and yet inseparable converging and diverging currents or associative and dissociative processes' (cited in Azarian, 2010: 327). As discussed throughout this book, relationships within networks can involve tensions, disagreements and disappointments (Bilecen, 2020), as well as power dynamics and exploitation (Del Real, 2019). As illustrated by Maryam's story, not all social ties are supportive and indeed some may be hostile, critical and obstructive. Nonetheless, Everett and Borgatti (2014) note that SNA research tends to overlook negative ties. The design of most network research studies is aimed at exploring functioning ties and hence risks ignoring relationships that have failed to function in some expected way, have broken down or been severed (Everett and Borgatti, 2014). As discussed in more detail in Chapter 3, my work seeks to use rich, qualitative methods to understand and make sense of complex relationships, including negative ties.

Throughout this book, avoiding 'network' simply as a metaphor, I draw on concepts derived from SNA and my rich data to explore how participants, such as Maryam, tell their stories and narrate the meaning, perception and presentation of particular relationships with significant others, including negative ties. I consider how these social ties came about (their antecedents), the various roles they play in the lives of my participants and how these relationships may encourage, enable or indeed hinder particular actions (their consequences). In so doing, I aim to understand networks as complex, spatially dispersed, differentiated and dynamic webs of interpersonal relationships. Moreover, rather than taking for granted the social capital inherent in these networks, as discussed in the next section, I aim to interrogate the flow of resources between social ties.

Networks and resources: beyond the bonding and bridging capital dichotomy

As mentioned earlier, migrant networks are often depicted in the literature as sources of valuable resources in enabling the migration process (Massey and España, 1987) and supporting migrants in the destination society (Haug, 2008). However, rather than being simply taken for granted, detailed analysis is required to assess the particular kinds of resources that may flow between specific social ties. For example, it has been suggested that networks may operate as 'boutiques not general stores' (Wellman, 1979). In other words, particular relationships may offer specialist sorts of support. Hence, someone who provides emotional support, such as a close friend, may not provide small favours such as lending a household appliance – more likely to be sought from a neighbour. Therefore, beyond any generalised notion of 'a network', it is necessary to examine the specific resources circulating among particular social ties.

The flow of resources through migrant networks is frequently analysed through the lens of social capital (Sommer and Gamper, 2021). Indeed, as noted earlier in Maryam's story, the term social capital has become ubiquitous in certain circles – "my friends call me social capital". In conceptualising migrant capital, researchers have often drawn on the work of the American political scientist Robert Putnam and the French sociologist Pierre Bourdieu (for an overview see Ryan, Erel and D'Angelo, 2015; Keskiner, Eve and Ryan, 2022).

Although neither a migration scholar nor a social network analyst, Putnam has proven to be extremely influential among migration researchers (for a discussion see Erel, 2010). Putnam's (2000) distinction between bonding – 'ties to people who are like me in some important way' – and bridging – 'people who are unlike me in some important way' – has been taken up in many migration studies (for example, Nannestad et al, 2008; Lancee, 2010). Within that body of scholarship, there is a marked tendency to define 'like' and 'unlike' along ethnic lines. For example: 'We define bridging ties as relations that cut across the ethnic divide and bonding ties as those within the same ethnic group, operationalizing these as intra-ethnic and intra-ethnic friendships, respectively' (Lancee and Hartung, 2012: 41).

However, the extent to which homophilous, co-ethnic ties are necessarily a source of bonding capital, while ties to non-co-ethnics are a source of bridging capital, cannot be assumed. Such narrow dichotomous constructions limit our understanding of what is actually going on within networks (Geys and Murdoch, 2010; Patulny, 2015; Ryan, et al, 2015; Keskiner et al, 2022).

As I have argued at length over the last decade or more (Ryan, 2011a; 2016), the conflation of tie strength, content and direction is problematic for a number of reasons. Firstly, it means that the structure of a tie is assumed largely on the basis of its content. So, ties to relatives are assumed to be strong, while ties to so-called 'natives' are assumed to be weak. Secondly, the resources available within the tie are also assumed. Thus, it is implied that ties to co-ethnics generate a particular set of resources, whereas ties to other ethnic groups, especially the 'native' population, generate different, and more valuable, resources. But, it is necessary to critically assess and differentiate these ties. Not all ties to so-called 'natives' are the same and neither can they be assumed to offer access to valuable resources (Ryan, 2016; see also Kalter and Kogan, 2014; Gericke et al, 2018; Bernhard, 2020; Lang et al, 2022; Rezai and Keskiner, 2022). Indeed, within super-diverse places, the notion of who is actually 'native' is open to discussion (Crul and Schneider, 2010).

Janine Dahinden (2016) has cautioned against the use of a priori ethnic categories when doing network research with migrants. Starting with fixed ethnic categories may shape but also limit the data that are generated. She argues, instead, that a network lens allows researchers to begin by examining the extent and range of social ties without grouping these into 'co-ethnics' or non-migrants (Dahinden, 2016).

As Wellman notes:

> The utility of the network perspective is that it does not take as its starting point putative solidarities – local or kin – nor does it seek primarily to find and explain the persistence of solidary sentiments. … Instead, social network analysis is principally concerned with delineating structures of relationships and flows of activities. (Wellman, 1979: 1203)

Hence, migration researchers should be wary of a priori assumptions about ethnic solidarities and avoid framing research questions about social ties through ethnic categories (Wimmer, 2004). As highlighted throughout this book, and suggested in Maryam's story earlier, identifications and affiliations are complex and multidimensional. Adopting an intersectional lens (Phoenix and Bauer, 2012; Mirza, 2013; Collins and Bilge, 2020) allows diverse aspects of identity, beyond ethnic homophily, to come to the fore, including religion, sexuality, class and gender, among others. As I discuss in more detail in Chapter 3, rather than imposing a priori ethnic or migrant categories, participants should be free to tell their network stories in their own words and to name and group their social relationships in ways that are meaningful to them (Ryan, 2021).

Of course, throughout this discussion, one has to avoid the assumption that networks are coterminous with social capital (Reimers et al, 2008). Simply knowing someone, or even being related to them, does not mean they will share resources with you (Smith, 2005). As Nan Lin (2000) argues, we need to differentiate between the resources existing within network ties and those that can be mobilised. Attempting to theorise migrants' resources, many researchers have turned to Bourdieu for a more nuanced understanding of networks and different forms of capital (for example, Erel, 2010; Nowicka, 2013; Kim, 2019).

Far from taking networks for granted, Bourdieu (1986) highlights the opportunities and obstacles to access different kinds of networks and to convert resources into particular kinds of valuable capital. Bourdieu argues that networking is 'the product of endless effort' required 'in order to produce and reproduce lasting, useful relationships that can secure material or symbolic profits' (Bourdieu, 1986: 52). Moreover, Goulbourne et al (2010: 28) observe that Bourdieu conveys an understanding of social capital that considers 'factors of social class, dominance and conflict'. Hence, Bourdieu's analysis is useful to understand power dynamics and how networks may also operate as exclusionary mechanisms. For example, in his essay on forms of capital, Bourdieu (1986) clearly outlines how networks can be used by elite groups to maintain their privilege. While such 'closed networks' (Coleman, 1988) may be high in trust and reciprocity, they are also very difficult for newcomers to penetrate (Bourdieu, 1986; see also Behtoui, 2022; Eve, 2022).

Bourdieu's theoretical framework has been taken up by researchers to explore the barriers that migrants may encounter in attempting to transfer their knowledge and qualifications (cultural capital) from one society to another (Cederberg, 2015). As shown by Kelly and Lusis (2006), in a study of Filipinos in Canada, migrants may experience discrimination, deskilling and downward labour market mobility as their qualifications and experience are devalued within the destination society (see also Erel and Ryan, 2019; Behtoui, 2022). Earlier, we saw how Maryam's cultural capital was not recognised and she faced deskilling. In Chapter 5, we will discuss the strategies she adopted to convert her cultural capital into social and economic capital.

In contexts of exclusion and discrimination, competition for scarce resources may mean that actors have to be careful with whom they share valuable information, for example about job opportunities. As Sandra Susan Smith (2005) has demonstrated in her work with poor urban African-Americans, the extent to which people are willing to share information about job vacancies, even among close network ties, is mediated by a range of complex factors, including a balance of risk and reputation.

In theorising how resources, especially jobs, flow through network ties, few have been more influential than the economic sociologist Mark Granovetter. Writing 50 years ago, Granovetter distinguished between weak and strong ties on the basis of 'a combination of the amount of time, the emotional intensity, the intimacy (mutual confiding) and the reciprocal services which characterise the tie' (1973: 1361). Strong ties are associated with high levels of frequency, intensity and intimacy (1362). People involved in strong ties, because they know each other well, may be motivated to help each other and share resources. However, as they move in similar circles, they are likely to know similar sorts of information, for example, about job vacancies. By contrast, 'those to whom we are weakly tied are more likely to move in circles different from our own and will thus have access to information different from that which we receive' (1973: 1371). Consequently, such ties are important for 'mobility opportunities' (1373). These individuals are likely to be 'only marginally included in [our] current network of contacts' and may include a former colleague or employer with whom we have only 'sporadic contact' (1973: 1371).

In later work, Granovetter (1983) acknowledged that not all weak ties were equally valuable. He emphasised that weak ties are most useful when they bridge 'substantial social distance' (1983: 209); in other words, when the person to whom we are tied weakly is well placed in the 'occupational structure' (1983: 209) and has access to relevant and reliable information about opportunities within that structure.

I have found Granovetter's conceptual framework useful in my own analysis of how resources flow through migrant networks (Ryan, 2011a). Moreover, I build upon his theorisation in three key ways. Firstly, in terms of tie direction, Granovetter argues that weak ties are more valuable if they link people from different social locations. For those in the lower social groups, he suggests, weak ties may not work as bridges at all but merely link the acquaintances of one's friends and relatives (1983: 208). In my view, this observation suggests the need to differentiate between horizontal and vertical weak ties. Referring to all such contacts simply as 'weak ties' confuses the different resources that these may be able to generate and transmit (Ryan, 2011a). Therefore, I distinguish weak ties horizontally (ties to people of a similar social position) and vertically (ties to people in higher social positions). Social connections may be most beneficial when connecting to people in advantageous or influential social positions, which I term 'vertical ties' (Ryan, 2016).

Secondly, going beyond Granovetter himself but instead focusing on how his work is often applied by migration scholars, I consider the content of these ties. Although Granovetter was not writing about migrants, his work is often cited by migration researchers (for example, Sanders et al, 2002; Patulny and Svendsen, 2007; Harvey, 2008; Lancee, 2010). Among many migration scholars, ethnic categories tend to be imposed on the strong tie/weak tie distinction, such that strong ties are defined as co-ethnics and weak ties are defined as 'natives' (for example, Lancee and Hartung, 2012;

Damstra and Tillie, 2016). There is a risk here of a reductive approach, such that the complexity and dynamism of networks become simplified into binary categories. My research explores tie content and in so doing I show that vertical ties need not be with 'natives'. Other migrants and indeed co-ethnics, provided they are located in advantageous social positions, and willing to share resources, can also serve as vertical ties (Ryan, 2011a; 2016; 2022). Therefore, as explored in more detail in Chapter 5, we need to avoid narrow reductive approaches that impute associations between tie content, direction and strength.

Thirdly, I suggest that the importance of tie 'weakness' may have been oversimplified. Ties that are too weak may lack the necessary trust to motivate the sharing of resources (Sanders et al, 2002). Thus, I propose that vertical ties, which bridge social distance, do not necessarily have to be weak (Ryan, 2016). On the contrary, these vertical ties may be most useful if, as well as spanning social distance, they also involve some level of trust, mutuality and reciprocity. Furthermore, adopting a temporal perspective, as discussed in Chapter 6, more attention is needed to the life cycle of social ties. Thus, I argue that a rigid distinction between static strong and weak ties is unhelpful because these ties form part of a dynamic continuum of relationships, ebbing and flowing over time (Ryan, 2022).

Hence, in analysing migrant networks, more attention is needed to the dynamic relationships between alters in order to understand what resources are actually mobilised and how such interpersonal connections may change (Ryan, 2016). Therefore, research on migrants' networks needs to take account of dynamism over time, as discussed in the next section.

Dynamism and change over time

There is growing interest in the dynamics of migrants' networks of relationships over time (Schapendonk, 2015; Ryan and D'Angelo, 2018; Kindler, 2021; Lubbers et al, 2021; Mazzucato, 2021; Sommer and Gamper, 2021). As suggested by Maryam's story, at the start of this chapter, the extent, range and content of her social ties changed enormously during the ten years from her arrival to when I first met her. Thus, the social ties that migrants may rely upon when they first move to a new society are rarely fixed and static. I am interested in the antecedents of social ties: how ties are formed in the first place and how they evolve. Some ties may weaken and fade, while others grow stronger and endure over time.

Understanding antecedents demands due attention to the spatio-temporal contexts of when, where and with whom particular ties emerge (Erel and Ryan, 2019). As discussed in detail in Chapters 4, 6 and 7, this is especially salient in the case of migrants who move to a new location and are embedding relationally in new connections – making new friends in new places – while simultaneously negotiating relational embedding at a distance in the origin country (Ryan and Mulholland, 2015).

SNA scholars have long been mindful that studying 'a network' risks offering a snapshot of a set of relationships at a particular point in time (Conway, 2014). Snijders (2005: 216) reminds us that the notion that dynamic social phenomena resulted from 'a continuous time-process, even though observations are made at discrete time points, was already proposed by Coleman (1964)'. As Bidart and Lavenu point out, 'personal networks have a history. The form and structure they show today result from a construction elaborated over time' (2005: 360). In addition, Lubbers et al (2021) argue that while descriptions of structural change over time may give an insight into dynamic processes, these do not reveal the dyadic processes (between alters) that are underlying wider, aggregate results. Hence, rather than focusing on the 'existence of ties', more attention is needed to the dynamic content of specific ties and how these evolve over time (Lubbers et al, 2021).

The challenge of how to research change over time has been a particular focus of my research (Ryan and D'Angelo, 2018). Understanding dynamism within networks means taking account of temporality and how that intersects with spatiality (Erel and Ryan, 2019). However, Barbara Adam has noted the difficulty for social researchers in 'taking time seriously' (2000: 126). When time is included in social studies, it tends to be regarded simply as 'the neutral medium in which events take place' (2000: 126). In my work, I have found useful Glen Elder's (1994) notion of life course to make sense of biographical time and how that is situated within wider historical contexts. Throughout this book, I consider how a life course perspective can generate insights into the dynamism of relationality. The methodological challenges of studying network dynamism will be discussed in Chapter 3, but, in this chapter, I focus on the conceptual innovations necessary to analyse social ties and the flow of resources over time.

Within SNA, one of the most influential studies of change over time was conducted in France by Bidart and Lavenu (2005). Based on repeated interviews over several years, the study mapped the changing composition of networks as participants' life circumstances evolved over time: 'Little by little, in the course of a lifetime, ties are woven, some relationships intertwine, others become distant and fade away' (Bidart and Lavenu, 2005: 360). Following the experiences of young people, Bidart and Lavenu observed how relationships emerged in specific environments such as college or the workplace and hence were associated with particular moments in time.

Although their participants were not migrants, some did move to other cities to study or for work. Hence, Bidart and Lavenu were able to analyse the impact of mobility on networks: 'Geographical mobility first produces a significant decline in the number of network members but over time new ties are created in the new environment' (2005: 373). Key life stages also bring about changes to the network size and composition. For example, moving in with a partner 'greatly limits sociability' (2005: 368). While the birth of child can also diminish network size as people have less time to socialise, these new phases of life can also bring about opportunities to forge new ties, for example with other parents (2005: 364).

Similarly, in Canada, Wellman and Wortley have highlighted how network roles and resources may reflect specific life stages and sociocultural gender norms. For example, they found that women, particularly those who have children, tend to be the main providers of emotional support and caring for others in their networks, including men, children and other women. 'Women – especially those who are full-time homemakers (and not doing paid work) – help each other with childcare, spousal care, and gender-linked domestic chores. Because homemaking is a lonely, gruelling business without institutional support, these network members support each other in their work even when they are not intimate' (Wellman and Wortley, 1990: 579). Through this caring work, women often build up links with other women in the area, including neighbours, as well as maintaining kinship ties to siblings, parents and other relatives (see also Bott, 1957). Thus, women tend to be the network linchpins or, as cited in a study from Israel, the 'foreign ministers' who create and maintain relationships on behalf of the couple/family unit (Spalter, 2010).

Although these findings are not based on international migrants, nonetheless, it can be revealing to bring together insights from research with non-migrants to understand patterns of sociality and network composition through life course dynamics. It is imperative for researchers to avoid the pitfall of migrant exceptionalism. As Eve (2022) notes, there is a tendency for researchers to analyse international migrants' networks in isolation and hence to attribute all their network characteristics to their migratory experiences. I have found that drawing on classic social network studies, such as those by Bott, Wellman, Bidart and Lavenu, can be useful when analysing dynamics within migrants' network stories, over time, and thus revealing gendered networking patterns, for example around child-based sociality within local neighbours (Ryan, 2007a).

Exploring how ties emerge, endure or fade over time also raises important questions about the opportunities but also the obstacles that may be encountered in forging new ties in new places (Gill and Bialski, 2011; Ryan, 2015a; Wessendorf and Phillimore, 2019; Bernhard, 2020; Speed et al, 2021). Migrants are not free to make new connections with whomsoever they choose in the destination society. As Alireza Behtoui (2022) has shown in his work with migrants in Sweden, processes of prejudice, stigmatisation and social exclusion influence the extent to which particular kinds of migrants can enter local forms of sociality. These points are taken up in more detail in Chapter 6 of this book.

In taking account of spatio-temporal dynamics (Erel and Ryan, 2019), it is necessary to understand not only how people change, as their needs, circumstances and relationships transform over time (Bidart and Lavenu, 2005), but also how the structural contexts around them are changing. Neighbourhoods, towns, cities and nation states are continually evolving and developing with consequences for their residents, including migrants. Indeed, migration itself may be a factor in those spatial transformations (Hickman and Mai, 2015; Schnell, Kohlbacher and Reeger, 2015; Ryan et al, 2021). For example, cities like London have been changed by historical waves of migration over centuries (Back and Sinha, 2018; Panayi, 2020) as well as by the institutional structures that seek to shape and contain those migratory movements (Yuval-Davis et al, 2019).

The concept of the life course helps to bring together individual biographies and wider sociohistorical structures: 'Time operates at both a sociohistorical and personal level' (Elder et al, 2003: 9). Through this principle of timing, Elder has argued that the 'same events or experiences may affect individuals in different ways depending on when they occur in the life course' (2003: 12). So, the personal time of an individual (for example, being a teenager, middle-aged or old-aged) needs to be contextualised in the specific context of historical time (for example, during a global economic recession, a pandemic or a war). Hence, as Elder et al argue, 'lives are influenced by an ever changing historical and biographical context' (2003: 7). But this is not to suggest that these experiences are negotiated by individuals alone. The principle of 'linked lives' is especially relevant to understand social networks within these temporally dynamic contexts: 'Lives are lived interdependently and socio-historical influences are expressed through this network of shared relationships' (Elder et al, 2003: 13). Hence, echoing earlier observations (Bott, 1957), we see again here the salience of networks as a meso level between the individual and wider sociohistorical structures. Thus, to borrow Bronfenbrenner's (1992) notion of an ecosystem, we can see how micro, meso and macro levels of social systems dynamically interact and shape each other.

In my own work, and in collaboration with colleagues, I have shown how analysing migrants' network stories through a life course perspective enables a deeper understanding of how interpersonal relationships are shaped by particular life stages such as, for example, parenthood (Ryan, 2007a; Ryan, 2018; Erel and Ryan, 2019) or post-retirement (Ryan et al, 2021), but also how these experiences need to be contextualised within specific sociohistorical events, such as a global economic recession or changing immigration regimes arising from Brexit (Kilkey and Ryan, 2021; Ryan et al, 2021) or a global pandemic (Kloc-Nowak and Ryan, 2022), that may rupture or reconfigure social ties.

As discussed in more detail in Chapter 3, undertaking interviews with participants from different waves of migration, as well as visualisation techniques and repeated interviews over several years, can be useful ways to research relational dynamics and changes in the composition and meaning of network ties. Using this approach, my work has also shown the ways in which perceptions of particular relationships can alter depending upon changing life circumstances, needs and expectations (Ryan et al, 2019). In analysing networks, a key focus of my recent work, as discussed in the next section, is how relationality is filtered through layers of perception and self-presentation.

Telling network stories: discursive devices and meaning making

As noted earlier, SNA has become increasingly associated with quantitative approaches influenced by advanced computational capacity and big data (Scott, 1988; Knox et al, 2006; Crossley and Edwards, 2016; Maltseva and Batageli, 2019; Tubaro et al, 2021). Consequently, SNA has developed into a quantitative approach 'with a language, toolkit and methodology which often seem alienating to more qualitatively oriented researchers' (Heath et al, 2009: 646). However, in propounding the virtues of SNA, I am not espousing a quantification of social ties analysed through graph theory or block modelling.

Indeed, following the cultural turn, there is growing interest in qualitative and mixed-methods approaches to networks (Bellotti, 2015; Crossley and Edwards, 2016). Moreover, there have been calls for more attention to meaning making and perception among some network scholars. Social networks can be understood as 'imaginary worlds that people create and then endeavour to live in' (Mehra et al, 2014: 3). While much social network research has 'focused on networks in their realist guise', far less attention has been paid to networks in their 'cognitive guise' (Mehra et al, 2014: 13).

Among migration scholars, there have been repeated calls for a 'renewed theoretical view' to enable a better understanding of 'how meaning-making unfolds within support relationships' (Bernhard, 2020: 2). Scholars point back to the work of Simmel, Goffman and White to offer theoretical insights into how meaning making plays out in migrant networks (see, for example, Bernhard, 2020). As I argue throughout this book, migration research needs to achieve more critical insights into the meaning, composition and dynamism of social ties. In seeking to go beyond taken-for-granted views of networks as fixed entities to be captured, studied and measured, I once again turn to classical network scholars.

It has long been noted by scholars, such as Burt (1992) and Krackhardt (1987), that the network data studied by researchers is not so much an accurate reflection of 'reality' as the product of perception and cognitive processes. However, as discussed earlier, recent developments in quantification and big data have meant that many SNA researchers are unable to see the micro details of personal perceptions amid the mass of whole network patterns (Crossley, 2015). By contrast, my own work draws on qualitative data and uses a critically reflexive approach to pay particular attention to intersubjectivity and how the notion of networks is perceived and constructed in interview encounters between myself and participants (Ryan et al, 2014; see discussion in Chapter 3).

Moreover, as suggested in a paper with Alessio D'Angelo, it is also necessary to pay attention to how participants present their networks to researchers. We argue that 'between perceptions and visualisation' of networks of relationships 'there is a further layer of complexity, what we call the presentation of the networked self' (D'Angelo and Ryan, 2021: 21). That means to say network data are not simply based on how participants 'perceive' their network ties, but also on how they decide to present them to interviewers in a research encounter. Inspired by Goffman (1978), we have argued that, in describing their networks, participants seek to present a particular image of themselves and their relationships (D'Angelo and Ryan, 2021). Nonetheless, that is not to suggest that networks can be simply depicted according to the whim of participants. The questions we ask, the visualisation tools we use as well as wider social discourses about social networks (Hogan et al, 2007; Healy, 2015) also shape how relational ties are configured in research settings (D'Angelo and Ryan, 2021). Pursuing this further, using the concept of 'stories', I reflect upon intersubjectivities and the ways in which participants and I engage in processes of co-constructing networks to make complex, diverse and dynamic relationships visible in particular ways – through words and pictures (Ryan, 2021).

To understand how participants talk about networks, I turn to the work of Ann Mische and Harrison White. While networks can be defined as 'sets of actors jointly positioned in relations to a given array of ties', Mische and Harrison argue that 'each type of tie is accompanied by a set of stories (along with associated discursive signals) that are held in play over longer or shorter periods of time' (1998: 703). Furthermore, it is not enough to simply argue that networks are 'constituted by stories' (Mische and White, 1998: 695); it is also necessary to understand how wider sociostructural contexts mediate those discursive processes. In other words, interactions occurring in network ties are shaped by what Mische and White call 'underlying socio-cultural patterning' (1998: 705).

One such sociocultural patterning is the 'explosion in the popularity of social networking sites' which have the capacity to 'alter the way in which people create, maintain, and leverage their social networks' (Borgatti et al, 2009: 895). As Healy has argued, 'The rapid development of computing power, the infrastructure of the Internet, and the protocols of the World Wide Web, together transformed the capacity to construct, visualize, analyze and build networked systems in practice. They were also accompanied by a major shift in the cultural salience of network imagery' (Healy, 2015: 186). Hence, researchers need to be mindful of how network content and structure, as well as people's understanding of what a network is, are being influenced by online sites. Social networking sites may impact on the 'performativity' of networks (Healy, 2015). In other words, online sites like LinkedIn actively encourage people to expand their social networks and, in so doing, these platforms are shaping what a network looks like and how it performs. Indeed, as discussed elsewhere (D'Angelo and Ryan, 2021), comparing our experiences of doing network research over many years, it is apparent that participants are far more aware of the concept of 'networks' than was the case 20 years ago. Thus, the way in which people describe their networks to researchers may be influenced by their perception of what a social network is meant to look like (that is, like on Facebook or LinkedIn). I argue that using the concept of storytelling (Ryan, 2021) may be helpful in attempting to understand how networks are perceived and presented by research participants. As observed in Maryam's story earlier, because of her work in London's large and vibrant voluntary sector, she was very familiar with the notion of social capital and presented herself as a skilled networker who was successfully forging links with diverse groups of people.

While scholars like Mische and White (1998) are interested in how storytelling occurs within networks, I want to go further and examine how networks themselves are constructed as dynamic discursive devices through the processes of telling stories and drawing pictures. Hence, I aim to contribute to SNA by exploring not only how networks are constituted by stories but also how they are framed within particular domains, including the interview encounter itself. In developing this approach, I draw upon concepts from narrative analysis.

In recent decades there has been a proliferation of writing on narrative analysis (Somers, 1994; De Fina, 2011; Rainbird, 2012; Ryan, 2015b; Azarian, 2017). Much of this work has focused on research interviews (Mason, 2004). The notion of telling stories, the interview as a story, has been particularly influential (Plummer, 2002). Narratives are 'interpretative devices through which people represent themselves, both to themselves and to others' (Mason, 2004: 165). Thus, narratives perform personal work – spelling out who I am and how I relate to other people. As Azarian notes, 'a story is primarily a justifying narrative' (2017: 692) which seeks to explain and rationalise a particular line of action.

But beyond the specificities of the interview encounter, these stories are situated in wider structural contexts. The work of Margaret Somers has been especially influential within sociology in understanding narratives as devices for making sense of individual experiences through relationality, that is, connecting to 'a social network of relationships' (1994: 616). Thus, she argues that 'narratives are constellations of relationships embedded in time and space' (Somers, 1994: 616).

Somers notes that while narratives have been used as a method to collect data (for example, by historians), there is need for deeper epistemological and ontological shifts to recognise that

> people make sense of what has happened and is happening to them by attempting to assemble or in some way to integrate these happenings within one or more narratives; and that people are guided to act in certain ways, and not others, on the basis of the projections, expectations, and memories derived from a multiplicity but ultimately limited repertoire of available social, public, and cultural narratives. (Somers, 1994: 614)

In other words, through narratives, we aim to make sense of our relationships, our place and identity in the social world. However, rather than simply individual stories, these narratives are framed by macro-structural contexts and meso-relational contexts. For example, as noted in our earlier discussion of Bott's study of couples in the 1950s, sociocultural norms and expectations about gender roles and identities were mediated through specific relational contexts (connectedness to kin, friends, work colleagues and neighbours).

Thus, it is important to contextualise narrative form, structure, content and meaning in wider sociocultural frameworks. In his pioneering approach to analysing participants' stories, Ken Plummer (2002) asked what the contingencies that shape story making are: the who, what, where, when, why and how of narratives. He argued that these questions can be answered on four interconnected levels. Firstly, the sociohistorical: how are the narratives situated in relation to wider historical factors and patterns in that society? Secondly, cultural: what cultural frames and dominant assumptions shape how narratives are constructed and told? Thirdly, contextual: to what audience and in what sort of encounter is the narrative being related? Finally, personal: what are the specific motivations, experiences and reflexivities that shape the stories being told?

Hence, although the individual narrative is usually presented and performed as a deeply personal story, specific to that one participant, nonetheless, individuals draw upon shared meanings and understandings to construct their personal stories (Rainbird, 2012). We do not construct narratives purely of our own making; our stories interact with and are shaped by the wider narratives circulating in the society around us. As discussed in later chapters, for some migrants, wider societal narratives may be significant and reflective of specific public and political discourses concerning immigration. Thus, narratives are not only about personal life experiences but also framed by particular sociohistorical settings. Thus, as Souto-Manning (2014: 162) has argued, 'narratives are a window into meaning-making processes in the "life-world" and can help us assess and understand institutional and power discourses in society in more concrete ways'. Earlier, Maryam mentioned being stuck in a "benefit trap". Her motivation to raise this issue may have been partly framed by wider societal discourses that depicted refugees as 'benefit scroungers' who abuse the welfare system (Mayblin, 2019). Mindful of these stereotypes, she sought to narrate, explain and justify why she found herself temporarily stuck in that "trap".

As noted earlier, researchers need to take time seriously (Adam, 2000). Spatio-temporal contexts present an important backdrop (Erel and Ryan, 2019) to how people tell network stories. In my work, I am conscious of how a migrant's story may be shaped by specific contextual factors including, for example, racist or anti-migrant rhetoric in the wider society at that time. This observation provides a more nuanced understanding of how migrants construct and present their network stories and, hence, may provide important insights into how relationships are made sense of, justified and explained. Hence, I suggest that rather than making invisible relationships visible (Conway, 2014), social network research is actually implicated in the co-construction of relationality, especially through visualisation tools (as discussed in the next chapter). Therefore, adopting a critically reflexive approach to qualitative SNA illustrates how networks are used as discursive devices to make sense of differentiated, dynamic and dispersed relationships (Ryan, 2021). But this process is not spontaneous. Rather, it is shaped by the tools we use and the questions we pose (D'Angelo and Ryan, 2021). In telling network stories, participants seek to construct a coherent narrative with which they are comfortable. Therefore, I propose that, instead of taking networks for granted, using the conceptual framework of 'telling network stories' can help migration scholars to gain deeper understanding of how personal networks are presented, constructed and interpreted within the research process.

Conclusion

This chapter has summarised how my research, as well as collaborations with colleagues, has sought to advance the field of qualitative SNA in migration studies, not simply as a methodology but as an epistemological approach informed by classic network theorists. While recognising some of the specificities of international migration, I have also shown how earlier studies of social networks, involving non-migrants, can add useful insights about relational ties and so help to avoid simplistic migrant exceptionalism. Building upon this earlier work, the chapter has set out my conceptual framework of 'telling network stories', which underpins this book. Moreover,

I have suggested how this approach can help to tackle some of the persistent challenges in how social networks are studied within migration research.

Firstly, I have sought to overcome the metaphoric use of networks (Knox et al, 2006; Ryan and Dahinden, 2021). While networks are often used in vague ways within migration research, I have proposed the framework of telling network stories to go beyond mere metaphors and offer insights into complex relationality. In developing this approach, I draw upon the rich legacy and well-stocked toolbox of SNA to go beyond a generalised notion of the 'migrant network', and gain deeper and more nuanced understandings of the meanings and make-up of interpersonal relationality. This approach allows analysis of how specific social ties, situated at the meso level, may mediate between the individual migrant and macro-social structure, helping to avoid methodological individualism and structural determinism.

Secondly, although turning to SNA, I have sought an alternative to the dominance of graph theory, block modelling and the quantification of big data which have become so influential in network analysis (Tubaro et al, 2021). Instead, I have highlighted the particular benefits of qualitative network analysis to understand relational meanings, emotions and tensions, including negative ties, as well as power dynamics, discrimination and experiences of exclusion. Furthermore, I have explored intersubjectivity and how the meaning of relationality gets filtered through processes of perception and self-presentation (D'Angelo and Ryan, 2021). Therefore, in contrast to the objectification of network data, the framework of telling network stories focuses on dynamic discursive devices.

Thirdly, I have critically interrogated the intricate relationship between networks and social capital (Erel, 2010; Goulbourne et al, 2010). Instead of taking social capital for granted, it is necessary to explore the opportunities and obstacles that migrants encounter in trying to convert, access and share specific kinds of resources in order to generate capital in particular contexts. Rather than a priori, homophilous and essentialised ethnic categories of bonding and bridging, this chapter summarised my contribution to analysing the complexity of tie strength, direction and composition. In so doing, as further explored in later chapters, I suggested that network stories can provide insights into the contingency of resources flowing through a continuum of dynamic relational ties.

Fourthly, in addressing the persistent challenge of how to research change over time (Adam, 2000; Collins and Shubin, 2015; King and Della Puppa, 2021), I have sought to understand how social ties emerge and evolve within spatio-temporal dynamics. Far from being static, webs of relationships, in both the destination society but also in the origin country, ebb and flow through different life course stages, framed by dynamic sociohistorical contexts (Elder et al, 2003). Network stories present rich and multi-layered accounts of dynamic, messy relationality. Beyond any simple linearity, these stories illustrate how social ties form, sustain, fracture, mend, fade or endure over time. The methods associated with this approach, including longitudinal and visual research, will be discussed further in the next chapter.

While this chapter focused on conceptual and epistemological innovations, the following chapter turns to methodology and how I have researched migrant networks over the last two decades, and how my practical approach to researching personal networks through stories and pictures has emerged over time.

3

Researching Migration and Networks: Empirical and Methodological Innovations

Having discussed the conceptualisation of networks, and explored my epistemological contribution, in the previous chapter, now, this chapter turns to methodology and the techniques that underpin my empirical research. The overall goal of this book is to present my approach to doing qualitative SNA in migration research, through the technique of telling relational stories and drawing pictures of interpersonal connections. This chapter summarises how that approach evolved slowly over the last 20 years of research with migrants.[1]

As discussed in the introductory chapter, my work focuses primarily on London, a city shaped by centuries of migration (Back & Sinha, 2018; Panayi, 2020), to where I moved in the 1990s. Working with migrants who arrived in London at different historical periods draws attention not only to place but also to change over time (Massey, 2007). As argued elsewhere, 'Migration not only involves spatial but also temporal movement. Migrants are not only moving between countries, they are also negotiating these environments over time' (Ryan, Lopez Rodriguez and Trevena, 2016). However, as noted by other scholars, it is notoriously difficult to research temporal dynamism (Adam, 2000; McKie et al, 2002; Collins and Shubin, 2015; King and Della Puppa, 2021; Lubbers et al, 2021). Hence, the first aim of this chapter is to discuss my attempts to research change over time. Influenced by Elder's work, I approach time in two ways: first, by drawing on a large corpus of qualitative data collected with migrants who arrived at different historical times, and second, by using longitudinal approaches to reinterview some migrants on several occasions to understand changes in biographical time.

In bringing together migrant stories from across a wide range of research projects, over many years, I faced the challenge of how to present these rich and varied stories in a meaningful way that conveys the diversity of experiences, while being engaging and digestible for readers. Thus, the second aim of this chapter is to explore the use of case studies or thick descriptions (see Thomson, 2007; Phoenix and Brannen, 2014; Stanley, 2015), in making sense of a large and diverse data sets.

Although interviewing individual migrants, it is apparent that their stories present complex relationalities. As Elder also notes, individuals do not experience sociohistorical contexts as isolated actors. The notion of 'linked lives' (Elder et al, 2003) highlights the salience of interpersonal relationships in individual biographies. As discussed in the previous chapter, building on this notion of linked lives, and inspired by earlier scholars like Bott (1957) and Boyd (1989), I have long been interested in how networks can play a mediating role between individual migrants and macro spatio-temporal contexts (Ryan, 2004). However, rather than attempting to quantify migrant networks, I apply a qualitative approach and an interpretive lens to bring into focus performative and perceptual dimensions of how personal networks are presented through narratives.

Narratives are devices for making sense of individual experiences through relationality (Somers, 1994). Migrant stories usually involve a host of characters who perform varied roles in encouraging, enabling or even hindering migration processes. I argue that these stories offer valuable insights into complex, dynamic relationality and so provide more nuanced understanding of networks of interpersonal relationships in contexts of migration. Therefore, the third aim of this chapter is to explain the use of oral narratives (stories) and visualisation techniques (pictures) in researching migrant networks. Later, I present the story and sociogram of Adrianna to illustrate that discussion.

However, asking people to tell their stories raises questions about memory and recall, requiring reflection on how stories are told and retold to specific audiences (Plummer, 2002). Furthermore, because I have worked with participants from different intersectional backgrounds of class, religion, nationality and so on, I have become more reflexive about my positionality. I am both an audience and an active participant in the co-production of network stories and pictures. How does my own migrant background, as well as my life stage, gender, class and so on, impact upon my relationships with participants? Hence, the fourth aim of this chapter is to discuss the value of critical self-reflexivity in research processes.

In the next section I begin by describing how I reanalysed the large corpus of qualitative data and selected specific case studies.

Making decisions about how to analyse the enlarged corpus of data

As mentioned in Chapter 1, in spring/summer 2020, during the COVID-19 pandemic and the UK national lockdown, I reread and reanalysed my combined corpus of data. While my goal was to read all the transcripts, I had to make some selections, especially across studies that had involved multiple teams and where data were collected in different geographical locations. Hence, I focused on interviews I had done myself in London.[2]

In approaching the reanalysis of such a large corpus of data, I was guided, but not limited, by the following five overarching research questions. These questions had also informed most of the original research projects:

1. What roles do network actors play in stories of migration decision making and processes of arrival in new destinations?
2. How do networks feature in accounts of initial encounters in London and navigating new and sometimes hostile environments?
3. How do networks of social ties feature in descriptions of accessing the labour market initially and employment trajectories over time and what can be learned about the flow of resources through these ties?
4. How are networks implicated in narratives of family formation and dynamism through different life course stages?
5. How are long-distance kinship and friendship relationships narrated and what can we learn about the ebb and flow of these ties over time?

I took the decision to reread all the transcripts, rather than working from my previous analysis (that is, existing NVivo nodes and reports), partly because it felt like the right thing to do in order to enhance the quality of the book but also, on a purely pragmatic basis, because the pandemic and the associated nationwide lockdown meant that all travel and holiday plans were cancelled and hence I had some unexpected time on my hands. Rereading whole transcripts brought me back to the original narrative, the story in its entirety, as told by each participant. This was necessary for the conceptual lens of 'telling network stories', as explained in the previous chapter. I thus analysed each transcript (and any related sociogram) as a specific unit of data.

Then, as a second step, I looked across the enlarged corpus of data and identified emerging themes informed by the research questions outlined previously. This allowed similarities as well differences across the data set to emerge more clearly, such as highlighting the significance of specific temporal contexts or immigration routes. Clearly, many of my studies had been designed to focus on migrants from particular countries or religious backgrounds, or those who migrated at a particular period in history, such as 'post-World War II' or 'post-EU accession' (see the Appendix for details). However, bringing all the data together from across these varied studies enabled me to look beyond the limits of an ethnic lens (Dahinden, 2016). Thus, I was able to explore how specific experiences, such as, for example, making new friends, engaging in child-based sociality or negotiating long-distance family dynamics, were discussed by all the diverse participants.

Looking across the combined data suggested the different roles of network actors in migration decision making, and choice of destination, for participants of varied ages, family situations and countries of origin, as well as the period in history at which they had migrated. Many had migrated while young and single, others as part of a family unit; some came to marry, others to study, and a few arrived as refugees. Moreover, avoiding any simple linearity, migration was not a one-off event but, in many cases, involved movement back and forth over time. Analysing across such a range of experiences illustrated the varied ways in which social ties appear to facilitate and support, or even constrain, migration aspirations and trajectories.

Confronted by such a large and diverse qualitative data set, I faced challenges about how to present the data in a meaningful way. One strategy may have been to quantify the data and attach numerical significance to specific patterns. For example, what percentage of participants used weak ties to gain new job opportunities? However, as discussed in Chapter 2, such quantification of network data risks simplifying complex and dynamic interpersonal relationships. Reducing relationality to measurable outcomes obscures the nuances of meaning, expectations, obligations, trust, interpretation and decision making. To convey the richness, nuances and dynamics of these narratives, I decided to present thick descriptions.

Thick descriptions

Although thick descriptions may take different formats, Joseph Ponterotto focuses on the most common usage in the social sciences: 'long quotes from the participants or excerpts of interviewer–interview dialogue' (2006: 547). However, that is not to imply that thick descriptions are simply long passages of quotations: 'thick description involves much more than amassing great detail: It speaks to context and meaning as well as interpreting participant intentions in their behaviours and actions' (Ponterotto, 2006: 541). Although he did not invent this approach, Denzin (2001) is credited with popularising the use of 'thick descriptions': 'A thick description ... does more than record what a person is doing. It goes beyond mere fact and surface appearances. It presents detail, context, emotion, and the webs of social relationships that join persons to one another' (Denzin, 1989: 83; cited in Ponterotto, 2006). Moreover, going beyond a lengthy account of what someone said, thick descriptions involve thick interpretation that enable insights into thick meaning. As Ponterotto goes on to explain, 'Thick meaning of findings leads readers to a sense of versimilitude, wherein they can cognitively and emotively "place" themselves within the research context' (2006: 543).

While thick descriptions appealed to me and fitted well with my aim of 'telling network stories' (Ryan, 2021), given the sheer number of participants in my combined data set, I faced the challenge of which participants to focus upon. In her insightful paper, *The Qualitative Longitudinal Case History* (2007), Rachel Thomson provides a useful account of processes that often remain hidden, how researchers make decisions about which participants to select for detailed discussion. That paper helped me to think through the process of how to move from a very large qualitative data set involving over 200 participants to select some for more in-depth discussion, while also acknowledging potential ethical issues. Thomson describes the process of immersing herself in the data. I too did that and it took many months from April to August 2020. Like Thomson, I too undertook the time-consuming procedure of 'analysing each interview in its own right' (2007: 574) and then a second step of exploring connections across the interviews.

My aim was not to undertake a comparative analysis. I did not seek to compare migrant nurses from the 1950s with women migrants in the financial sector in the 2000s to produce typologies of female migrants. Instead, I am inspired by Thomson's approach of avoiding the terminology of typologies and comparison and instead placing stories 'in conversation with each other' (2007: 575). This approach allows the specificities of each participant's story to be appreciated in its own right, in line with narrative approaches, while at the same time allowing a conversation with how other participants articulated similar or different experiences. This aims to avoid a reductive approach to the data, while enabling the processing and presentation of the large data set to be more manageable. Hence, it may be interesting to hear how a female migrant from the 1960s, for example, talked about transnational kinship networks, alongside a 21st-century male migrant talking about his transnational networks in the age of new communication technologies. But this is not to suggest a reductive comparison of traditional letters versus contemporary WhatsApp group chats (as discussed in Chapter 7). The richness of the individual stories enables a deeper understanding of the nature of those long-distance relationships, their situatedness within a life course and the kinds of resources (emotional, informational or material) being exchanged between long-distance ties.

Thomson demonstrates that, by bringing detailed case descriptions 'into conversation', she 'sought to find ways of identifying analytic patterns at a higher level of abstraction/generality' (2007: 577). In a similar way, returning to the example of transnational network ties, I sought to show patterns of relationality. For example, why might some long-distance friendship ties wane, despite the prevalence of new technologies and enhanced opportunities for sustained communication? How might transnational kinship ties transform over time, through the life course, with changing care needs of aged parents? Bringing diverse narratives into conversation allowed me to explore a range of transnational networks to bring deeper understanding to these relational, spatio-temporal dynamics.

So, how does one select which participants to focus upon for thick descriptions? While seeking to avoid a reductive ethnic lens, I was keen to discuss how discrimination was articulated and navigated in contexts of racialisation. Because of the nature of my previous studies, most participants are White and European. But I have also undertaken studies with more diverse participants. Hence, although the numbers are smaller, I was keen to include the voices of the African Caribbean, Asian, Middle Eastern and African participants. I was keen to select some male, as well as female, participants, though overall I have fewer men in my studies. Therefore, readers may notice that some men, especially from racialised groups, are cited a good deal. By contrast, among the more numerous female participants, especially Irish[3] and Polish, I draw upon a larger pool of participants. I have not done a direct gender or ethnic comparison, partly because the numbers are far too skewed but also because, as noted previously, my aim here is not to undertake a comparative analysis.

I was keen to illustrate how Black and/or Muslim participants may have specific experiences based on racism, including Islamophobia. But I also tried to avoid the limitations of the ethnic lens (Dahinden, 2016). So, I also discuss my diverse participants through shared themes such as, for example, employment, family, friendship and transnational relations. I hope that where issues of racism or religious discrimination are key to understanding those experiences, I acknowledge them. But I was wary of discussing Black participants only through a lens of racism or Muslim participants only through the lens of Islamophobia (Meer and Modood, 2012). To do so would be to contain their stories in negative accounts of victimisation and overlook the range and diversity of their rich narratives (Back, 2015).

I also sought to include thick descriptions for migrants who arrived at different periods in time. My participants had migrated from the 1940s to the 2010s and, given my use of the life course perspective (Elder et al, 2003), I wanted to explore how the temporal context may shape experiences. While referring to decades of arrival, I realise that these are not necessarily meaningful categories. For example, arriving in the early 1940s – in the middle of a war – would be a different experience from arriving in the late 1940s, post-war. So, using decades to capture time is not always helpful but it does provide some context to readers.

The thick descriptions included in this book are not intended to be representative. They are selected to illustrate diverse experiences of participants from varied time periods, ages, countries of origin, immigration routes, occupations and family life stages. Beyond mere description, however, and in line with Denzin (2001), these extended examples are framed by my meaning making. So, the end result is an edited, 'crafted' story (White and Drew, 2011) informed by my network analysis.

Thomson (2007) addresses the ethical challenges associated with thick descriptions that reveal a good deal of information about a particular individual. This approach may risk revealing so many details about the person that, even though pseudonymised, they could be identifiable to someone who can piece together the clues. However, I am aware that thorough anonymisation, removing all identifiers, including place names, may diminish the meaning of the story. So, I have tried to strike a careful balance of protecting identity, while presenting sufficient information to be meaningful. The ethical challenges of anonymisation become even more apparent when it comes to network visualisation tools, as discussed later in this chapter. The discussion so far points to my active role not only in data collection but also in decision making about analysis and presentation of findings. I now turn to discuss reflexivity and the research process.

Reflexivity

Interviewing participants is never about simply 'extracting' information as if data were simply waiting there to be 'collected' or 'captured' (White and Drew, 2011). Interviews are a performance and involve dynamic presentations of self. I apply a reflexive approach to critically scrutinise shifting and multi-layered positionalities in research processes. As discussed in the previous chapter, the ways in which participants tell their stories are shaped by numerous contextual factors, not least the interview encounter itself (Plummer, 2002). Hence, it is necessary to pay due attention to where, when and by whom interviews are conducted. The questions we ask shape the answers we receive. Moreover, the ways in which we present ourselves to participants, and who they perceive us to be, impact on the relational dynamics of the interview (Nowicka and Ryan, 2015).

There are ongoing calls 'for researchers to be reflexive and transparent about how their backgrounds, positionalities, and histories inform their work' (Collier and Muneri, 2016: 640). While many migration scholars develop a speciality with a particular migrant population, I have undertaken research with diverse migrants. Interviewing migrants from different countries has the potential to complicate the ethnic exceptionalism that marks some migration research (Schiller and Çağlar, 2009; Amelina and Faist, 2012; Dahinden, 2016). Nonetheless, interviewing migrants from different national backgrounds poses challenges. For instance, limitations associated with language skills[4] and country-specific expertise may serve to undermine researcher 'authority' (Mauthner and Doucet, 2003). Elsewhere, I have reflected upon the challenges and opportunities of researching within, as well as across, diverse intersectional identities (Ryan, 2015c; Nowicka and Ryan, 2015). Instead of a simple, fixed binary of insiders versus outsiders, I suggest that interview processes should be understood in terms of the dynamic rhythms of multi-positionalities. Such an approach enables researchers to be reflexive about the instability and contingency of empathy, understanding and rapport, and how these need to be continually negotiated across layers of power differentials (Ryan, 2015c).

That is not to promote reflexivity as self-indulgent narcissism where the research becomes a form of catharsis for the researcher (Pillow, 2003). Pillow advocates 'reflexivities of discomfort' (2003: 188) which, rather than highlighting similarities with participants, continually explore 'power relations' and the tenuousness and situatedness of knowledge. In this way, reflexivity demands 'ongoing critique of all of our research attempts, recognising that none of our attempts can claim the innocence of success' (Pillow, 2003: 188). Thus, as Collier and Muneri have argued in their research in Kenya and Zimbabwe, reflexivity goes beyond 'confessing lists of identity positions', such as nationality or ethnic background, and instead seeks to address how these positions 'frame, constrain, and enable research and praxis' (2016: 640).

I will never know what it is like to be a Black man being beaten up at a train station (Howard's story) or a refugee woman fleeing Somalia (Maryam's story). But I should not assume that I can automatically know how an Irish woman migrant will feel and think just because I am an Irish woman migrant (Ryan, 2008a; Ryan, 2015c). Moreover, it is important not to define these interview participants through a narrow ethnic lens. To do so simplifies and rarefies their positionalities.

Rather than assuming that migrants arrive in the destination country with a clear and fixed sense of ethnic or national identity, it has been argued that 'we-ness' may emerge as a constructed identification through the migration experience (Portes and Sensenbrenner, 1993: 1328). Thus, it is more useful to begin by asking how identities and affiliations are constructed and negotiated through the migratory experience (Gray, 2004; Ryan, 2010). Andreas Wimmer reminds us that 'members of an ethnic group might not share a specific culture, might not privilege each other in their everyday networking practice and thus not form a "community," and might not agree on the relevance of ethnic categories and thus not carry a common identity' (2009: 252).

Moreover, national affiliations may interact with other facets of identity such as gender or religion to create marked differentiation in how identities are experienced and expressed (Bhopal and Preston, 2012; Mirza, 2013). Hence, far from being fixed, stand-alone dimensions of who we are, ethnicity, nationality, gender, sexuality, age, class, religion and so on are ingredients in complex and active intersections of identities. As Ann Phoenix and Elaine Bauer observe, viewing narratives through an intersectional lens 'draws attention to the importance of treating categories and identities in non-essentialist ways' (2012: 493). Furthermore, it is necessary to understand how these intersectional experiences are situated within time and place and shaped by specific power structures (Bhopal and Preston, 2012; Mirza, 2013).

Of course, it is not easy to predict how one will be placed by research participants (Ryan and Golden, 2006). The interview encounter is not only a process of individual 'identity work' but also of mutual identity co-construction. Far from being stable, these identities may be re-formed and reshaped throughout the encounter as various verbal and non-verbal clues are used to piece together a sense of the other actor (Botterill, 2015; Leung, 2015). Razon and Ross (2012) refer to the fluidity of identities throughout the research encounter: a dance in which both parties attempt to size up each other. The metaphor of 'dance' helps us to reflect upon the intricate rhythms of shifting positionalities through the interview encounter (Ryan, 2015c[5]). While sometimes I appear to have much in common with participants (gender, age, nationality, parenthood, professional status), at other times, I appear to have very little in common at all, except that we are both migrants. Our shared experiences may seem to bring us closer together, without claiming any simplistic notion of insider status. At other times, we may appear less close as divergent life experiences may create a gulf between us. But these positions are rarely fixed as we weave around each other through the dance of the interview encounter. Reflecting upon and being aware of these dynamics can help to create empathy and rapport, while at the same time being sensitive to the power differentials at play. Thus, as Pillow (2003) reminds us, reflexivity should not result in our claiming the 'innocence of success'.

My use of critical reflexivity also influences how I do social network research and in particular my approach to interview encounters with participants when mapping their social ties. As discussed in Chapter 2, the relationship between the interviewer and interviewee – both playing roles as performer and audience – shape how stories are told, interpreted and understood (Plummer, 2002). 'Storytelling is a prime site for identity negotiation' and in the interview encounter 'the kinds of identities people present crucially depend on who they understand their interlocutors to be' (De Fina, 2011: 30). As discussed in the previous chapter, in analysing 'network stories', I am interested in how networks are co-constructed by interviewer and interviewee through words and visual images within interview contexts. Network data are not generated in a vacuum. In the next section, I consider how the visual tools, as well as the interview questions, shape the kinds of data that participants present (D'Angelo and Ryan, 2021).

Asking questions about social ties

At the start of my career, when I first started to undertake oral history interviews with older migrants (Ryan, 2003), I did not adopt a network lens. Instead, my interest in networks grew out of how participants spoke about their significant relationships with friends and relatives. I soon became aware that individual migration stories were very much relational narratives (see also Mason, 2004).

In my subsequent studies, I began to frame research questions specifically around networks of relationships. While the language of networks has entered popular discourse in recent years thanks to social media platforms like Facebook (Healy, 2015), that was certainly not the case in the past. When I first started to explore interpersonal ties in research interviews, I tended to avoid the technical language of networks, which was largely unfamiliar to participants.

Based on my previous experience of survey design (Ryan et al, 2006), I tended to ask very specific questions about forms of support.[6] So, for instance, I asked questions like: did anyone help you?; what kinds of help did particular people give you?; who did you ask for advice?; did someone help you to find a job?; who were your friends?; did you make new friends?; did you stay in touch with relatives back in your country? In answering these questions, I noticed that people often told stories of intricate relationships involving numerous characters, sometimes funny or moving incidents, occasionally a confusing sequence of events, but rarely a specific account of a particular individual fulfilling neatly assigned network roles. Furthermore, I observed that these intricate stories sometimes included descriptions of tensions, disagreements and ruptured relationships. This feature of narratives may be especially important for understanding negative social ties.

As noted in Chapter 2, research on social networks, including migrant networks, tends to focus upon positive forms of support such as sources of information about jobs or offers of accommodation. Research questions that ask 'who advised you?', 'who encouraged you?' or 'to whom did you turn for information?' tend to reinforce a focus on supportive network ties. As a result, less attention is paid to so-called 'negative ties' (Hosnedlová, 2017). Of course, when the focus of research is specifically about abuse, for example in studies about online bullying, then clearly there are questions about negative relationships. But, in the main, in research on social networks more broadly, there has been a tendency to overlook negative ties (Everett and Borgatti, 2014). That is not to suggest that networks are always assumed to be entirely positive. Obviously, there is acknowledgement of tensions within networks such as, for instance, pressures on migrants to remit back to kinship networks in the country of origin (Boccagni, 2015). Moreover, the so-called 'dark side' of social capital, that may channel migrants into low-paid jobs in ethnic industries, has also been researched (Anthias and Cederberg, 2009; see discussion in Chapter 5).

Nonetheless, research with traditional network methods, such as name generators, suggests that few people actually mention their negative ties (Hosnedlová, 2017). Indeed, how to research so-called 'invisible ties' (Felder, 2020) remains a challenge for network scholars. Thus, some ties, including negative ties, may be 'missing data', latent ties that are not reported in surveys or traditional network instruments (Hosnedlová, 2017). Moreover, in SNA, where ties are usually quantified and aggregated, the existence of a single negative tie may be overlooked or its significance underestimated (Everett and Borgatti, 2014). Nonetheless, even one negative tie can be extremely influential if that person is encountered regularly, for example in the domestic setting. Of course, it is important to distinguish between tensions and disagreements on the one hand, and relationships that are actually abusive and harmful on the other hand, while acknowledging that such distinctions may not always be clear-cut (Hosnedlová, 2017). Not all negative ties have the same impact and it is necessary to consider the power dynamics within particular relationships. For instance, a conflictual relationship with a manager at work may be detrimental for career progression (Labianca et al, 1998).

This is where I have found the approach of telling network stories especially useful. In recounting their migration narratives, it is remarkable how often relational tensions, difficulties and disagreements were mentioned. While completely ruptured relationships may not be apparent in traditional network methods, as further discussed later, these may feature in biographical interviews. One reason for this apparent inconsistency is that biographical narratives are often plot – and character – driven (Somers, 1994), and thus, difficult, tense and even abusive relationships may emerge as significant at a particular period in one's life. By contrast, network research often focuses not only on positive relationships but also on current ties. Therefore, negative ties may be omitted either because they are not seen as relevant or because the relationship has completely ended.

Nonetheless, any research that focuses on narratives of relationality has to take account of memory and how particular social ties are remembered retrospectively. Hence, trying to generate data on networks is usually hampered by challenges of memory and recall (Merluzzi and Burt, 2013). This raises questions about how to research changing relationships over time.

I am interested in processes of remembering and retelling the past, acknowledging that those two processes are not identical. Oral narratives involve not only memory work but also decisions about sharing and censoring (Chamberlain, 1997). What is told is not necessarily all that is remembered. In her research with Bengali migrants in the East End of London, Katy Gardner (1999) refers to participants' 'narratives' or 'stories' rather than their 'memories' because, she argues, we can never know for sure what someone remembers. We only know what they choose to tell us.

I am aware that participants were not living records of historical events. Memory is the raw material of oral history but remembering is not a passive process (Thomson, 2019). Stories of the past are influenced, at least in part, by present contexts (Thomson, 2019). As Ritivoi (2002) argues, our stories of the past are constructed not only in relation to the present time and present selves but also in relation to present location. Moreover, Julia Brannen notes that 'life stories' are not neatly created through a clear chronology of events but interspersed with evaluation which is 'recounted from present time perspectives and with hindsight' (2013: para. 2.3). Indeed, lived experience 'is inevitably at times "messy" and hard to explain' (Ritivoi, 2002: 61). In her research with Barbadian migrants, Mary Chamberlain (1997) also noted that the oral narratives were not linear but 'mixed up' circular stories of family relationships often told without reference to specific years or dates. Hence, narratives may be more plot-driven than chronologically framed (Somers, 1994).

I am aware that, like Rachel Thomson, I 'forged a longitudinal account' (Thomson, 2007: 574), informed by my use of Elder's life course framework, around key life events such as migration, work, family formation and ageing. But that is not to suggest a simple linear notion of key life stages through time. The life course framework has been criticised for being overly linear (Collins and Shubin, 2015). I am mindful of this critique. Moreover, it is important to avoid heteronormative assumptions of key life stages such as marriage and parenthood (Botterill, 2014; Harris et al, 2020). Therefore, while drawing on the life course perspective, the stories presented in this book also show messy, uneven and sometimes circular accounts that challenge linear approaches to change over time.

Moreover, it is necessary to understand how personal stories are situated within and framed by dynamic socio-temporal contexts. Hence, while interested in character-driven network stories, I also try to understand the historical contexts within which these stories were situated. Therefore, I did intervene in narratives, sometimes, to seek clarity and understand the connections between the assorted cast of characters and the time period within which particular events unfolded. Another way in which I sought to understand the complexity of temporal dynamics was through follow-up interviews over extended periods of time.

Repeat interviewing over time

Reflecting on the past raises the challenge of recall, described already, so a different approach is to reinterview people at different stages in their lives to understand their experiences, attitudes and relationships at particular moments in time. The advantages of following up participants through qualitative longitudinal research (QLR) have been well established (Thomson and McLeod, 2015). While a one-off interview encounter may represent a snapshot frozen in time, repeated interviews over time may help to illuminate some of the spatio-temporal dynamics that shape individual narratives. Reinterviewing participants over time 'enables accounts to be collected as biographically transformative experiences are lived through and/or reflected upon and narrated' (Miller, 2015: 293). In so doing, we can gain an insight into 'the recursive, shifting and uneven ways in which identities take shape and in which we come to recognise and represent ourselves as certain kinds of people' (McLeod, 2003: 206).

For example, the plans and aspirations of young, single migrants may change significantly after they become parents. Moreover, the expectations of migrants in the aftermath of EU accession, and expansion of freedom of movement rights, may have been dramatically altered by the onset of Brexit a decade later (Erel and Ryan, 2019; Kilkey and Ryan, 2021; Mulholland and Ryan, 2022). As Tina Miller notes, QLR facilitates 'the establishment of an ongoing research relationship and "rapport" and the accessing of fluid and time-sensitive accounts of individual experiences, leading to a more nuanced understanding of temporal subjectivities' (2015: 293).

Nonetheless, repeat interviews raise a number of ethical and methodological challenges (see Ryan et al, 2016). For example, repeated interviews with participants may foster trust and encourage the sharing of more intimate information than a one-off interview between perfect strangers (Henderson et al, 2012). This compounds the anonymisation challenge, discussed earlier, and adds to the ethical sensitivities required in presenting such rich, detailed data about individual participants. Moreover, there are practical challenges to conducting QLR, especially over extended periods of time beyond the life of a specific research grant. As Farrall et al note, 'Attrition represents a significant obstacle to overcome in any longitudinal research project' (2016: 287). This is especially the case in qualitative studies that have a small sample to begin with and hence attrition can pose a real challenge over time. Without additional funding, it can be especially hard to maintain contact with participants over an extended period. One way in which I have sought to address that challenge is through adopting asynchronous methods of data collection.

The process of conducting interviews via email is emerging as a serious research method in the social sciences (Fritz and Vandermause, 2018). Unlike email surveys, interviewing via email is 'semi-structured in nature and involves multiple e-mail exchanges between the interviewer and interviewee over an extended period of time' (Meho, 2006: 1284). Emailing a series of questions to research participants allows them to respond in their own time, according to their schedule, as well as to reflect on and consider their answers before replying (Burns, 2010; Gibson, 2010). A key practical benefit of email-based research is its low cost, especially when one has no funding to support travel or transcription costs. However, some would question if this is a 'proper' interview method (for a discussion see Burns, 2010). Without face-to-face encounters, it is difficult to establish trust and rapport with participants (Meho, 2006). This was less of a problem in my studies because, in both studies where I used this method, I had already met all the participants in earlier phases of the research. Hence, I was building on rapport already established, albeit several years earlier, in face-to-face encounters.

Therefore, through my research career, I have used a range of methods to generate data about personal relationships, including semi-structured interviews, oral history and biography interviews, as well as some asynchronous approaches. These diverse experiences have informed how my approach to doing network research has emerged and developed in recent years.

Sociograms and interviews

In a number of different research projects, I have used sociograms embedded within in-depth interviews (Ryan et al, 2014; Ryan and D'Angelo, 2018; Ryan, 2021). In this section, I explain how my use of sociograms evolved across several different studies. I highlight the advantages but also the challenges of using this visualisation technique and the associated ethical issues (Tubaro et al, 2016; D'Angelo and Ryan, 2021; Tubaro et al, 2021).

As noted in Chapter 2, there have been calls for migration researchers to go beyond simplistic, metaphorical use of 'network' (Ryan and Dahinden, 2021), and instead to delve into the conceptual and methodological toolbox of SNA, including visualisation tools. As Bettina Hollstein notes, network visualisation is useful for collecting qualitative data and, when used in combination with in-depth interviews, enables the researcher to go beyond a 'merely metaphorical reference to the term network' (2011: 15). Thus, applying visualisation techniques adds depth and detail to accounts of interpersonal relationships. In fact, sociograms have a long history in network analysis and can be traced back to the pioneering work of Morena and Northway in the 1930s–40s (Freeman, 2000; Scott, 2011). Nonetheless, until recently, network visualisation has been underutilised (Conway, 2014). Over the last decade or so, developments in computer software packages, such as Pajek and Krackplot, have enabled more sophisticated graphics to build multi-layered visualisations of networks (Tubaro et al, 2016).

Therefore, it may be tempting to suggest that traditional pencil drawings of ego networks have become obsolete. Nevertheless, some researchers continue to use these simple visual tools, partly because they have the distinct advantage of being completed by participants during the interview – rather than post hoc in a computer lab (Ryan et al, 2014; Altissimo, 2016; Herz and Altissimo, 2021; Ryan, 2021).

The simplicity of Mary Northway's original 'target' design sociogram makes it ideal for generating data 'in an intuitive and easy way' (Carrasco et al, 2008: 9). Visualisation during interviews not only adds valuable detail on the size and structure of ego networks but also serves as a useful way of prompting memories and stories about particular relationships and for checking certain measures such as interpersonal closeness (Hogan et al, 2007; Bellotti, 2015). As Merluzzi and Burt (2013) note, researching networks involves a high level of memory work by participants. Remembering names and relationships, on the spot, can be burdensome. The graphical representation of relationships functions as a cognitive aid which helps to keep track of various ties discussed in the interview (Bellotti, 2015). In this way, these visual images also provide a 'strong stimulus for the production of narratives' (Hollstein, 2011: 15). I have found this to be the case in my own research, where completing the sociogram prompted participants to relate stories about specific alters and social ties that had not emerged in the earlier interview discussion.

But that is not to suggest that sociograms can accurately 'capture' networks in a tangible way. As noted in the previous chapter, network scholars such as Burt (1992) and Krackhardt (1987) already cautioned that network data should not be assumed to be an accurate reflection of 'reality' but rather as a product of perception and cognitive processes. Network data are not generated in a vacuum. The layout and design of the sociogram are important as these may influence how data are represented (Huang et al, 2007). In addition, the questions asked by the interviewer may influence how the network is visually depicted and verbally explained (Samuelsson et al, 1996).

Moreover, sociograms have been criticised for offering a snapshot of network composition at a moment in time (Conway, 2014; Tubaro et al, 2016), and therefore not useful for understanding dynamism over time. Nonetheless, as discussed elsewhere (D'Angelo and Ryan, 2021), combining a sociogram with an interview enables that dynamism to unfold through the narrative. Changing relations with friends, partners or work colleagues are woven through the narrative. The placing of alters is not only visible but also audible. The time taken, the hesitancy, forgetting, omitting and remembering alters, moving people around the sociogram and explaining that process become an important aspect of the data (Ryan et al, 2014; Ryan, 2021). These processes would not be apparent if the sociogram was completed alone, online or compiled post hoc by the researcher based on interview data.

Although I was aware of sociograms from the classic work of Barry Wellman (1984), I only began to use them in my research around 2012.[7] In a study with Jon Mulholland, assisted by PhD student Agnes Agoston, we used paper-based sociograms to visualise the social ties of highly skilled French migrants in London (Ryan, et al, 2014). This followed a simple paper-based design adapted from Wellman (see the image in Chua, Madej and Wellman, 2011) and Hersberger (2003). Participants wrote their contacts on a target diagram consisting of seven concentric circles, representing degrees of closeness,[8] divided into four quadrants labelled as friends, family, work, neighbours/hobbies/others (see the figures that follow). While the use of seven circles was inspired by Herberger (2003), I found that design rather cumbersome as participants often struggled to distinguish between so many circles. Therefore, I adapted and simplified the design to just three concentric circles in a subsequent study with Polish migrants (Ryan, 2016). In both studies, sociograms were embedded in an in-depth, face-to-face interview. The paper-based visual tool was introduced about 15 minutes into the interview. In most cases, it took participants about 20 minutes to complete the sociograms. After completing the sociogram, usually when the participant indicated that they could not think of anyone else to add, the interview continued with other related topics. The sociogram remained on the table, within view, and it was notable that participants frequently remembered other people and added them to the visual image. Thus, the oral interview and the visual picture were closely interconnected and informed each other in the generation of data.

Because I used 'free listing' (Widmer, 2006) participants could name as many or as few alters as they wished, so no limits were placed on the number of people included on the image. This resulted in a wide range of completed pictures (see examples throughout this book), with some participants naming large numbers of alters, while others named fewer. Of course, I was not interested in comparing the sociograms or in quantifying the number of ties. Instead, using a narrative approach, each sociogram and accompanying interview were analysed together as a set of data (see Ryan, 2021). Moreover, because I am interested in the individual style of each sociogram, I retain the original drawing and do not standardize using network software such as Vennmaker, for example.

I read and coded each interview transcript and sociogram together side by side. Unlike studies where sociograms are produced outside of an interview (see Bellotti, 2015), I used sociograms as completely integrated aspects of the interviews; therefore, story and picture were entirely interrelated. For example, the analysis process revealed how themes emerging in the interview, such as job seeking, prompted stories about particular alters who might be then hurriedly added to the sociogram. Alternatively, the act of completing the sociogram prompted participants to suddenly relate a story about a particular alter. It was not uncommon for participants to talk aloud and explain their decision-making process as they populated the sociograms, deciding who to add and who to omit. For example, in placing alters on the sociograms, Karina carefully weighed up the trustworthiness of specific individuals: "Maria is lovely but she's flighty so I would not count on her". Similarly, Irène deliberated about where on the sociogram to put her British in-laws. She seemed to feel an obligation to include them but also to accurately reflect their lukewarm relationship. In the end, after some reflection, she decided: "Pfff, I'll put them – let's be diplomatic".

The analysis, informed by critical reflexivity, also revealed my own role in probing for more information about particular alters or asking why some people who had seemed to be significant in a particular time, such as old friends in the origin country, had not been added to the sociogram. In answering such a question, Karina further elaborated that she was "terrible" at maintaining contact with long-distance friends; she had not made the effort to stay in touch with them. Thus, the analytical process explored not only the themes arising from the data but also the process of how that data were co-produced in the interview encounter.

Further exploring this theme, in the next section, I consider how generating network data needs to take account of processes of self-presentation.

The presentation of the network self

In a paper co-authored with Alessio D'Angelo (2021), we draw on Goffman to help us think through the methodological, epistemological and ethical issues arising from visualising social networks. We argued that between the participants' perception of their social ties and the ways in which those ties are visualised on paper, there is an important, though often overlooked, additional step – that is, the presentation of the network self. In other words, far from simply 'capturing' a network through visualisation techniques, researcher and participant are engaging in processes of co-constructing how that network looks. While the interviewer designs the questions and the visual tool and hence plays a key role in shaping how networks are defined within research processes, the participant seeks to present a particular self-image through descriptions of their interpersonal relationships. Nonetheless, the unfamiliarity of the sociogram may mean that participants are surprised by how the completed picture looks. Ewa, a participant in the Polish study, seemed genuinely surprised to observe that her sociogram consisted almost entirely of people living in England: "oh my goodness, it's all England". This prompted her to reflect aloud about her ties to Poland: "just thinking if I still maintain really close friendships in Poland". After some reflection, she added some people: "Actually, I'm not fair, I should put them in here" (adding cousins/aunts in Poland to the sociogram).

The mismatch between the image they sought to portray and the visualised image on the paper in front of them (D'Angelo and Ryan, 2021) can raise ethical concerns as it may expose participants to unexpected and uncomfortable results (Tubaro et al, 2021). When Adele, a participant in the French study, was visualising her network, she populated the picture with numerous social ties including a wide circle of friends (Ryan et al, 2014). Later in the course of the interview, she discussed the appeal of living in London and emphasised how the cosmopolitanism of the city especially attracted her. She spoke very positively about the diversity of ethnicities, cuisines, languages and music that make up London society. However, when attention was drawn back to the completed sociogram on the table, Adele seemed shocked and uncomfortable to observe that the social ties visualised in her network were entirely European and mostly French, Spanish and Italian. The cosmopolitan diversity of London did not feature at all in her personal network. There was an embarrassed silence. This was uncomfortable for both the researcher and the participant (Ryan et al, 2014).

As discussed elsewhere, asking a participant to visualise their relationships on paper carries particular ethical responsibilities over and above a more familiar oral question and answer interview format (Tubaro, et al 2021). The visualised image may show their social connections in a way that participants had not anticipated, as illustrated by the case of Adele. Therefore, great sensitivity is needed when using the method and it behoves researchers to pay attention to how the participant is reacting to the emerging picture. It may be necessary to create additional space for the participant to reflect and talk upon their reactions, if appropriate (D'Angelo and Ryan, 2021).

To further illustrate my framework of telling network stories and highlight the value of including a sociogram within in-depth interviews, I now present a thick description – Adrianna's story.

Adrianna's story

Adrianna, a law graduate, came to London in 1999 with the intention of learning English before returning to Poland to qualify as a lawyer: "I thought it would be nice to come to the UK just for a year to learn a bit of language since I couldn't speak any English at all". As this move occurred before Poland joined the EU and its citizens gained access to freedom of movement, Adrianna required a visa and so registered with a language school. Thus, her narrative unfolded within specific socio-temporal contexts and associated immigration regulations.

Social ties enabled Adrianna's move to London: "a friend from high school, came to the UK four years earlier, helped me with finding accommodation and finding a school where I could do a course". Unable to speak any English, Adrianna relied entirely on Polish networks to find work as a cleaner: "word of mouth through a friend who just stopped being a cleaner who moved to another position". This pattern of people finding replacements to take over jobs, especially as they moved to better jobs, was common among participants.

Although ethnic networks can result in clustering in niche jobs (Anthias and Cederberg, 2009), because of English language barriers, Adrianna had no option but to rely on these networks. Despite being a university graduate, Adrianna experienced downward occupational mobility by becoming a cleaner: "obviously I couldn't ask really for more bearing in mind that I wasn't able to speak any English … I looked at it, it's a temporary measure. It's not like I'm doing it forever".

However, Adrianna's migration project soon changed as she "met a boy". The boyfriend, now husband, was a refugee from a Middle Eastern country who had no plans to return to his country of origin or to move to Poland. So, according to Adrianna's narrative, remaining in London now began to seem more likely. As she laughingly added: "I never managed to buy the return ticket".

Adrianna described how her own aspirations changed: "I worked as a cleaner for a couple of years while I was going to school to learn, trying to learn the language and then when I felt more confident, I thought well maybe it's time I do something else … I better get a proper job". Deskilling may be overcome if migrants can access appropriate language support and training opportunities (Trevena, 2013; Parutis, 2014). According to the level of available resources, networks can support occupational mobility (Ryan, 2016; Badwi et al, 2018). However, accessing resource-rich networks can be challenging for migrants. Among Adrianna's initial contacts in London, domestic cleaning was the most common occupation. Cleaners usually work alone and rarely come into contact with anyone apart from their employers. It is possible that these employers may be beneficial in some way and could serve as vertical weak ties. Although Adrianna worked in affluent households in a part of North London famous for celebrity residents, it seems that no employer offered to help her get a better job. Thus, it should not be inferred that knowing affluent people will necessarily result in shared resources.

Adrianna decided to gain new experience through volunteering: "I found a charity and I thought that's something that relates to my degree so I decided to become a volunteer". For two years, she volunteered at the charity several times a week, while working as a cleaner and studying English. Adrianna said it was very hard work but her husband was a huge source of support and encouragement: "he would support me through the bad days and good days – he always believed in me".

Volunteering gave Adrianna access to new opportunities: "I met a lot of really nice people and they were very supportive as well so I would say I learned a lot from them". At the charity, Adrianna met a Cypriot woman who was to become a major influence on her career development: "We worked very closely. I was doing admin … she would try to get me involved.

It wasn't just photocopying or sending a letter, she wanted me to learn something from this experience". This Cypriot woman fulfils many of the characteristics of a 'vertical weak tie' (see Chapter 2) who imparted valuable information and opportunities to Adrianna. When the charity advertised a paid job, Adrianna was encouraged to apply: "I was successful and I've been there ever since, which is nearly ten years". Over that time, her role has expanded and she is now the senior administrator for the large charity. Having built her career, Adrianna was keen to help other Polish migrants and started volunteering every weekend at a Polish Saturday school.

Adrianna's story illustrates many of the themes introduced in Chapter 2 and further elaborated in later chapters. In some ways, her story appears to confirm a linear trajectory: from initial dependency on dense co-ethnic ties, for low-skilled cleaning jobs, to a gradual expansion of ties to access bridging social capital through a weak tie in a professional occupation, who helped Adrianna to get a "proper job" commensurate with her qualifications. However, beyond this simple linearity, using network stories, including visualisation, suggests a more nuanced picture of relationality.

Her well-populated sociogram (see Figure 3.1) suggests numerous ties across several locations. Adrianna took great care over the picture, seemed keen to be as accurate as possible and was concerned about missing people out: "Oh gosh, suddenly I can't remember". After more than 15 years in London, her sociogram illustrated the enduring importance of Polish networks both locally in London and transnationally to family and friends in Poland. Moreover, the sociogram, coupled with her rich narrative, presented a story of how relationships evolve over time. Over the years, her weak tie, to the Cypriot woman at work, developed into a "close friend", emphasised by an added circle around the initials 'MS': "a lady I consider a really, really good friend ... She's an incredible person and as a friend she has always your best interests". This story indicates how weak ties change over time and may, in certain circumstances, even become strong ties. The sociogram also suggested marked continuity in friendship groups, as several of Adrianna's London friends were people she initially met in 1999 on her English language course. Completing the sociogram prompted reflections about time constraints and investment in friendships: "life here is very demanding sometimes – we don't have time to socialise and even going for a cup of coffee". Her narrative emphasised the centrality of her husband ('AG' on the sociograms), who was her primary source of emotional and practical support.

As illustrated by this thick description of Adrianna, analysing network stories through words and pictures offers insights into dynamic interpersonal relationships, flows of resources and the relative social location of actors, situated within and framed by specific socio-temporal contexts. These themes will be revisited throughout this book.

Figure 3.1: Adrianna's sociogram

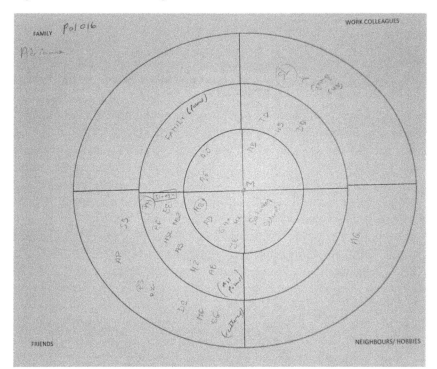

Conclusion

In this and the previous chapter, I set out my epistemological, empirical and methodological approach. Through the conceptual framework of 'telling network stories' (Ryan, 2021), I am interested in how personal networks are co-constructed by interviewer and interviewee within research contexts, informed by particular spatio-temporal settings.

This chapter had four aims. Firstly, I have sought to contribute to techniques for researching change over time. Drawing on Elder's life course framework, but mindful of avoiding simple linearity, I have adopted two related techniques. Engaging with participants who migrated in different periods, from the 1940s through to the 2010s, I have sought to understand the salience of historical time. Furthermore, by reinterviewing particular participants repeatedly over many years, I have sought to understand changes through biographical time. In so doing, I aimed to show the interconnectedness of macro, spatio-temporal contexts and micro, biographical life experiences and the mediating role of relational ties.

No new data were collected for this book. Instead, I revisited and synthesised qualitative data generated over 20 years of my migration research in London (see the Appendix). By describing the process of reanalysing that combined data set and the challenge of how to present the data in meaningful and digestible ways to readers, using thick descriptions, this chapter's second aim was to contribute to empirical, methodological and analytical techniques associated with revisiting existing data sets. As it is increasingly difficult to obtain research funding to generate new data, there may be advantages to revisiting existing data sets through different lenses to gain new insights.

Thirdly, building on the conceptual framework of telling network stories, presented in Chapter 2, this chapter described how that approach can be used in practice by using a combination of oral narratives (stories) and visual techniques (pictures). Far from approaching networks as a fixed entity to be captured and measured, I use an interpretivist framework to understand how networks are perceived and presented by research particulars. Moreover, I am interested in the dynamic, intersubjective interactions between participants and myself through which data are presented, generated and crafted (White and Drew, 2011; D'Angelo and Ryan, 2021).

Finally, this chapter adopted an intersectional lens to address multi-positionalities and the ethics of reflexivity in the research process. There is growing interest in the ethical dimensions of social network research (Tubaro, et al, 2021). However, rather than reflexivity as a form of self-indulgent narcissism on the part of the researcher (Pillow, 2003), I argue that considering how data were generated, including the complexities, confusions, emotions and messiness, is an important aspect of the research process (Ryan, 2008a).

Having explained my methods, the next chapter presents my analysis of narratives of arrival and discusses how participants relate their migration decision making and the journey process through stories of interpersonal relationships.

4

Social Networks and Stories of Arrival

Introduction

As Barry Wellman (1997) has noted, social network research can be polarised into quantification of social ties at one end of the spectrum and metaphorical descriptions at the other end. Similarly, in migration studies, research that, on the one hand, seeks to measure migrant networks, by counting ties, or, on the other hand, merely refers to the role of networks in some vague, metaphorical way, each risks simplifying complex and dynamic relationships. Indeed, merely describing the existence of ties tells us very little about how they may be implicated in migration decision-making processes. Hence, it may be misleading to simply infer causality between pre-existing network ties and migration (D'Angelo and Ryan, 2021).

Drawing on the framework of 'telling network stories', this chapter's primary aim is to contribute to deeper explorations and understandings of the multidimensional, messy and nuanced role of different relational ties in narratives of migration decision making and arrival in London. Following Borgatti et al (2009), I seek to *analyse* rather than merely *describe* social ties. Moreover, as discussed in Chapter 2, networks are a product of perception and cognitive processes (Krackhardt, 1987). Analysing network stories, I am interested in how participants perceive and present various social connections and narrate how these relationships may have shaped their migration projects.

In so doing, the chapter's second aim is to go beyond the merely 'metaphorical' use of networks within migration studies (Bilecen et al, 2018), to gain nuanced understandings not only of the meaning of relationships, but also the varied actors involved and the roles they play within network stories, as well as the sorts of resources that seem to be accessed and shared. My diverse participants present opportunities to analyse different arrival routes, including, for example, students, family migrants, intra-company transferees (ICTs), refugees and those directly recruited from abroad. Many, though not all, had pre-existing ties to friends or relatives in London. Using rich narratives, including thick descriptions, I explore how migration decision making can involve varied and even competing interpersonal relationships. Therefore, the chapter challenges simplistic assumptions about the apparent lure of strong ties, or the role of dyadic weak ties, as well as offering insights into negative ties and fleeting ties in migration processes.

Thirdly, this chapter aims is to understand change over time. The varied entry routes of my participants over more than seven decades, from the 1940s to the 2010s, demonstrates changing immigration processes over time. Plummer (2002) notes that personal stories are framed by particular sociopolitical contexts. As the stories in this chapter indicate, the role of relational ties, and the resources circulating therein, may vary through different historical periods and routes of arrival. For example, it is interesting to consider if the rise of the internet has changed the role of interpersonal networks in stories of migration decision making and planning.

We begin with Howard's story of arrival, which highlights many themes that will be explored through this chapter.

Howard's story

I met Howard in 2019, when he was 82 years old, as part of a study on ageing, care and migration.[1] During the interview, he explained how and why he migrated to London 60 years earlier. In 1956, while working in a sugar cane factory in Guyana, Howard was persuaded by his uncle to seek new opportunities in England.

> 'I had no intention or had never thought about coming here. But one day an uncle of mine, he's roughly about two years older than me, we got chatting and he says: "Would you like to go to England?" "England, what for?" He said "Well there's lots of opportunities over there that you can't get here". ... I was about 19 at the time. And he says "There's lot of entertainment over there, you know, which we don't have here and you can get work and the money is good and all that". ... So, I thought that sounds like fun, yeah, let's go for it.' (Howard, 1950s)

It is noteworthy that Howard tells the story through seemingly verbatim extracts of conversation from six decades earlier. This is, of course, probably a well-honed story retold many times over the years. I am not seeking to assess the veracity of the account. Instead, my interest is how the story is presented to convey the role of social ties in migration processes. As noted earlier, narratives can be driven more by plot and characters than by accurate details (Somers, 1994).

Howard related how his parents "were shocked" about his decision to move to London. Nonetheless, they agreed that he could go if it was what he really wanted. Although Howard had a steady job and lived a comfortable life with his parents, his uncle encouraged him to move halfway across the world to London in pursuit of fun and adventure. This story shows the persuasive power of particular social ties in migration narratives. It is likely, of course, that this youthful uncle, who was in his early 20s, wanted to go and needed companionship. Shortly afterwards, the two young men set off on the long ocean voyage: "being a young person, it was a bit frightening, you know, but luckily I had my uncle with me and we both supported each other". Before leaving home, Howard wrote to his close friend, Andy, who had moved to London sometime earlier. Andy agreed to meet them upon their arrival.

As Plummer (2002) reminds us, stories need to be understood within specific sociohistorical contexts. In the 1950s, because of the colonial legacy, Guyanese citizens were officially 'British subjects' and could travel to, and work in, Britain without visas. Moreover, English was the official language of Guyana. Thus, although geographically far away, Britain seemed culturally close. However, the reality of Britain was often different from expectations, as Howard recounted: "when I landed at Euston and Andy came to meet me, he says 'Welcome to London'. I says 'This is London?' He said 'Yes, why?' I said 'Man, look at this place, it's all black and filthy, cold, wet, damp'. I was shocked".

Andy appears in the story as a reliable friend who helped Howard and his uncle to find accommodation. The continued support of Andy proved invaluable because, shortly after arrival, the uncle went off to live with other friends, leaving 19-year-old Howard alone in an unfamiliar city. This story illustrates that while migration is framed by wider sociopolitical structures, it may be also enacted within dynamic social relationships of friends and relatives. Despite a seemingly strong kinship tie, the relationship with Howard's uncle proved fragile and unreliable. Thus, as discussed later, one cannot assume that trusted levels of support flow through kinship ties.

Howard's early experiences in London did not match his expectations and, when winter arrived, he felt miserable and, missing home comforts, moved back to Guyana. However, after a few months, he started to feel bored and decided to return to London. Howard's arrival story illustrates many themes that will be further developed through this chapter. In addition, we will return to hear more from Howard in later chapters.

Contextualising the lure of strong ties

Like Howard, many participants recounted how ties to close relatives or friends seemed to influence decision making. Bernadette was attending a technical college in Ireland, training to be a secretary, in the 1950s. Her friend, Lizzy, had gone to train as a nurse in England: "Then the letters came and for nine months I was bombarded with letters telling me of the glories of [hospital] and I then decided that I was following her over here".

In this narrative, it seems that Bernadette, rather like Howard, had little intention of migrating. In both cases, the decision of these teenagers to pack up and move to Britain seemed to be guided largely by one influential actor in their network. While Howard was guided by his young uncle, for Bernadette, being "bombarded" with letters from her friend Lizzie seems to have been pivotal in shaping her plans. The encouragement, example and support of a strong tie were often highly influential in stories of migration.

Among the more recent migrants, a similar pattern of influential actors seems to be apparent. Sonia, from Poland, described how her friend encouraged her to move to London: "so my friend was living here for two years already and she said 'come and visit, try to get the job – if you can't, at least you improve your English, and then we'll see how it goes'". Sonia travelled to London for a visit in 2004 and enjoyed the experience so much that she returned in 2005 with a view to staying longer and exploring opportunities for study and work.

Marika narrated how, in 2004, aged 18 years old, she decided to move to London:

> 'I actually just finished my studies in Poland and my friend, she was really fixed on, you know, coming to London, so I decided yeah, why not. And we travelled together and she was studying History and Spanish. When I arrived, I wasn't really sure which university ... she chose [University in London] and so I thought, why not, let's try. And this is how I ended up at the same university.' (Marika, Poland, 2000s)

Although 50 years after Howard's and Bernadette's migrations, these stories show remarkable similarity and reveal the enduring influence of close friends in shaping migration decision making. Marika, like Howard, was encouraged to accompany someone who was determined to migrate to London. While Sonia, like Bernadette, was attracted to join a close friend who was already in Britain.

As discussed elsewhere (Ryan, 2008b; Ryan et al 2008), many of the migrants I interviewed, across numerous studies, had at least one pre-existing tie in London, usually to a friend but sometimes also a relative. However, it would be simplistic to explain migration purely in terms of the lure of strong social ties. Contextual factors also need to be taken into consideration as options to migrate are framed by wider geopolitical factors. Immigration regimes change over time in ways that can close down or open up routes for migrants. Before Poland joined the EU in 2004, migration to Britain required a particular set of strategies and support systems.

Mateusz initially visited London for a "gap year" in 1995. Returning to Poland to complete his degree, he was determined to move back to London as soon as possible: "In 1998, I left immediately after I was done with my degree in Psychology. I didn't feel like I wanted an adult life in Poland … and the struggles which I thought went with it, you know". However, in order to secure his immigration status in Britain, Mateusz had to register with a language school:

> '[Y]ou know, we're talking about 1998 so it was very different immigration status to what it is now … One had to manoeuvre, you know, and one could not always tell the whole truth … crossing the border every time and having to explain yourself – "I'm here to study English", "how much longer you want to study English?" I never did study English really – it was always, to be honest, the deposit paid to the school, numerous school of languages, you know, *Mickey Mouse School of Languages*, which sort of allowed me to return time and time again.' (Mateusz, Poland, 1990s)

This narrative paints a vivid picture of navigating border crossings before Polish citizens gained EU freedom of movement. Mateusz never attended the language school; instead, he worked without documents in the shadow economy. Although he presented his migration narrative as an individual story of adventure and self-discovery, it emerged that he did have an important set of social ties in London who helped and supported his migration. During his first visit in 1995, he rented a room from a Polish landlady and her British husband. Upon returning in 1998, he had arranged to live with them again. By now they had become like a "pseudo-family". We will return to Mateusz's story in later chapters to see how his network enabled him to navigate changing immigration regimes and develop a career in London.

The backdrop of wider sociocultural contexts in framing migration stories is also apparent in the case of Oliwia: "I was finishing my second degree in Poland, there was not really much to do, like my country had nothing to offer and a couple of my friends were already here and obviously they were saying how amazing it is". In addition to the lure of strong ties, Oliwia suggests other reasons for wanting to leave rural Poland where her family owned a farm:

> 'I always wanted more from life … Growing up on a farm, my parents had a really hard life … I didn't see them enjoying life and they never had time for it. They had to work … and you wake up one day and you're 80 and your life is gone, and you've never seen anything and

you've never done anything and actually who are you? You know, you just worked, just married whoever came along, in Poland, you just have to marry because then you are, you got that stigma. It's, I think, it's probably similar in Ireland.' (Oliwia, Poland, 2000s)

This narrative suggests an interplay of factors. Although initially Oliwia suggested that her migration was largely influenced by her friends who told her how "amazing" London was, later her narrative revealed a more nuanced picture as she sought to avoid the hard life of her farming parents. It was interesting that Oliwia, knowing I was Irish, made this direct comparison with rural life and expectations of marriage in Ireland. Indeed, her story chimes with many of my Irish interviewees, albeit from an earlier generation. The interplay of networks, job opportunities and the desire to escape a life of hardship was also narrated by Deirdre, an Irish migrant from the 1940s: "my sister went nursing to England and then my other sister followed her there ... I joined her to take up nursing as well because you didn't want to stay around there and just marry a farmer and work hard all your life". There is remarkable similarity in the story of Deirdre, who left Ireland in the 1940s, and Oliwia, who left Poland in the 2000s. Both women migrated with the lively encouragement of siblings or friends who had already moved abroad. Both were drawn by the promised opportunities and quality of life awaiting them in Britain. While, at first glance, the migration narratives of Oliwia and Deirdre appear to evidence the lure of strong ties (friends and kin), on deeper probing it becomes apparent that these network stories are framed by wider sociohistorical contexts (Plummer, 2002). These narratives vividly reveal the salience of structural factors in the origin country. The prospects for women in rural, farming communities appeared limited, and so migration was also motivated, in part, by an active decision to reject married life and hard work on a farm. Therefore, without wishing to deny the lure of strong ties, one needs to be cautious in drawing a simple conclusion about their causal role in migration.

Moreover, it would be simplistic to assume that strong ties only operate in one direction, as so-called 'pull factors'. Kathleen's story, presented in the introductory chapter, illustrates how she felt torn between her cousin and sister who wanted her to join them in London and her older sister who tried to encourage her to remain in Ireland. The older sister even found Kathleen a local job in the hope of persuading her to stay. Kathleen's story suggests how migrants may need to navigate competing influences, reminding us that 'a network' is not a singular entity operating in one direction.

My framework of telling network stories provides insights into the meaning, emotions and aspirations of migration and, in so doing, enables a deeper understanding of the complex interpersonal relationships within particular social ties, as revealed by Emer's story. Emer moved from Ireland to train as a nurse in London in 1955. Although she had an aunt who was a nurse in the city, Emer explained her dislike of this relative: "she wasn't a very nice woman". Although this aunt tried to persuade her niece into a particular hospital, Emer narrated her own sense of agency, as a rebellious teenager, who rejected this advice and applied independently to a different hospital. This narrative suggests some caution in drawing simple causality between social ties and outcomes. On the surface, it would be easy to conclude that Emer went to London and became a nurse because of the influence of a strong tie between aunt and niece. But Emer herself rejected that association and instead sought to assert her own preferences in opposition to the influence of an aunt whom she disliked. In this way, nuanced network stories allow perceptions and interpretations of interpersonal relationships to emerge beyond superficial descriptions and implied causality.

While ties to siblings, cousins and friends feature prominently in many narratives, there are also indications of the ways in which 'weak ties' may shape migration decision making.

Weak ties – though often in tandem with strong ties

In Barbados in 1957 a young woman named Phyllis had no thoughts of migration, when she went to a recruitment office to enquire about local jobs:

> 'There was a gentleman there that knew my family. He said "Listen, do you want to go to England?" At the time, I knew nothing about this emigration to England – I had never even heard about it. So, he said "You go over that side to that table and you put your name down over there, you register there", and that was how I get to England.' (Phyllis, Barbados, 1950s)

In the 1950s recruitment from the Caribbean to Britain mostly involved men (Brannen et al, 2016), so, it is hardly surprising that Phyllis had not considered this option for herself. The recruitment officer, who knew her family and so could be considered a weak tie, appears to have been instrumental in persuading Phyllis to sign up for a job in Britain. Once she signed up, Phyllis recounted how the process moved quite swiftly: "Then a few days later I got the letter to be ready to come to England and I didn't even know where I was going". Phyllis described how her sudden departure surprised her family, especially her grandmother who was shocked and saddened by the decision: "When I told my grandmother that I was going she said, 'Are you mad? Are you going to England, that cold place – what are you going there for'?"

Phyllis was assigned a job with British Transport based in the English Midlands where she knew no one and where there were very few other Black people at that time. Soon afterwards, Phyllis left the Midlands and moved to London to join a fellow Barbadian. Phyllis's story chimes with the experiences of other Caribbean migrants from that era who went to a particular location because of a job but later relocated to be near friends or relatives (Phoenix and Brannen, 2014; Chamberlain, 2017; Bauer, 2018). So even when networks do not influence the initial migration, they may be a factor in subsequent location selection. Phyllis's contact in London was not a close friend, but a young man whose mother, a neighbour in Barbados, had asked Phyllis to connect with and keep in touch. Interestingly, Phyllis later married that young man.

Phyllis's migration story illustrates the different roles of key players: a weak tie (family friend/recruitment officer), her grandmother, a neighbour and a male friend (later to become her husband). A similar interconnected web of relationships is apparent in Dymphna's migration story.

Using an oral history approach (see Chapter 3), I asked Dymphna to "tell me about how you came to London to train as a nurse". In response, she narrated a long and detailed story. In 1951 Dymphna's life was rocked by the sudden death of her beloved father. The family was left in reduced financial circumstances and her widowed mother struggled to cope. Aged 17, Dymphna realised she would have to quit education and get a job to support the family. There were no job opportunities in their village in Ireland. A neighbour, whose daughter was nursing in Britain, suggested Dymphna should consider that option: "one day, Maureen's mother (you see Maureen there in the photo), … 'Why don't you go nursing,' she said. … And then Dr Mac came down and he said he would ring the hospital where Maureen had put in her application form".

In this short extract from her story, we can already see a cast of characters coming into play. A friend, Maureen, appears not only as an actor in the initial migration story but is also present in the room during the interview through her photograph on the mantelpiece. The photo symbolises Maureen's enduring importance as someone to whom, over 50 years later, Dymphna still felt an emotional attachment. However, it is not Maureen but her mother who actively encourages Dymphna to apply for nursing in London. Dymphna, still grieving her father, seems unsure how to proceed. At this point a weak tie enters the plot. In 1950s rural Ireland, few people held more influence than the local doctor. This influential character seems to play the classic role of a weak tie: not an intimate family friend or relative but rather a more distant contact (Granovetter, 1973). Moreover, as discussed in Chapter 2, this type of person can be considered a vertical weak tie (Ryan, 2011a) because of their valuable expertise and the capacity to span social distance in order to access professional contacts beyond the reach of other network members. Furthermore, his willingness to share those resources (social capital) is apparent in the fact that he made the very expensive international phone call to the London hospital.

Nonetheless, as noted elsewhere (Ryan, 2022), although influential sources of valuable social capital, weak ties should not be understood as detached from wider social connections. In the cases of Dymphna and Phyllis, the weak tie was someone known to the family and hence trusted to give reliable information and advice. My analysis suggests that weak ties may be nested within wider webs of relationships (Ryan, 2016; 2022). In other words, rather than viewing a weak tie as a single, isolated dyadic relationship (Granovetter, 1973), it may be useful to explore how some weak ties are situated within a broader network. In so doing, one may gain insight into why weak ties are motivated to share their social capital by offering help, advice and assistance. This issue is further explored in Chapter 5.

It would be misleading to imply that migrations were simply motivated by economic factors. Indeed, as the stories so far reveal, migration decision making was also informed by relationality, fun and adventure. Moreover, as discussed in the next section, narratives often describe how relationships, including romantic ties, may be woven into migration stories alongside economic and wider structural factors.

Romance and marriage migration: looking beyond dyads

Among my participants, both male and female, there are examples of migration motivated, at least in part, by romance.[2] Daragh, from Ireland, who will be discussed in more detail in Chapter 5, recounted how he moved to London to be reunited with the English girlfriend he met while travelling in Australia. Catriona, also discussed in more detail in a later chapter, narrated her migration primarily as a desire to join her Irish boyfriend who was studying at a university on the south coast of England. Martyna met her London-based boyfriend during his frequent visits back home to Poland. For a while, the couple commuted back and forth but then Martyna explained how she decided to join him in London to give the relationship a chance to develop. At that time, she arrived with open plans, unsure how the relationship would proceed. All three examples mentioned here benefited from immigration rights that enabled them to move to Britain with open plans to see if a relationship would work out.

Several participants explained their arrival in Britain through family reunion routes. For example, Reema arrived from Pakistan in the 1970s to join her husband; similarly, Jennah moved from India in the 1990s to join her husband. We will return to their stories in later chapters. Simply referring to people as marriage migrants or saying that someone's migration was motivated by romance actually tells us very little about the complexity of their particular situation. The risk of labelling their migration as 'romance' or 'marriage' is that it focuses only on a dyadic tie between two people. Adopting a networks lens, as Wellman (1979) notes, allows us to look beyond mere dyads to understand how even the most intimate of relations are situated within wider webs of interpersonal connections. I argue that network stories can illustrate how relationships are rarely about just two people and indeed romantic ties may involve complex negotiations among multiple actors.

Wiktoria's migration story began when, as a student in Poland, she was invited to visit London for a holiday in 2005: "a friend lived here and she suggested that I could come and visit her for the summer holiday". So here we see the direct role of an alter (a friend) in encouraging mobility, albeit an extended holiday. But, as the story unfolds, another significant character enters the plot. During the holiday in London, Wiktoria met a Turkish young man and started a romance. Over the following years, Wiktoria narrated a complex story of moving back and forth between London and Poland, which I found difficult to follow in the interview. Rereading the transcript, I was struck by how often I interrupted the story to try to clarify some temporal sequencing. As discussed in Chapter 2, plot-driven narratives may not follow a clear chronological sequence (Somers, 1994). In 2008 the couple had a baby. However, rather than cementing their commitment together in London, the birth of the baby instead prompted Wiktoria to return to Poland to be close to her own parents for help with childcare. Her lack of support networks in London markedly contrasted with the ready availability of networks in Poland and underlines the enduring salience of propinquity for hands-on care, especially childcare (Ryan, 2007a).

Nevertheless, it gradually became apparent that long-distance separation strained the marriage. Wiktoria hoped the situation could have been resolved by her husband moving to Poland, but he considered this to be unrealistic as he did not speak Polish and was unlikely to get the kind of well-paid job he enjoyed in London. So, in 2011, after six years of transnational mobility, Wiktoria decided to settle in London. However, she explained, this decision came at a cost and, as the mother of a 3-year-old, she found herself bereft of networks: "I was missing that support, and my husband was working long hours, so basically I was left alone with my son, just a bit exhausting".

Wiktoria's story suggests the complexity and even the potential competition between social ties within a network. While wanting to create a family unit with her husband and son, she also wanted to avail of the emotional and practical support of her parents and extended family. Wiktoria felt torn between the most salient people in her life: her husband and her parents. She tried to overcome this dilemma by travelling back and forth and spending time with both sets of ties. But this was exhausting, disruptive and ultimately unsustainable, especially as her son got older and schooling became a consideration. Her story illustrates the immense emotional strain that Wiktoria endured for several years and how her migration decision making was defined not so much by her own aspirations but rather by the needs and priorities of other people, especially her husband and her son.

Like Wiktoria, the story of Chantal, an IT engineer from France, illustrates how family migration strategies may involve competing priorities and obligations among kinship ties and highly gendered caring roles. Chantal's husband, also French, was transferred by his bank from Paris to London and initially he commuted weekly between the two cities, on the Eurostar train. Meanwhile, Chantal maintained her job and their son attended school in Paris. However, over several years, it became apparent that commuting was unsustainable. So, in 1996, Chantal made the decision to leave her job in France and move, with their son, to join the husband in London. This was a difficult decision for Chantal and involved considerable sacrifice on her part. As noted elsewhere in the literature, it is often women who have to adjust their own careers to fit into family migration plans (Ackers, 2004; Kofman et al, 2005). Moreover, Chantal was leaving dense networks to arrive in a context where she knew no one except her husband. This lack of local connections proved to be a serious problem when the couple's second child was born with a life-threatening illness. Bereft of support networks in London, Chantal turned to her family who lived in the south of France and drew on her parents for hands-on care. She remarked: "At least when I was with my parents, there were three people to look after the two children". This was necessary because her husband "was working like mad".

Chantal's narrative again highlights the salience of relationality but also propinquity in migration stories. Her husband, school-age son, seriously ill baby and her parents are not only key players in Chantal's story, but also frame her migratory movements. While initially she did not move – rather, it was her husband who commuted – ultimately, it was Chantal who needed to uproot and relocate to address the needs of others, firstly moving to London to join her husband, but becoming a regular commuter, flying to the south of France, to avail of hands-on support from her parents. Moreover, Chantal's story highlights the ways in which relationships, and the associated flow resources, are connected to specific places: London, Paris and the more distant south of France, with implications for travel and related costs.

Clearly, migration motives are multi-layered and, as seen in the case of Wiktoria and Chantal, may change over time, especially if migrants move back and forth. Therefore, it is important to avoid a simple linear view of migration trajectories. Moreover, as discussed earlier in the case of Mateusz, personal migration narratives need to be understood within shifting geopolitical contexts. These points are well illustrated in the story of Parisa. Born in Iran, Parisa initially moved to London in the 1970s as a student.

She met and married a British man and so, although initially motivated by study, her migration narrative became a story of romance. She and her husband then returned to Iran where they lived for several years and had two children. However, following the Revolution in 1979, they decided to flee the country. Parisa explained how their return to Britain was expected to be temporary:

> '[T]hat was a joke for us Iranians, no one believed that the Revolution would last. We came here in 1980 – we felt that things would settle down in Iran. We felt that things would return to normal. For example, we left our car in the garage thinking that we would go back soon when things settled.' (Parisa, Iran, 1980s)

As noted in the previous chapter, narratives often include specific details to conjure up a vivid picture of past events and capture a palpable sense of emotion (Somers, 1994). Leaving the family car in the garage powerfully evokes an expectation of imminent return. Parisa's story is very much a relational narrative (Mason, 2004). Her husband and children are key players in her story. She vividly described their challenges in trying to adjust to life in London. Having fled their house and spacious garden in Teheran, she said their lives became "miniaturised" in a small London flat with no garden and she experienced a "kind of depression". In an effort to forge new relationships, she joined other Iranian refugees in setting up a "Persian Saturday school" where their children could maintain links with the language and culture. Through volunteering at this school, Parisa gradually created a network of friends and began to build a new life in London. The role of relationality in migrants' stories of embedding (Mulholland and Ryan, 2022) in London will be discussed further in Chapter 6.

So far, we have focused on positive, supportive relationships to people who encouraged or enabled migration. But social ties are not necessarily positive and it is important to also address the role of so-called negative ties.

Negative ties

As noted in Chapter 3, research on social networks, especially using standard techniques such as surveys and name generators, tend to focus on positive ties – in other words, relationships that provide practical support. Moreover, in researching migrant networks, questions that ask 'who encouraged or enabled your migration?' tend to elicit information about positive ties. Researchers need to pay more attention to so-called 'negative ties' (Everett and Borgatti, 2014). Negative ties cover a spectrum of relationships, including people we dislike or disagree with, as well as those who may do us serious harm (Labianca, et al, 1998; Del Real, 2019). In telling their migration stories, my participants often mentioned conflictual relationships. Their decisions to migrate may involve a web of different actors including some who supported them and others who sought to constrain them. These stories can reveal insights into the power dynamics underpinning particular relationships.

Rukhsana, originally from Afghanistan, arrived in London in the early 1990s as a marriage migrant. Her husband, also Afghan, had lived in Britain for many years. She explained how the marriage came about:

> 'My husband lived here before me. His family was friends with my family. His brother came to my home and asked for me to marry his brother in London. It was an arranged marriage. I never met him. I only saw a photo. I often think why did I accept that? I am an educated lady. ... I thought I could study in London.' (Rukhsana, Afghanistan, 1990s)

Thus, although Rukhsana migrated through marriage, her desire to move to London was also motivated by aspirations to study and develop a career. She did not know her husband, had no contacts in Britain and was entering a completely unfamiliar situation. Her brother-in-law, who brokered the marriage, travelled with her to London and continued to live with the couple, where he proved to be a controlling influence. The marriage was unhappy. Rukhsana described how the brothers blocked her opportunities to study or work. Because she had no money, no access to resources outside the home and little understanding of her rights, Rukhsana felt trapped. The negative tie to both her husband and his brother proved to be an extremely powerful relationship that sought to control every aspect of her life. Without any local networks of friends or relatives, she suffered from isolation and loneliness. Rukhsana seemed keen to tell me this story. Surviving abuse and escaping from the marriage framed her narrative. When I met her in 2010, she was working with other abuse survivors and clearly felt it was necessary for women to talk about their experiences. We will return to Rukhsana's story in a later chapter to see how she managed to forge new networks and rebuild her life.

While in some cases, like Rukhsana's, participants appear willing to talk about negative ties, in other cases, it may remain unspoken with just an occasional hint to an untold story. In the case of Gabi, a participant from Poland, the role of a negative tie in influencing her migration decision making only emerged very slowly through her story.

Gabi initially described her migration from Poland through a narrative of adventure but also personal growth and development. A graduate, she had previously worked in the USA in a hotel and developed her English language skills to a high level of proficiency. However, immigration regimes provided a crucial framing context to her story: "in America, getting Green Card is really hard. … I was told that getting Green Card is going to take like years because I don't have any relatives in America". By contrast, in the UK, because of EU freedom of movement, at that time, she could work without visa restrictions. Moreover, social ties also were significant as Gabi had a close friend in London who offered a place to stay: "I can come and stay with my friend for a month".

When I met her in 2014, Gabi had lived in London for eight years and was working as an accountant. Thus, at first glance, it seems that she had made a pragmatic decision based on career aspirations, language skills, immigration regimes and the support of a good friend. Only later in the interview did Gabi mention that she used to be married in Poland. She then explained how the desire to leave this marriage motivated her migration: "I was in a relationship at that time. I wanted to separate and I thought if I stay in the UK … it's going to be easier for us to separate". The desire to escape this negative tie (an unhappy marriage in Poland) was clearly a very significant factor in Gabi's story but was not mentioned in her initial presentation of the migration story. Towards the end of the interview, Gabi revealed that since ending her marriage, she had come out as a lesbian. This example illustrates how negative ties may be relevant in migration stories but may be harder to discover if people are reluctant to discuss them.

The case of Rukhsana and Gabi both involved ex-husbands as negative ties, but of course negative ties may take many forms, including exploitative employers, as discussed in Chapter 5.

But, as noted earlier, the influence of networks cannot be looked at in isolation from other wider macro factors. In recent years, with the rise of the internet, have interpersonal ties become less salient in migration decision making and processes?

Enter the internet – replacing the need for social networks?

Given rapid advances in online technology and the proliferation of job search engines, it may be tempting to assume that social networks are now less relevant in migration planning. It has been suggested that social media require us to 'rethink' international migration and social networks (Dekker and Engbersen, 2014: 405). Participants across several of my projects had migrated to study at British universities. They found courses online and often arrived without any pre-existing networks. For example, Desmond, from Ireland, applied to do a postgraduate qualification at a British university in the early 2000s. He was attracted by the course and had no prior connections with anyone there: "I went by myself, didn't know anybody".

Moreover, several participants had used the internet to explore UK job opportunities and even to find employment before leaving their home country. As noted by Janta and Ladkin (2013: 242), 'the online environment enables migrants to have better access and be more in control of their choices in the labour market'.

Agnieszka arrived in London alone and didn't know anyone; nonetheless, she felt "secure, 100 per cent" because she found her care-sector job[3] before departing from Poland: "The interview was carried out in Poland. I knew I was going to have accommodation guaranteed and maybe that's why I chose this job, because it was easy to come here". Similarly, Justyna was also recruited from Poland to work in a British care home in the early 2000s. Having never been in Britain before, she was uncertain what to expect but she was assured by the offer of a job and accommodation. However, upon arrival at the care home, Justyna realised it was located in a remote rural area, removed from the kinds of entertainment facilities and cultural amenities she had associated with life in Britain. Justyna felt lonely and moved to London at the first available opportunity. For Justyna, the absence of any pre-existing networks in Britain meant that she had not been able to seek advice from trustworthy sources before taking a job in such a rural location.

As clearly shown earlier in Phyllis's story of leaving Barbados in the 1950s, long before the internet, the direct recruitment of migrants from abroad to fill particular gaps in the British labour market has a long history. Direct recruitment has the advantage of providing migrants with the security of pre-arranged jobs and often help with accommodation. Nevertheless, without any pre-existing networks, as sources of local knowledge, migrants, especially those who arrive alone, may risk loneliness, isolation and unexpected challenges in unfamiliar environments (Ryan, 2022).

For those seeking particular career development opportunities, finding the right job online, in preparation for migration, can be a protracted process (Janta and Ladkin, 2013). Damien, originally from France but living in Luxembourg for many years, arranged his relocation to London in 2007 via internet job searches. Despite having an offer of permanent employment in Luxembourg, Damien was determined to move to London, "as I am working in financial services, and for me it was a logical step to come to London, as it is one of the international capitals of finance". Nonetheless, he did not want to move until he found "the right job". So, from his base in Luxembourg, he used the internet and uploaded his CV to sites such as "Monster.co.uk". This process proved surprisingly slow and frustrating for Damien but eventually he did manage to obtain a short-term contract in London. As an EU national, he did not need a visa, at that time, so a short-term contract was no barrier to his migration. Hence, on the surface at least, Damien's experiences might suggest that networks were irrelevant to this job search. However, Damien's story revealed the enduring role of interpersonal networks, especially in the world of finance in the City of London, as will be discussed in more detail in Chapter 5.

While participants like Damien, Agnieszka and Justyna relied entirely on internet advertisements and remote recruitment, internet job searches can be used in conjunction with, and supported by, one's existing social network. For instance, seeing a job advertisement online, someone may then draw on his/her network to elicit additional information or advice to support the application (Kuhn and Mansour, 2014). As well as being used to supplement established ties, the internet can also be used to grow and develop one's web of connections. Hence, rather than replacing interpersonal networks as a route to migration, the internet enables people to expand their social contacts through a range of networking sites such as LinkedIn (Garg and Telang, 2018). My data include several stories that illustrate how internet searches were used in conjunction with interpersonal ties to facilitate migration.

Seamus, a university graduate from Ireland, described using websites to scope out the employment situation in London, and obtain information about job opportunities and salary scales: "checked a few websites, saw all the jobs there." As a trained teacher, Seamus focused his search on education-related job sites: "I used the *Times* Education Supplement website". While still in Ireland, he applied for several jobs and was invited for two interviews. He flew to London for the interviews and was offered a job at the second school to which he applied. A few months later, in summer 2012, he relocated to London secure in the knowledge that he had a full-time job, in his chosen profession. At first glance, this story seems to suggest that personal networks have now become irrelevant, at least for highly qualified migrants, because they can secure employment via the internet. However, looking more closely at Seamus's migration narrative reveals a more nuanced picture. Social ties were fundamental to his decision to move to London. His girlfriend had just obtained a place at a London university and she persuaded Seamus, who only had a part-time, temporary teaching job in Ireland, to accompany her. Moreover, Seamus's brother lived in London and provided initial accommodation. Seamus also had several Irish friends who had already migrated to London and who provided practical advice, for instance, about transportation costs and routes across the city. This was useful because Seamus had completely underestimated the time and costs associated with his daily commute to work across the city. So, while his actual job was obtained via the internet, it would be misleading to discount the indirect role of networks in encouraging and enabling his migration. Hence, despite advances in new technology, we can see some enduring patterns in how personal ties, alongside formal recruitment channels, may continue to shape migration decision making and processes.

Of course, beyond facilitating initial migration, the internet and other communication technologies play other roles, especially in enabling migrants to maintain spatially dispersed networks of relationships, as discussed in detail in Chapter 7.

Fragile, fleeting and loose connections

As noted in the previous section, some participants arrived alone without any pre-existing social ties. However, it was not always so clear-cut to decide if someone had pre-existing connections. Some contacts were so fleeting and fragile that it could be misleading to describe them as social ties.

Like Justyna and Agnieszka discussed previously, Ewa also arrived from Poland in the early 2000s, with a pre-arranged job and accommodation in a social care setting. But, unlike them, she did have a contact in London: "my brother's friend who met me in the station and said 'hi, welcome to London' and that was all. I really was alone". As a newcomer, Ewa was expecting some support from her brother's friend. But the simple existence of this pre-existing tie tells us little about the meaning of that relationship. Ewa's narrative suggests that this person offered no support and was actually a source of disappointment. As discussed in Chapter 2, social networks should not be conflated with social capital (Reimer et al, 2008). Social contacts may not be willing to share resources with recently arrived migrants. Among my data, there are several similar examples of pre-existing social ties who failed to live up to expectations.

Izabela initially came in London in 2004 aged 18 to make some money before returning to Poland to attend university. Her decision to move to London alone, without a pre-arranged job, needs to be understood within the context of EU freedom of movement and the culture of migration in Poland: "I come from a very, very small town in Poland and in my home town there is no one left". Because of this high outward migration, especially to Britain, at that time, Izabela was aware of many people who had moved to London: "I know them, like I know their name or I know who they are, but they are not my friends". Rather like Ewa's brother's friend, these indirect connections are not necessarily reliable sources of support, as Izabela soon found out:

> '[A] friend of a friend of a friend of a friend took me for two days. I was supposed to stay there longer but somebody found out that I was there so he had to kick me out. And then I found another friend of a friend of a friend of a friend.' (Izabela, Poland, 2000s)

This "friend of a friend" was illegally subletting his spare bedroom to Izabela and, once discovered by the landlord, she was forced to leave immediately.

While quantitative SNA often counts the number of ties in a network, one should be cautious about inferring access to social capital merely based on the existence of a connection between two alters (Ryan and D'Angelo, 2018). As argued elsewhere, more attention is needed to the nature of the relationship, the relative social location of the actors and the realisable resources (Ryan, 2011a). Network stories, as well as highlighting the role of significant, influential actors, may also include 'bit players', in minor roles, such as passing acquaintances. While such minor players may not appear significant and could be discounted from a network analysis, their existence can also reveal insights into the kinds of support and resources that migrants relied upon. Izabela's "friend of a friend of a friend" underlines the absence of reliable and trustworthy actors in her London network.

In their study of migrant newcomers in Birmingham and Luton, Wessendorf and Phillimore (2019) observed the salience of fleeting encounters and casual acquaintances. Beyond the strong ties much written about in the migration literature, Wessendorf and Phillimore note that brief encounters can also be a valuable source of information and support during the initial weeks and months post-arrival in a new place. Indeed, as my analysis shows, it may not be the strength of the connection or the length of its duration that matters but rather the quality of the resources flowing through that tie (Ryan, 2016). Some casual acquaintances may not be able or willing to share social capital with newly arrived migrants, such as Ewa's brother's friend. By contrast, other participants described casual acquaintances who were kind, supportive and willing to help but who, unfortunately, did not have access to valuable resources. For example, Marek, a Polish participant in my original 2006–7 research project (Ryan et al, 2008), observed that his circle of acquaintances did not possess any of the relevant knowledge that he needed to navigate his way through British society:

> 'I didn't have here in London people, if I had a problem, for example … to sort out at an institution, to go somewhere, sort something out … I never had a person, who I could ask, who could tell me: "you'll do it like that and everything will be okay". No … all the people, I was surrounded by, didn't have a clue about anything.' (Marek, Poland, 2000s)

Having connections to people who not only possess but willingly share social capital, including valuable information, is clearly advantageous. Colette moved from Paris to London in 2000. Her primary motivation was to develop a career in banking. Upon arrival on the Eurostar train, she had no job and was unsure how long she would stay in London. Although she had no close friends in London, she had some business acquaintances:

> 'So I just asked my colleagues in London and said "I want to come to work in London – how do I do it? And basically they said "send

me your CV, I know someone in a recruiting agency, I'll send it to them". ... one of my contacts who used to work for [xxx bank], an English guy, sent my CV and then the agency said "Right, we want to have you on our books, so come and see us and then we'll try".' (Colette, France, 2000s)

Weak ties to acquaintances may be beneficial in providing access to information that is otherwise beyond one's reach (Granovetter, 1973). In an earlier section of this chapter, the stories of Dymphna and Phyllis illustrated how weak ties in the origin country can facilitate migration. In Colette's case, weak ties in the destination society proved to be significant. Of course, not all weak ties are equally valuable; social location matters (Ryan, 2011a; 2016). Marek described how his acquaintances "didn't have a clue" and so can be interpreted as 'horizontal ties', occupying a similar social position to himself; their access to resources, including local knowledge, was no better than his own. By contrast, Colette's pre-existing weak ties can be described as 'vertical' (Ryan, 2011a), as they occupied established positions within the banking sector and possessed valuable social capital (local knowledge) which, at that time, was unfamiliar to her. Therefore, while casual, fleeting and weak connections can be important within migrants' stories of arrival, we need to look not only at the strength of the relationship but also at the flow of realisable resources in order to understand what is going on between those social ties (Ryan, 2011a).

Moreover, it is apparent that relationships evolve and change over time. Some fleeting ties are short-lived and do not endure, while others may strengthen and develop into stronger ties. Among my data, there were several examples of how casual acquaintances can blossom into lasting friendships through shared experience of migration. Having made up his mind to migrate, Patryk described how he had unexpectedly bumped into an acquaintance in Poland who was also planning to move to London. Through their experience of migration, they forged a bond of friendship in London and even shared accommodation. Similarly, Blaithin, when planning to leave Ireland to study at a London university, "happened to chat with a girl" in Dublin who was also about to move to London. The two young women decided to share a flat together and became good friends. These stories suggest how migration may 'throw together' people who are not otherwise friends. In the case of both Blaithin and Patryk, these casual acquaintances did not influence their decision to migrate. Nonetheless, because they were planning to move to the same city around the same time, they forged mutually supportive and perhaps pragmatic relationships, including renting accommodation together.

So far, we have focused on a range of migration stories, including students, those who were directly recruited into new jobs and people who arrived through family reunion. Of course, there are other types of migrants who arrive via different routes. In Chapter 2 we heard the story of Maryam who arrived as a refugee from Somalia, and we will return to her experiences in later chapters. But at the more privileged end of the migration spectrum, let's consider the case of ICTs who arrive on ex-patriot[4] contracts.

Organisational ties – Information and communication technology

Having focused on ties between people, it is also important to consider the role of structures and institutions within networks. As noted in Chapter 2, drawing on actor network theory (ANT), some scholars argue that organisations, such as a university or a firm, should also be included in our analysis of networks (Herz and Altissimo, 2021). Within the body of literature on business networks, much has been written about the role of firms and the salience of organisational ties. Indeed, organisational ties are defined in different ways to include, for example, the relationship between a particular individual and an organisation – such as an employee and a firm (Nunes, 2014) – or the working relationships between staff within a firm (Van Kessel et al, 2014) or connections between different companies (Retzer et al, 2012; Kawai, 2012). Among my data, several participants had migrated through ICTs. Hence, an organisation had been crucial not only in shaping but also facilitating migration. Nonetheless, as argued elsewhere (Ryan and Mulholland, 2014a), we should not assume that this form of mobility is necessarily easy and seamless.

Florin arrived in London from France in 2010 through an ICT: "It had been proposed to me to be located in London, doing the same job I was doing in Paris but based in the UK". Although proposed by his company and hence not self-initiated, this relocation to London suited Florin's long-term career goals. Thus, he was open to the suggestion because he was already thinking about gaining international experience and hoped eventually to move further afield, such as New York. Therefore, the relocation to London seemed an attractive first step. Both Florin and his wife had previously spent a year in London as students, learning English, so the city felt familiar. As part of the transfer package, his employers arranged a relocation company, which not only organised the move but also helped to find accommodation in London for Florin and his family. On the surface, this sounds like a highly privileged and well-managed migration. However, a separate interview with Florin's wife, Martine, suggested that the move was less straightforward than expected.

Martine narrated how the process of settling their three children into school had been challenging and quite stressful. Once again, it is apparent that women do much of the emotional labour in managing family migration processes (Ackers, 2004; Kofman et al, 2005). Moreover, Florin worked long hours and so Martine was alone most of the day. Without pre-existing networks, Martine described feeling lonely in London. Once the children had settled, she hoped to return to paid employment: "I don't want to stay at home at all". Having worked as a teacher in France, she hoped to find work in one of the many French language schools in London. Indeed, based on information she had received through her networks back in France, including people who previously lived in London, she had expected to find a job as a French language teacher relatively easily: "I was thinking I could find a job more easily because we had friends also, they came three or four years ago and she was a primary school teacher like me and she found it really easy". However, for whatever reason, Martine did not find the process easy and was feeling frustrated by her continued failure to find a job. This example suggests how information circulating through friendship networks may be less than accurate and can generate false expectations. In the absence of any organisational ties of her own with London schools, Martine lacked insider knowledge about how to navigate the job scene. While her husband's career was flying, her own seemed to have stalled: "that was the most disappointment for me". However, at the time of interview, Martine and Florin had been in London for less than a year and, as will be discussed in later chapters, network composition, and the opportunities therein, may change considerably over time.

One such interesting example of change over time is demonstrated by Izabela. As noted earlier, she initially arrived in London in 2004 and relied on very fragile and loose connections to "a friend of a friend" to access insecure accommodation. After such a difficult situation, Izabela was determined that her next migration experience would be more positive. Having returned to Poland to complete her studies, she later got a job in a multi-national corporation in Warsaw. When the opportunity arose for an intra-company transfer to London, she seized the chance. Thus, her second migration was facilitated through organisational ties and she arrived in the city with a secure job and good salary. When I met her in 2014, she was very happy with the move. Her transition over ten years from low skilled to highly skilled, from waitress to analyst, reveals the necessity of taking a long-term view to understand how migrants' experiences evolve over time. Those changes and the role of networks in migrants' developing opportunities and strategies over time will be discussed in the next chapter.

Conclusion

Focusing on stories of arrival, this chapter has sought to contribute to network analysis within migration research by providing nuanced understanding of dynamic interpersonal relationships, the resources flowing between them and their relative social location within specific social contexts. In so doing,

I have sought to go beyond a narrow quantification of ties, and implied causality, at one end of the spectrum and a vague metaphorical notion of 'network' at the other end.

Through the use of network stories, I argue, one can gain better insight into entangled relationality including how negative ties, fleeting acquaintances, weak ties as well as strong kinship and friendship ties may feature in migrants' decisions to move and the resources that enable them to do so. Rather than direct causality, this approach suggests how actors' migration decisions and processes are situated within diverse webs of social ties that offer varied and even, at times, contradictory influences.

Moreover, it is important to pay attention to sociostructural contexts. As this chapter has shown, migration stories are not only located in particular webs of relationships, but also framed by macro spatio-temporal contexts (Erel and Ryan, 2019). Drawing on the stories of participants who migrated from different countries, during different decades, reveals some significant changes over time, such as shifting immigration regulations and the rise of the internet. Nonetheless, analysing these diverse narratives also suggests some enduring continuities, including the salience of interpersonal relationships, in framing migration decisions and processes.

While this chapter has focused on stories of arrival, of course, networks are dynamic over time and through different life course stages. The social ties that are important at the point of migration may channel migrants into particular kinds of jobs (Keskiner et al, 2022). In order to enhance labour market mobility, overcome discrimination and build their careers, post-arrival, migrants may need to forge new social ties with access to beneficial resources (Ryan, 2016). In the following chapter, using oral history interviews as well as qualitative longitudinal methods, and network visualisation, I explore stories of evolving experiences and relationality, especially in relation to the sphere of employment.

5

Employment, Deskilling and Reskilling: Revisiting Strong and Weak Ties

Having examined initial migration plans and stories of arrival in Chapter 4, the focus now shifts to networks and employment seeking post-arrival. Within migration studies, there has been considerable interest in the role of migrant networks in accessing employment (Massey, 1986; Boyd, 1989; Curran et al, 2005, to name a few). Moreover, there has been much discussion about the benefits but also the potential disadvantages of co-ethnic ties in facilitating labour market access (Smith, 2005; Nannestad et al, 2008). Over-reliance on ethnic-specific networks may result in a funnelling effect into niche jobs, downward mobility and economic disadvantage, as well as possible exploitation (Anthias and Cederberg, 2009; Thondhlana, Madziva and McGrath, 2016). Drawing on social network literature, some migration scholars have examined the importance of weak ties in helping migrants to forge more diverse and advantageous social connections as a way of increasing job opportunities (Lancee, 2010; Ryan, 2011a; Patulny, 2015; Gericke et al, 2018; Bernhard, 2020). Weak ties are often configured in the migration literature as bridging ethnicity – that is, ties to people outside the ethnic enclave (Lancee and Hartung, 2012; Damstra and Tillie, 2016).

My work has cautioned against a reductive approach that conflates tie strength with ethnic composition (Ryan, 2011a; 2016). As noted in Chapter 2, it cannot be assumed that ties to co-ethnics are necessarily strong, while ties to so-called 'natives' are necessarily weak. Moreover, the social capital inhering in these ties cannot be taken for granted. Instead, it is important to look more closely at the relationships between people and the kinds of resources flowing between them. Furthermore, as my research over many years has shown, not all 'weak ties' are beneficial. Simply forging diverse social connections is no guarantee of enhancing employment opportunities. As discussed in Chapter 2, my work draws on network theorists such as Granovetter, Burt and Lin to critically interrogate what is meant by *weak* ties. Analysing relative social location, I have differentiated between horizontal and vertical weak ties (Ryan, 2011a). In other words, weak ties are more likely to be advantageous if connections are vertical (that is, to those in a higher social position). Therefore, building upon my existing work (Ryan, 2022), the first aim of this chapter is to analyse stories of job seeking in order to gain more nuanced understanding of the relative social location, flow of resources, as well as perceived trust and relationality between 'weakly' connected actors.

Researchers, especially when using surveys, often ask about the direct consequences of a particular tie in accessing a job – for example, 'did anyone help you to get a job?' (for a discussion see the chapter by Ryan, Keskiner and Eve, 2022). But such a narrow view of labour market access risks simplifying the diverse, complex and often indirect roles of social ties. Some sectors, such as banking and business, actively facilitate networking to forge career-enhancing social capital. In other areas of work, such as public-sector jobs like teaching, where recruitment seems to be open and transparent, networks appear to play a less direct role (Ryan, 2022). Hence, drawing on the narratives of participants across a wide range of occupations (including cleaners, teachers, nurses, construction workers, bankers and so on), this chapter's second aim is to further network analysis by exploring how social ties may operate, both directly and indirectly, across different employment sectors.

Moreover, it is necessary to pay attention to changing employment experiences over time (King and Della Puppa, 2021). Getting a job is not a once-off event. The job that a migrant gets upon arrival in a country, and the networks drawn upon to do so, may give little indication of how employment develops over time. Thus, for example, the extent to which initial experiences of deskilling can be overcome may depend, at least in part, on how cultural and social capital can be mobilised (Kelly and Lusis, 2006; Erel, 2010; Badwi et al, 2018). Using oral history narratives, as well as repeated interviews over a number of years, the third aim of this chapter is to explore employment trajectories over time and the varied roles of networks in those dynamic processes.

In addition, informed by Elder's (1994) life course framework, this chapter further aims to understand temporal change by analysing key life events, like becoming a parent, especially in the case of women. Particularly in historical periods when access to formal childcare provision was limited, combining paid work and family life may depend upon the support of networks. Hence, a fourth aim of the chapter is to analyse participants' stories of managing childcare through networks of family, friends and neighbours and, in so doing, to consider the salience of propinquity for hands-on care.

An unusual feature of my data set is its enormous diversity. I analyse narratives and network visualisations from participants who migrated from different countries, through varied immigration routes and across a wide range of decades from the 1940s to the 2010s. In so doing, the chapter's final aim is to consider how class, gender, ethnicity and religion intersect, within sociohistorical contexts, in ways that impact upon opportunities to build employment-related networks.

But first, I begin with Daragh's story.

Daragh's story

Daragh, a university graduate in his 30s, had been working in sales in Ireland but derived little satisfaction from that job. Sometime earlier, he had met an English woman while travelling in Australia. After returning to their respective countries, they visited each other for occasional weekends. Daragh decided to move to London in 2005, for a trial period, to see if the relationship might develop. Indeed, the couple married a few years later. Thus, Daragh's migration was motivated both by romance and the chance to explore new career opportunities.

Having been a keen sportsman in Ireland, Daragh quickly joined a Gaelic sports club in London. He described the club as a "good network" and a source of information about "flats, houses, and you know, contacts"; he added: "that was my initial footing". Through these Irish contacts, he could easily get a job in construction. Daragh described how intra-ethnic obligations were entrenched in the sports club: "people have been here for 50 years – it's just so ingrained into them to help and support the Irish". However, after working in construction in Australia and America, Daragh was "determined not to do that". Reliance on co-ethnic networks may result in an occupational "mobility trap" (Anthias and Cederberg, 2009; Kalter and Kogan, 2014). Instead, as a graduate, Daragh was keen to use his move to London to develop a professional career. Thus, even when access to particular kinds of jobs is available through ethnic networks, some migrants, especially those with 'a strategic advantage' (Harvey, 2008: 453), such as higher qualifications, may wish to avoid these routes and explore other options.

Interestingly, however, Daragh turned to another set of social ties to find his first job in London: "my wife knew people in this media agency, she said, 'why don't you call them?' ... I went into that appointment that my wife's people set up for me directly, and they offered me the job on the day, yeah, I just took it". These contacts in the media agency did not know Daragh personally and may be regarded as classic weak ties. Moreover, because of their position within the occupational hierarchy, these ties may be defined as vertical weak ties that spanned social distance (Ryan, 2011a). Trust is usually a necessary dimension of business relations (Burt, 2009) and, as Granovetter (1983) notes, 'reputation' is critical in job recommendations. But Daragh did not know directly any of these media agency contacts. Thus, it was trust between his wife and her social contacts that secured a good recommendation for Daragh. Hence, as Sandra Susan Smith has observed, 'reputation is at least in part the product of one's network of relations' (2005: 5).

Despite enjoying the job, Daragh could not envisage a permanent career in the media. Several members of his family in Ireland were teachers and, as he explained, "I always kind of did feel that, deep down, my calling was to teaching". Unsure how to access teaching in the British context, a kinship tie proved to be highly significant: "a cousin of mine was in the middle of her PGCE[1] ... I never knew of that avenue into teaching ... as soon as I started talking to her, I knew that's what I wanted to do. So, I applied for the PGCE".

With the support of his wife, who was in well-paid employment, Daragh was able to quit his job and become a full-time student. Having completed his PGCE, he found a permanent job as a teacher quite easily, in a local primary school, without the use of networks. Because of the shortage of teachers in Britain, and the high turnover of staff, especially in London, as well as open recruitment practices within the public sector, it seems that networks are not necessary for these professional jobs. However, as shown by the advice Daragh received from a strong tie, his cousin, the wider example of his many relatives who are also teachers and the practical support provided by his wife, it is apparent that networks supported his career move, in indirect ways. Thus, it is necessary to consider the broader, and perhaps more indirect, role that social ties may play in facilitating access to the particular labour markets (Ryan, 2022).

Daragh's story is of interest because of his experience across several different sectors – construction, media and teaching. His narrative illustrates the diverse ways in which networks may operate as sources of information, recommendations and direct job offers. Moreover, his account indicates dynamism over time as migrants may weave in and out of ethnic networks, including strong kinship ties and weak ties, at various points in their career trajectories depending on what other opportunities and resources are available to them. Many of the points raised by Daragh will be picked up throughout this chapter.

Being a 'good networker': the direct and overt role of networks in London's financial district

There have been calls for more comparative research to understand how networks may operate across different labour markets (Toma, 2016). As a teacher working in the public sector, Daragh did not appear to need networks to access employment. All public sector jobs must be advertised and appointment processes need to be transparent (see also Lang et al, 2022). By contrast, within the private sector, it is apparent that networks remain important, especially when it comes to recommendations based on trust and reputation (Beaverstock, 2005; Smith, 2005; Burt, 2009).

Damien moved to London in 2007 to take up a job in financial technology. As noted in Chapter 4, while based in Luxembourg, he had used online search engines to find a job offer in London. After moving to London, he began to understand why his online search had proven so slow, as he observed that interpersonal networks were crucial for career advancement in London's financial sector:

'People just want the approval by somebody else that you can work in London ... I've noticed here particularly people work on recommendations – it's very important that people who can back you up and say: "okay, I know this guy and I worked with him, he always has done a good job there" and it eases things a lot.' (Damien, Luxembourg, 2000s)

Armed with this knowledge, Damien described how he built up business networks in order to advance his career: "So I really increased the number of people I knew in my business environment here in London". He explained how these business networks could lead to job opportunities: "oh yes, I know this person. Are you interested" or "I can match you if you want to?" Indeed, Damien's next job move came about directly through weak ties developed from business contacts. Bourdieu (1986) calls attention to the effort required to build and maintain networks. Damien explained: "you have to know how to maintain your networking; you have to spend some time doing that".

While benefiting from his newly formed social connections, Damien also noted the downside of London's business networks: "you still have all the old school boys, which is very strong, all the membership clubs which can be very exclusive". This description suggests a form of 'network closure' (Coleman, 1988), based on dense, privileged 'old school' ties. These membership clubs illustrate how networks can operate to reproduce class privilege and power (Bourdieu, 1986). Thus, Damien's observations draw attention to the exclusionary potential of networks (Borgatti et al, 2009) in ways that seek to protect class privilege (Goulbourne et al, 2010). For a migrant, like Damien, an outsider, keen to develop his career in the City of London, it can be challenging to penetrate such networks.

Similarly, Irène, who worked as a lawyer in a large firm in the City of London, noted: "The City is a very close-knit world". Thus, in order to penetrate that world, it is necessary to expend effort to build up a client base: "the way to get the clients is to network". But doing so required considerable effort: "it is not always easy and sometimes these sorts of things take time".

Nevertheless, the financial sector needs to facilitate networking in order to generate new business opportunities (Beaverstock and Smith, 1996). Several participants in the private sector, explained that networking was fundamental to their jobs. Given its importance within the business world, companies organised social activities to facilitate networking. Celine, a French woman who had worked in London's financial sector for 30 years, explained that banks arranged "institutional networking" through lunches, dinners and cocktail parties.

However, the simple act of meeting people over drinks did not necessarily lead to business relationships. Some participants drew attention to the need for networking skills to forge more meaningful and trusting connections, beyond merely fleeting encounters. For example, Irène described herself as having good networking skills: "I was also lucky enough to have people skills which opened the doors to me quite quickly ... I enjoy the networking and I enjoy working the room".

As discussed in Chapter 2, adopting a narrative approach to analyse networks helps to reveal presentations of self. Throughout the interview, Irène presented herself as an accomplished networker who had the required skills to build up a large number of clients. This presentation of the networked self (D'Angelo and Ryan, 2021) needs to be understood within the specific context of London's business district. As noted, narratives do not emerge in a vacuum but are shaped by particular sociocultural contexts (Somers, 1994; Plummer, 2002). Within the City of London, networking was a prized activity and hence being a good networker was a valued accomplishment. Thus, the ways in which networking was perceived across different employment sectors may help explain, in part, how participants narrated their network stories during our interview encounters.

Colette, introduced in the previous chapter, arrived in London on the Eurostar train from Paris without a job but, through valuable business connections, she developed a career in banking. Colette's narrative underlined not only the role of networking in building and sustaining her career but also the global reach of those connections: "investment banking, you know, it's all over the world so I have a web of people that I know". Much of this global networking took place online: "I actually find Facebook a very powerful tool in terms of building relationships with someone you've never met but you work with". However, Colette also explained the role of propinquity, especially for face-to-face encounters within London's financial district:

'Canary Wharf is like a little village and you see the same people ... you see people around and "oh how is it going?", "how's your job?",

"I'm being made redundant next month", "well, okay, drop me an email because I might have something". And it's, you know, you always meet someone who knows someone who needs a job.' (Colette, France, 2000s)

As a director within a global financial institution, Colette was the most senior professional I interviewed. Given her position, it is clear that she acted as an influential vertical weak tie for others: "A friend contacted me last year saying 'a friend of mine wants some information on what you do on [particular financial product]. She has an interview but she's not very knowledgeable'. I met the person and I said 'right, this is how you need to prepare your interview'". This anecdote describes a classic weak tie according to Granovetter's (1973) original definition. Colette did not know the job seeker. She was a friend of a friend. Thus, there was only an indirect connection between these two women. In fact, the friend who contacted Colette could be seen as a broker (Burt, 2009) who brought about the introduction between two previously unconnected individuals. This is similar to the earlier story of Daragh's wife who brokered an introduction to people within the media agency.

While many participants described their efforts to access a beneficial weak tie, Colette was precisely this kind of influential person in a position to impart valuable know-how. Her story challenges the rather simplistic assumptions that beneficial weak ties necessarily involve 'natives'. Colette was a migrant, albeit a privileged one. As argued elsewhere (Ryan 2011a), the value of a tie lies not in its ethnic composition but rather in its ability to bridge social distance and share beneficial resources. Moreover, her story sheds light on the possible motivations for someone to share resources with an acquaintance to whom they are only weakly connected. Colette invested time and energy in building connections because she regarded the circulation of information as the life blood of the financial sector. So, taking time to talk to someone about a job interview, although not in her bank, seemed natural to Colette. Moreover, she was probably also motivated because the request came initially through her friend. Thus, as discussed elsewhere, weak ties should not be seen as isolated dyads, involving just two actors, but rather as part of wider webs of relationships (Ryan, 2022).

For migrants, especially newcomers, weak ties can provide valuable work-related know-how and insider knowledge that might not be otherwise available. In the absence of such weak ties, migrants may struggle, at least initially, to understand new systems. Having, so far, focused on participants who secured professional jobs commensurate with their qualifications, the next section turns to participants who had difficulty achieving their desired employment goals.

Converting cultural capital and the role of weak ties

Catriona, discussed in the introductory chapter of this book, obtained a degree from an Irish university and, in 2006, decided to join her boyfriend, who was a university student in a small city on the English south coast: "he was over here and he was enjoying it, and being apart was tough, so yeah, it seemed like a very straightforward option". While romance could be seen as her primary motivation for migrating, she also expected to find work in her chosen field.

Catriona's narrative revealed her surprise when problems began to arise: "I wasn't anticipating a problem at this point. I was merrily applying for jobs and I got a letter back saying 'No, we can't recognise your qualification'". She explained that the difficulty related to a specialist teaching qualification that "did not transfer" between the Irish and British contexts.[2] Catriona was advised of the need to retrain. She felt like a "door was closing" and navigating the requirements was like a "minefield" of bureaucracy. Later, she discovered there were ways to navigate the system which would have allowed her to teach while seeking professional recognition. However, that route had not been presented to her at the time: "Now I've lived longer in England, I realise that there were alternatives but I just didn't know people … because I was an outsider". Catriona lacked insider connections. Despite having access to a ready-made social network of her boyfriend and his student friends, they did not have the necessary knowledge to help: "none of us were in the system. And it's amazing how many questions you can ask and still not have the important information".

Catriona's experience illustrates how being a newcomer, and not knowing anyone who can provide insider knowledge, can make administrative systems seem impenetrable. Her story recalls the earlier account of Marek from Poland who, in Chapter 4, explained that all the people in his social circle "didn't have a clue" about how systems worked. In both cases, networks of acquaintances can be seen as horizontal ties, occupying a similar social position, and hence unable to provide valuable "know-how". Out of desperation, Catriona got a job in a shop. A number of years later, she relocated to London and began to do a professional doctorate in Educational Psychology. In a later chapter, we return to Catriona's story to explore how networks can evolve over time.

As noted in Chapter 2, network theory requires not only an analysis of the consequences of social ties but also of their antecedents (Borgatti and Ofem, 2010). It is necessary to understand where social ties come from. How do new relationships develop in the first place? What are the particular social ambiences that facilitate new social connections (Eve, 2002; 2022)? Forging links to people with beneficial knowledge, 'insider know-how', may be challenging for newly arrived migrants, especially those in low-skilled jobs, or with limited language skills, with few opportunities to meet new people (Behtoui, 2022).

Mateusz, introduced in Chapter 4, arrived in London in 1998, before Poland joined the EU, and hence without freedom of movement rights. Mateusz was initially only able to work informally in catering. However, he developed a supportive relationship with his Polish landlady and her British husband. The landlady had lived in Britain for decades and worked within the health sector. Mateusz described how this woman helped him to gain a bursary to study nursing and thus regularise his immigration status, while also gaining access to a new career. It is noteworthy that Mateusz's landlady, while spanning social distance, providing access to valuable know-how, and hence, fulfilling the criteria of a vertical weak tie, was a co-ethnic, a fellow Pole. Thus, contrary to how weak ties are conceptualised in much of the migration literature, it can be misleading to define these beneficial connections as necessarily involving the 'native population'. As shown with Colette earlier, vertical ties can connect to influential migrants.

Moreover, in Mateusz's narrative, the weak tie with his landlady, and her husband, gradually strengthened into friendship, illustrating the significance of dynamism over time. When visualising his network of relationships, it was noteworthy that Mateusz placed this older couple close to the centre of the sociogram. Having started out as landlords, over time they had become "super friends" and like his family in London.

The antecedents and dynamics of a weak tie are also apparent in Ewa's story, which unfolded through repeated interviews over many years. Arriving from Poland with a Master's degree in 2002, at a time before Poland joined the EU, Ewa needed a visa to work in the UK. Initially, she worked as a carer, while perfecting her English language fluency. However, she was determined to get a better job commensurate with her qualifications. When we met in 2006, Ewa had moved from a carer to a clerical job. On reconnecting with her in 2014, I discovered that Ewa's career had developed significantly and she was employed as a senior statistician for a large company. Although this trajectory from carer to statistician had been long and arduous, requiring tremendous effort on Ewa's part, including undertaking several courses to update her skills, her narrative highlighted the practical support she received from her former boss in the care sector. Ewa gave a detailed example of how her former boss had helped with filling in job application forms and explaining how to answer questions on equal opportunities:

> 'I looked at the question, "what does equal opportunity policy mean to you?" What am I expected to answer? … Everybody expects you to tell a story about what the policy is about. You would never guess it. And my director at the time, I asked her about it. I said openly I would like to understand it, I will always fail on it and she actually

explained to me all the English idea about it and then I wrote my answer and she actually said "no, let's sit down. You are thinking the right thing but you are not wording it as it's expected". So those things were extremely helpful. I was extremely lucky … a few people in my life who spent time and gave some energy and the skills to explain me about how things work.' (Ewa, Poland, 2000s)

Although it may not seem like a big deal to sit down and explain to someone what is expected on a job application form in relation to equal opportunities, for Ewa this was precious information about the "English idea". This was not about language or formal policies, but about the cultural codes, the insider know-how of what is expected (Cederberg, 2015). This story is similar to that described by Colette earlier, where she took time to explain particular products and processes to someone who was going for a job interview. In each case, the weak tie was not a direct route to a job but instead provided valuable know-how to indirectly support job seeking.

Ewa's connection to her boss can be regarded as a vertical weak tie to someone who was willing to share knowledge and help Ewa apply for a new job. The boss realised that Ewa was over-qualified for her current role and had the talent and ambition to develop her career. It seems an act of pure altruism on the part of an employer to help someone apply for a job at a different organisation. Unlike Colette, who helped a friend of a friend, someone she did not know directly, Ewa had an established, trusting relationship with her boss. Thus, 'likeability' may be a fact here (Rezai and Keskiner, 2022) as her boss liked and wanted to support Ewa. The fact that they subsequently went on to become friends suggests that likeability may well have been a motivating factor. As Ewa populated her sociogram in 2014, I observed with interest that this former boss now appeared in the inner friendship circle.

Of course, it would be misleading to suggest that all weak ties transform into strong ties. Some weak ties, although helpful at a particular moment in time, may be fleeting. Sylwia, a Psychology graduate from Poland, initially experienced deskilling and got a job delivering sandwiches to London offices. Embarking upon a Master's programme, she met a senior academic who became important to Sylwia's career trajectory. Through this academic, Sylwia got the chance to work as an assistant on a research project which "opened doors" to a new career. Nonetheless, when populating her sociogram, I was interested to observe that this helpful academic was conspicuously absent. When I asked about this former weak tie, Sylwia simply said they had lost touch. As discussed in Chapter 3, combining in-depth interviews with sociograms helped to provide significant insights into the meaning and dynamism of particular relationships. This proved to be especially helpful in understanding the complexity of 'weak ties'. As noted earlier, rather than regarding weak and strong ties as binary opposites, it may be more useful to conceptualise them along a continuum of dynamic relationships that ebb and flow over time. Some weak ties may fade away quickly, while others endure and may even transform into friendships (Ryan, 2016; Ryan, 2022).

The participants in my studies were drawn from different occupations and diverse skill sets. Moreover, adopting a temporal lens, it is apparent that their employment trajectories changed over time. Cultural capital does not always travel well across national borders (Erel, 2010; Erel and Ryan, 2019). Hence, some migrants experience deskilling and downward mobility. However, the jobs they did upon arrival in London did not necessarily reflect the kinds of jobs they were doing ten years later. Some who began in low-paid, insecure jobs managed to transition into skilled occupations. As shown here, and in the earlier discussion of Adrianna's move from being a cleaner to a senior administrator (Chapter 3), networks were often crucial to stories of career progression. Thus, it is important to follow trajectories over time. In so doing, we also see that boundaries between so-called skilled and unskilled migrants may be quite blurry and should not be treated as fixed categories. However, for some migrants, obstacles in the labour market may be harder to overcome, especially in contexts of racist discrimination.

Drawing on social ties to navigate hostile working environments

Social ties do not operate in a vacuum but rather need to be understood within specific socioeconomic contexts including structural racism (Smith, 2005; Reynolds, 2013). Opportunities to convert and accumulate cultural capital, such as qualifications and work experience, are shaped by racialising discourses and practices (Madziva et al, 2016; Badwi et al, 2018). Adopting an intersectional lens allows us to see how particular social categorisations interact in ways that may empower or further marginalise individuals (Phoenix and Pattynama, 2006).

As discussed in the previous chapter, many migrants, especially from former colonies, were directly recruited into the British labour market in the post-war era. Despite being invited to come to Britain to work, upon arrival, they often encountered explicit forms of racism and hostility (James, 1992; James and Harris, 1993; Webster, 2005).

Phyllis, introduced in Chapter 4, was recruited from Barbados to work for British Transport in the Midlands. Feeling lonely and isolated there, Phyllis later moved to London where she retrained as a nurse. Her narrative included several incidents of overt racism during her years as a nurse in the 1960s and 1970s: "I've been working as a nurse – occasionally you'd get the old, some of the older folks was cussing us: 'I don't want to see any Black faces in here' or 'Take your Black hands off me', and things like that".

Irish nurses reported similar experiences of anti-immigrant hostility during the same era. For example, Siobhan recounted how "a woman said to me one night, 'why don't you go back to your own country'". Similarly, Tricia heard a patient on the maternity say about the Irish "you should send them all back". However, on that occasion another nurse retorted: "you better hurry up and have your baby because there will be no one to deliver it because it is all Irish here".

The ways in which migrants sought to navigate these hostile workplaces depended in part on the relationships they forged with work colleagues and managers. Workplace hostility was especially apparent in Hannah's story.

Hannah arrived from the Caribbean in 1965 to join her husband who had earlier migrated to London. Her first job in London was in a food production factory. But after a while on the factory floor the manager, realising that Hannah had experience of office work prior to migration, asked her to cover for a clerical worker who was off sick. Having got on well with colleagues prior to this change of role, Hannah's elevation from the production line to the office provoked overt racist reactions as members of the office staff complained to the manager:

> 'They went and said they can't work with me, they said they wouldn't work with me. That they don't like coloured people working in the office … I was really shocked … I was in tears because you know, I mean I don't know what prejudice is … We never heard that word. So, it was difficult for me – it was my first job and I started to cry when he told me.' (Hannah, Guyana, 1960s)

However, rather than agree to the colleagues' demands, Hannah's manager was supportive and encouraged her to remain in the job by saying: "Don't worry, if they want to go, they can go". So, Hannah took up the office job but, despite the manager's support, she found the atmosphere hard to endure and, shortly afterwards, she left. Hannah's experience shows how migrants' route from low-skilled to higher-skilled jobs may encounter opposition. While on the factory floor, she was well received by colleagues. But, as soon as she was promoted to a more senior and better-paid role, she met with overt hostility. Her colleagues can be seen as negative ties who tried to block her career progression. Thus, in exploring the role of networks, it is important not only to concentrate on positive, helpful and supportive ties but also to consider negative, abusive and obstructive social ties (Hosnedlová, 2017) who may have a detrimental impact on employment experiences (Labianca et al, 1998).

Grainne completed a secretarial course in Cork before migrating to London in 1974. She had secured an office job in Ireland but was encouraged "to go off to England" by her friend Ann. Their primary motivation seems to have been to have fun. Soon after arriving in London, the two friends decided to further their adventure by travelling in Asia for six months. Upon returning to London, Grainne was unsure what to do next and turned to her uncle for support. He invited her to move in with him while she looked for a job. It took Grainne some time to find a job due to the economic recession of the 1970s. Eventually, she responded to an advertisement for a nursing assistant in a home for people with severe disabilities. Despite her inexperience, Grainne got the job and although initially finding it physically and emotionally challenging, she soon began to enjoy the work. Observing her hard work and dedication, her supervisor encouraged Grainne to consider a career in nursing. However, Grainne was surprised to encounter a negative response at the interview for the nursing course:

> 'I went for the interview and I will always remember it, I was applying for registered nursing and this man said "who do you think you are, Irish people don't do that, they do enrolled nursing"; he said "you haven't even got O-Levels" and I said "no, but I've got a Leaving Certificate with four honours",[3] and he was just totally dismissive and wouldn't countenance having me training.' (Grainne, Ireland, 1970s)

This is an explicit example of non-recognition of cultural capital as the interviewer dismissed Grainne's educational qualifications, which were actually higher than the basic requirements. However, it appears this was not simply a misunderstanding by the interviewer. Grainne perceived the interviewer as having a prejudicial attitude towards Irish people's suitability for particular courses. Faced with such hostility, Grainne was unsure how to proceed. However, her supervisor offered to help in navigating the application process: "When my nursing officer heard about it she was furious and she encouraged me to appeal, which I did. I had another interview and then I was told, 'yes, you can do registered nursing'".

Thanks to the insider knowledge of this vertical weak tie, to her supervisor, Grainne discovered how to challenge the system by activating the appeals process. Without such active encouragement, this young migrant, who was unfamiliar with the system, would probably not have pursued nurse training. I asked Grainne about the supervisor: "she was English, she was one of these beautiful older women, very elegant". Interestingly, Grainne added that one of the other supervisors was Irish "but I didn't relate to her ... I just found her personality difficult". Thus, it was an older English woman who went out of her way to support and advise Grainne. While an Irish supervisor, a potential weak tie, was present, a lack of compatibility, or likeability, seems to have been a barrier to co-ethnic solidarity.

While acknowledging the prevalence of racism, adopting a networks lens also reveals the ways in which migrants may mobilise resources, through social ties, to navigate social exclusion and tackle discrimination, especially in work-related contexts.

Kathleen, whose story of arrival was discussed in detail in the introductory chapter to this book, migrated to London in 1949 to train as a nurse having been hired directly through an NHS recruitment drive in Ireland. Her sister Nora and a female cousin were already working in London. So, as well as a job and accommodation in the nurses home, Kathleen had a pre-existing cluster of close ties to help her when she arrived. However, like many Irish recruits in that era, Kathleen was confronted by anti-Irish hostility and prejudice (Walter and Hickman, 1997; Walter, 2001; Ryan, 2007b; Hickman and Ryan, 2020). She described the matron at the hospital as "a real Tartar". Because these young trainee nurses not only worked but also lived on the hospital premises, almost like a boarding school, the matron exerted tremendous control over all aspects of their lives.

> '[S]he didn't have a lot of time for Irish people – you knew the feeling, you were like something that came off the sole of her shoe. So, I showed her my papers and she said "oh I suppose you want to go to church". I said yes and she said "well you can go to church on your day off" ... So, I thought, I am not going to say anything but I will go to Portland Square and look for a transfer.' (Kathleen, Ireland, 1940s)

It took considerable courage for a young, newly arrived recruit to challenge the matron. Kathleen chose not to openly defy her boss but instead to go to nursing headquarters in Portland Square and seek a transfer to a different hospital. It was quite unusual at that time, according to my data, for any student nurse to take such drastic action, but Kathleen was supported in her decision by a strong tie: "my sister came with me". As mentioned in the earlier discussion of Kathleen's story, there was a strong bond between the two sisters. Nora was pivotal in Kathleen's decision to migrate to London. Moreover, because Nora had already been in London for some time and was regarded as clever ("She was as bright as a button, you know, she was great at school"), Kathleen drew upon this valuable source of advice and support to challenge the authority of the matron: "It was strange you know how things work out – I think if you fight for something hard enough something good comes out of it". Kathleen was transferred to another hospital and got on very well there.

The extent to which migrants can challenge overt racism often depended upon the resources available to them, especially their cultural and social capital (Erel, Reynolds and Kaptani, 2018). Lalima, a woman of Indian heritage, born and raised in Guyana, moved to London in 1969 to join her husband. He had been living in the UK for some time and had already bought a house in a suburb of South London. Lalima was from an affluent family and upon her marriage, she explained, she did not know how to cook because her family employed "people who used to cook". Lalima narrated how she had no intention of becoming a stay-at-home wife and was keen to find a job. She related the story of how her husband, who worked for a large company, asked if there was any job opportunity for his recently arrived wife: " 'My wife is here'. So, they said 'She speaks English?' He said: 'Yes, she speaks English' [laughs]. So, they said 'Okay, we can let her come and give her a test and we'll have an interview'".

Lalima was an experienced secretary. After training in secretarial college, she worked within the judicial system in Guyana. She drew on all this experience when she attended her first job interview in London, at her husband's place of work, armed with a reference from the Chief Justice of Guyana. "So, I walked in with my reference, and I took the test and spoke to them and the next morning she rang me and told me to go to this job in the library. It was a research library. So, I went there and I worked".

After working in the library for some years, Lalima applied for a job at a bank and worked there for the rest of her career. On the surface, it appears that Lalima did not encounter much racism. However, she recounted several incidents of racist abuse on the street and casual encounters on public transport. Nonetheless, within her career, it seems that Lalima was able to mobilise particular resources that helped to navigate the worst effects of racism. Her husband already owned a house and so, as discussed in Chapter 6, she was spared exposure to overt racism experienced by many participants who sought rented accommodation, especially in the 1950s and 1960s (Webster, 2005; Ryan, 2007b; Ryan et al, 2021). It is noteworthy that the first question the employers asked was whether or not she spoke English. Although English is the official language of Guyana, it should not be assumed that language fluency is necessarily recognised by employers (Madziva et al, 2016). As an educated woman, from an affluent background, Lalima was able to transport her cultural capital, in the form of qualifications and work experience, from Guyana to London, helped in part by her husband's professional connections but also by her impressive reference from a vertical weak tie, the Chief Justice of Guyana.

In Chapter 2, I presented the story of Maryam, who arrived from Somalia as a refugee in 1999. In contrast to Lalima, who was able to mobilise resources to successfully transfer her cultural capital and hence achieve equivalent occupational status in London, Maryam encountered considerable obstacles to transferring her cultural capital and realising her employment aspirations. Having done clerical work in Somalia, Maryam was advised by an employment agency to become a cleaner in London. As Umut Erel (2010) has argued, cultural capital cannot be simply packed up and transferred across borders in a rucksack. Instead, the recognition and accreditation of prior experience and qualifications may be framed by local requirements and regulations, but also by racialised stereotypes. Nonetheless, Maryam challenged and resisted this downward mobility and instead mobilised social capital through existing, and new, social connections to establish a career within the voluntary sector. As discussed earlier, networks were fundamental to Maryam's narrative as she forged horizontal and vertical ties both within and across ethnic groups. However, as noted, Maryam's inter-faith and interethnic work also sparked criticism from some co-religious who disagreed with her feminist activism and accused her of not being 'a good Muslim woman'. In a later chapter, we will hear more about Maryam's activism and how she mobilised her diverse social connections to challenge racism on a North London housing estate.

In this section, while noting the salience of positive social ties to help navigate and overcome the obstacles that newly arrived migrants may encounter, the impact of negative ties has also been noted. In the next section, we consider how negative co-ethnic ties, especially employers, may be associated with the so-called 'dark side' of social capital (Portes, 2000).

Co-ethnic negative social ties and the dark side of social capital

Earlier, in Daragh's story, we saw how networks associated with a Gaelic sports club, inscribed with high levels of ethnic solidarity and obligation, could offer job opportunities, especially within the construction sector. However, other migrants, particularly those from earlier generations, highlighted some of the negative aspects of such ethnic networks.

Barry was the oldest participant I interviewed. A lively 92-year-old, who arrived in Britain in 1949, his narrative was highly entertaining with songs and poems sprinkled throughout the interview. Like many Irishmen from that era (Cowley, 2011), Barry worked in construction and endured hard physical labour throughout his working life. Upon arrival in Britain, Barry and his friend Joe found work in a factory in Yorkshire:

> 'In the foundry. An open furnace ... Pig iron. I had overalls and they were full of holes, burned from the sparks flying out at me. My friend Joe came up with me, and he says "Barry, we'll pack it in". He said "You won't have a lung left in your body from all the sparks". We packed it in.' (Barry, Ireland, 1940s)

The two friends made their way to London and got jobs with Irish sub-contractors in the building sector. However, Barry asserted that these Irish employers exploited their workers while pocketing large profits:

> 'They were subbies [sub-contractors] … The wages I got from them, they were getting twice that amount from the main contractors. They were Irish. They were not nice at all. … Irish companies, you couldn't do enough for them … They exploited Irish workers, that is the truth, that is the truth.' (Barry)

The memory of this co-ethnic exploitation reminded Barry of a song which he suddenly started to sing in the interview:

> 'They sent me down to Cricklewood mixing sand, cement and lime,
> Oh Cricklewood, oh Cricklewood, you stole my youth away,
> I was young and foolish but you were old and grey …
> It was in the Crown we drank the sub, and drink it with good cheer,
> but now we're on the road again and damn and f… the beer [ends song laughing].'[4]

Barry's experience is not unique. As well as funnelling into low-paid, dead-end jobs (Madziva et al, 2016; Badwi et al, 2018), co-ethnic networks may take advantage of migrants through exploitative employment practices (Anthias and Cederberg, 2009). Thus, as Portes and Landolt (2000) remind us, the downside of social capital, arising from negative social ties, should not be overlooked. As discussed in previous chapters, within social network research there is a tendency to overlook or underestimate the impact of negative ties (Everett and Borgatti, 2014). However, in-depth narratives, such as Barry's story, can provide insights into negative, abusive and exploitative relationships within co-ethnic ties and their consequences for migrants' employment opportunities.

Moreover, drawing on rich oral history narratives may also provide insights into change over time. As illustrated by Barry's story of moving from Yorkshire to London, and indeed Phyllis's career change from the transport sector in the Midlands to nursing in London, employment trajectories develop spatially and temporally (King and Della Puppa, 2021). Thus, accessing the labour market is not a once-off process but may require ongoing strategies of mobilising capitals (Erel and Ryan, 2019). Moreover, adopting a life course lens, it is important to consider how family life stages may shape opportunities and obstacles to employment.

The role of networks in restarting careers at different family life stages

While many of my participants arrived in Britain as single young people, there were several who had migrated to join partners, usually husbands (such as Chantal in Chapter 4). Marriage and childcare responsibilities may impact on employment opportunities and trajectories.

Reema, originally from Pakistan, arrived in London in the early 1970s to join her husband. During those early years, she did not work outside the home but devoted her attention to her growing family. Over time, as her children got older and she became more familiar with the local environment, she began to look for other activities to pursue: "I got involved in the [local] Muslim Association and I started to do some teaching voluntarily".

Like Catriona and Maryam, mentioned earlier, Reema had difficulty transferring her cultural capital: "I had been a teacher before in Pakistan but when I came here my qualifications were not recognised". Volunteering in the Muslim Saturday school allowed her to gain additional teaching experience. Moreover, as her children were growing up and she had more time to focus on herself, Reema was able to undertake advanced studies: "I did my qualifications in 1987 to go into teaching and I have been a teacher for the last 23 years". Reema rose to the role of deputy head in a large secondary school. Her narrative highlighted the role of formal networks, such as community and faith organisations, not only as sources of support and encouragement for migrants, but also providing opportunities to develop skills and knowledge and hence reactivate and recalibrate cultural capital.

Wiktoria, introduced in Chapter 4, moved from Poland to London in 2011 to join her husband after many years of commuting back and forth with their young son. Initially, Wiktoria was entirely occupied with settling her son into his new environment:

> 'I came here ... I was concerned about my son settling in England because he didn't speak any English. So, I was kind of really focused on settling here, making sure he was alright ... and then, you know, after a while of doing nothing you kind of get used to it and it's really hard to take that first step. But luckily there was my volunteering that took me somewhere, where I am now.' (Wiktoria, Poland, 2000s)

Like Reema previously, it was volunteering in an education setting that helped Wiktoria make the transition from full-time mother to converting her cultural capital and starting a career. Wiktoria became a parent volunteer at her son's primary school. This proved to be a turning point for two reasons: firstly, the school provided access to local connections with other mothers – "really lovely friendships" – and secondly, it revealed new insights into the British educational system which had seemed incomprehensible to Wiktoria. Later, a part-time paid role became available: "I joined as a volunteer and I kind of got into it, then they were looking for a 'meal supervisor'. I applied and I got the job there. It was just five hours a week". With a Master's degree from a music academy in Poland, it is possible to see Wiktoria's job as a part-time meal supervisor as deskilling. But she did not see it like that. Her narrative positively asserted that the part-time job suited her and provided new insights into the British schooling system. Through this experience, she gradually found out how to apply for a graduate teacher training programme and when I interviewed her in 2014, she was in the process of training to become a teacher.

Reema and Wiktoria were highly qualified migrants who moved to Britain for family reasons. Although migrating at different times and through different routes, both found their prior qualifications did not easily convert to the local context. Volunteering introduced them to new networks, local knowledge and opportunities to gain valuable experience that paved the way for career activation as teachers. Local networks are also central to the stories of women migrants who re-entered the work force after becoming parents.

Bernadette, introduced in Chapter 4, migrated from Ireland to train as a nurse in the early 1950s. Upon marriage to an English man in 1957, she quit her job to become a full-time wife and mother, in line with social norms at the time. Some years later, Bernadette was encouraged back to work by Kate, a nursing friend: "When Michael, my third child, was 3 years old, Kate came around to the house and told me I was a lazy devil and why wasn't I getting back to work". As noted in Chapter 2, social networks can operate on the meso level mediating between macro-structural contexts and micro-level individual experiences. Hence, as Bott (1957) observed, wider social norms are mediated through the opinions and experiences of interpersonal networks of friends and relatives. Because her circle of nursing friends had all returned to work, after motherhood, Bernadette felt motivated to reject the full-time housewife and mother ethos of the late 1950s and early 1960s.

Moreover, the shift patterns of nurses, especially night work, enabled them to manage motherhood and employment in an era when formal childcare was almost non-existent (Ryan, 2007a). As well as encouragement from her friendship network, Bernadette's decision to return to nursing was enabled by strong kinship ties: her husband and mother-in-law:

> 'He [the husband] was always keen to let me do whatever I wanted. He was so supportive – when I was on early shifts I used to let Michael go over to my mother-in-law – she lived over in the next street, you see. And when I was on a late shift [the husband] would pick the kids up

from their grandmother and he would cook and do all the work and clean and everything else. So supportive!' (Bernadette, Ireland, 1950s)

Similarly, Fiona returned to nursing after the birth of her daughter in the 1960s and highlighted the invaluable role of local networks of support: "You're always juggling with your children, like I'd mind yours and you'd mind mine, I'll take them to school this week and you'll take them next week … You just accepted it. You weren't alone – everyone else was doing it". Like many other nurses I interviewed from that era, Fiona managed to combine work and family by mainly doing night shifts (Ryan, 2007a). This often meant snatching short periods of sleep during the day, while someone looked after her child: "an old lady who lived upstairs, she used to take Mary out for a walk in the pram. So, I got an hour's sleep when the child was taken out for a walk".

But Fiona was ambitious and sought to develop her career beyond part-time night shifts. When a full-time position came up, she realised the need for formal childcare. Her narrative clearly illustrates the role of local social ties:

'I met a friend of mine from County Clare[5] and I knew her daughter went to school with the daughter of a woman who had the one nursery in Tooting.[6] I asked my friend where that woman lived. So, I went to see her, told her my story, I desperately wanted this job and I didn't particularly like night duty … I went home and she rang that evening and said she would take my daughter. That was 38 years ago and we are friends ever since. I never forgot what she did for me.' (Fiona)

It is noteworthy how Fiona sought help from her friend, as a network broker, to span a structural hole (Burt, 2009) and reach the owner of the only nursery in the neighbourhood. Hence, that strong tie had valuable social capital, that is, access to the nursery owner, which her friend was willing to share with Fiona. The nursery owner, it turned out, was not only Irish, but also from the same county in the west of Ireland as Fiona. All three women in this network triad were Irish. It is impossible to know if that was a factor in the nursery owner's decision to help Fiona. It is possible that ethnic solidarity in this case may have combined with gender solidary as working mothers, in the 1960s when this was less usual, to activate support. In any case, the women became firm friends. Fiona got the job and developed her career into a senior managerial role. In addition to her strong local networks of female friendship and shared childcare arrangements, Fiona also mentioned the support from her husband: "he would cook … He'd clean up, tidy up".

Husbands' support, through hands-on practical work around the home, was mentioned by many of these pioneering career women. Like Bernadette and

Fiona, several nurses managed to combine work and motherhood by relying upon husbands as part of wider networks of support from female relatives, friends and neighbours. However, some couples appeared to form dyads who managed everything between themselves. In the 1950s, Una resumed her career as a staff nurse after her two children started school. She and her husband, a policeman, combined childcare through their shift patterns: "we never really depended on other people to look after our children". Her husband, who was present during the interview, chipped in: "we never made plans including somebody else".

Without networks of support, it was near impossible for women to combine paid work and childcare in the 1950s and 1960s. Eithne, a nurse from Dublin, was married to an English man who was a teacher. However, it was apparent from her narrative that his career took precedence over her own. Moreover, his career progression involved geographical mobility which caused the family to relocate several times. In one such move, the family ended up in a remote area of Yorkshire where Eithne knew nobody: "I got post-natal depression – I needed people, I really did". Deprived of support, she went back to her own family in Dublin, until she recovered, and later returned to her husband. When the children were at school, she resumed nursing but her husband was uncooperative:

'[I]t was a nightmare trying to fit in childcare as well, because my husband, being what he was, would go to meetings, forget the children were in the school yard, I would have the police come to me ... So, I just gave it up, I got a shop job, because it was 9 to 4, I could collect the children.' (Eithne, Ireland, 1950s)

In the absence of any support networks, and with the lack of cooperation from her husband, Eithne quit nursing entirely and worked around school hours in a local shop. Geographical mobility is an important feature of Eithne's story. Unlike Fiona or Bernadette, who had built up strong local support networks over many years of living in a neighbourhood, continued relocation associated with her husband's job made it impossible for Eithne to establish local networks. The role of propinquity and local networks will be discussed in more detail in the next chapter.

Conclusion

Drawing on the narratives of my diverse participants, and informed by a life course framework to understand sociohistorical contexts, this chapter aimed to contribute to understanding migrant networks in five particular ways.

Firstly, by looking across a wide range of employment from finance, to teaching and health care, to construction, I showed how networks may operate differently across particular sectors of the labour market. While in some sectors networks may lead directly to job opportunities, in other sectors, especially those with formal and transparent recruitment practices, networks may play indirect but nonetheless important roles. In this way, I complicate the notion of network consequences by going beyond assumptions of direct causality to explore stories of how social ties may operate indirectly to support employment strategies.

Secondly, using both in-depth interviews and network visualisation techniques, this chapter examined the meaning and dynamism of weak ties. I show how these ties need to be understood not simply by their ethnic composition but rather their relative social location (vertical or horizontal) and willingness to share valuable social resources, including information. While some of these ties are not only weak but also fleeting, others may endure and become stronger over time. Through this analysis, I advance understanding of weak and strong ties, not as polar opposites but as points along a dynamic 'continuum' (Bagchi, 2001: 37) as characters weave in and out of relational narratives over time (Ryan, 2022).

Thirdly, adopting a temporal lens, this chapter has helped to complicate understandings of migrant employment trajectories over time. While some clearly experienced deskilling, at least initially, these are not necessarily permanent situations and could be overcome with time. Hence, I caution against 'unskilled', 'skilled' and 'highly skilled' as fixed categories. The narratives in this chapter suggest the role of particular social ties in helping migrants to reactivate cultural capital and improve employment opportunities. However, that is not to assume that all social ties are supportive and, indeed, some work-based relations may be abusive and obstructive.

Fourthly, bringing together the narratives of diverse participants from a wide range of origin countries, this chapter has presented powerful stories of anti-migrant sentiment and workplace racism over many decades. Moreover, adopting an intersectional perspective and a networks lens, I have considered how migrants narrated mobilising support and resources to navigate and challenge employment discrimination. In several cases, strong ties, including kinship ties, as well as weak ties, appear to have played key roles in supporting and helping migrants to challenge or overcome workplace discrimination. In other cases, ethnic, migrant and faith-based associations provided valuable support.

Finally, utilising a life course perspective, and interviewing migrants of different ages and life stages, the chapter has shown that accessing the labour market is not a once-off event. Rather, it is an ongoing process that may involve breaks and re-entry, especially for women. As shown here, social ties may play key roles at different points in employment stories. Moreover, going beyond a metaphorical use of networks, I have sought to understand the role of particular social ties. Formal associations, kinship ties, strong friendship ties, as well as neighbours, may be crucial as sources of advice, information, support and practical hands-on care. This raises questions about propinquity. The ways in which migrants activate and access local forms of support will be discussed in detail in the next chapter.

6

Evolving Networks in Place over Time: A Life Course Lens

Introduction

Friendship is 'an important part of what makes us human' (Bunnell et al, 2012: 490). While sociologists in the past may have been guilty of ignoring friendship as a 'personal' rather than 'social' relationship (Eve, 2002), in recent decades there has been a proliferation of work on the sociology of friendship (for example, Pahl and Spencer, 2004; Pahl and Pevalin, 2005; Reynolds, 2012; Vincent et al 2018; May, 2019). Among social network researchers, there has also been increasing interest in examining the number and nature of friendship ties (Wang and Wellman, 2010). For migration scholars, while there has long been attention on kinship ties, recent decades have seen increasing attention on migrants' friendships (Kennedy, 2004; Conradson and Latham, 2005; Gill and Bialski, 2011; Ho, 2011; Bilecen, 2014; Ryan, 2015a; Robertson, 2018) and how migrants negotiate identities and attachments through relationality in new places (Butcher, 2010; Meier, 2014; Van Riemsdijk, 2014; Koelet, Van Mol and De Valk, 2017; Grzymala-Kazlowska, 2018) Of course, we must acknowledge 'the ambiguities of concepts of "friend" and "friendship" as culturally and historically situated, and potentially overlapping with relations of family, kin, colleagues and acquaintances' (Robertson, 2018: 543). As Ripley Smith (2013) observed in his analysis of refugee women's networks in the US, there may be cultural differences in how friendship is defined and understood. Therefore, it has been suggested that more research is needed in order to understand how mobility impacts on meaningful friendship relationships (Harris et al, 2020).

I have long been interested in how migrants make new friends in new places (Ryan, 2004; Ryan and Mulholland, 2014c; Ryan, 2015a). The first aim of this chapter is to take forward that work, drawing on the rich narratives of my diverse participants, by adding insights into the meaning of friendship ties and the varied ways in which new, local relationships are forged. As noted in Chapter 2, social network research is not simply about describing social ties but also analysing the antecedents and consequences of those relationships (Borgatti and Ofem, 2010). Hence, I consider how stories of friendship formations may indicate processes of embedding (Ryan and Mulholland, 2015; Mulholland and Ryan, 2022), suggesting the opportunities, as well as obstacles, for migrants to create attachments and belonging in particular places.

Deeper analysis of these interpersonal relationships can offer insights into why some people become friends and others do not (Azarian, 2010; Block and Grund, 2014) and thus reveal the relevance of homophily. Defined as the 'tendency for friendships to form between those who are alike in some designated respect' (Lazarsfeld and Merton, 1954: 23), homophily remains a powerful concept in network analysis. People who are friends tend to exhibit similarity in attitudes and behaviour (McPherson et al, 2001; Reynolds, 2012). However, there have also been important critiques of the homophily thesis (Berg and Sigona, 2013; Eve, 2022). Indeed, it is not always easy to unpick the extent to which people are attracted to those who are like themselves, in the first place, versus the role of social influence in how friends become more alike over time (De Klepper et al, 2010).

Moreover, the extent to which people are 'alike in some designated respect' cannot be reduced to one specific characteristic (Ryan, 2015a; Bilecen, 2021). Identities are complex and dynamic: 'people are inherently multidimensional, have many attributes and are members of multiple groups' (Block and Grund, 2014: 189). Therefore, a second aim of this chapter is to critique a one-dimensional notion of homophily. Drawing on the framework of telling network stories, I apply an intersectional lens to analyse the ways in which participants talked about and visualised the meaning and identity of friendship ties. I consider what network scholars refer to as 'preference and opportunity' (Block and Grund, 2014: 192) in friendship formations. In other words, forging new interpersonal ties is partly about individual preferences, based on social attraction or shared characteristics, for example, but also opportunity structures that shape the kinds of people with whom we interact regularly (Eve, 2022).

Of course, none of us, migrant or non-migrant, is free to make friends just as we choose. Friendship is a two-way process and requires mutual willingness to form a connection. Moreover, as discussed later, migrants may encounter hostility, especially in contexts of racism and stigmatisation (Behtoui, 2022). Thus, a third aim of this chapter is to consider 'network closure' (Coleman, 1988) as migrants recount experiences of exclusion but also mobilise resources to tackle such hostility.

Beyond a focus on how new friendships are established upon arrival in a new society, there have been calls to understand how meaning making unfolds (Bernhard, 2020) as relationships evolve and change over time (Lubbers et al, 2021). Using a life course perspective, this chapter's fourth aim is to take up those calls by focusing on the dynamism of friendship networks through key life events, including, for example, becoming a parent, divorce, ageing and bereavement. While transnational friendships will be discussed in Chapter 7, this chapter, drawing on longitudinal methods, including biographical interviews with older migrants, explores stories of how local friendships ebb and flow through the ageing process and how migrants negotiate network shrinkage. In so doing, I consider the relevance of propinquity for practical, hands-on support and exchange of small favours (Wellman, 1984). The chapter begins with Irène's story.

Irène's story

Irène moved from Paris to London in the 1990s. Having arrived in the UK as a student, and qualified at a British university, she briefly returned to France, but then decided there were more opportunities to build her career as a corporate lawyer in London. Irene was interviewed three times over a seven-year period. The final interview took place in 2018 to gauge her views on Brexit (see Chapter 8). She was first interviewed in 2011 and again in 2013, when the sociogram was completed (see Figure 6.1). At that time, she was married, living in south-east London and on a career break while rearing her three children. Having lived in London for almost 20 years, she reflected on how her relationships had evolved over time and through different life stages:

> 'So, you do make a lot of friends at university ... then when you work, it's very difficult ... So, making friends was a much slower progress during my working years, very slow ... in the third circle of life, when I had the children, you open up a completely different world ... which I hadn't realised existed.' (Irène, France, 1990s)

Universities offer multiple opportunities for friendship making (Ho, 2011; Bilecen, 2014; Robertson, 2018). As a newly arrived student, Irène interacted and socialised regularly with young people who were open to forming new friendships.

However, the transition to work changed patterns of interaction. Irène's professional work environment actively promoted networking and, as discussed in Chapter 5, she considered herself to be a skilled networker. Nonetheless, despite the events organised by her law firm, the people she socialised with did not become friends. One reason for this, according to Irène, was because English people are "extremely superficial". She explained that it was difficult to get to know English people and get close to them. Hence, despite having an English husband, whom she met at university, Irène had few English friends. The challenge of making friends with English people was raised by many participants, as discussed throughout this chapter.

Most of Irène's friends were French. However, she was keen to distance herself from the so-called 'French bubble' of wealthy families who congregate in Kensington around the French school.[1] She remarked: "these people are living in France ... that is not me". Irène considered herself to be settled into a multicultural, local neighbourhood in south-east London.

Irène's embedding in her local neighbourhood seemed to be forged through child-based sociality (Ryan and Mulholland, 2015). Taking a career break facilitated her engagement in local play groups, such as mother and toddler clubs, where she got to know other local mothers. Over time, she said, these mothers became her "best friends". Interestingly,

Figure 6.1: Irène's sociogram

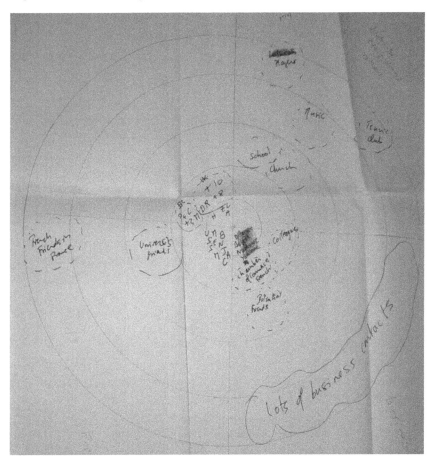

most of those local mothers were French. Irène explained that after having children, she felt "naturally" drawn to French mothers. This was motivated in part by language, so her children could play with other French-speaking children.

As discussed in Chapter 3, representing networks visually, through a sociogram, in an interview context can spark self-reflection among participants. As she populated the sociogram and observed how French her networks seemed to be, Irène paused for a moment and then added an Australian and a Greek friend. Interview encounters involve 'presentation of the networked self' (D'Angelo and Ryan, 2021). Having previously criticised French people who live in the Kensington 'bubble', perhaps by adding two non-French friends Irène wanted to avoid the impression that she also lived in a French bubble. Combining interview narratives with a sociogram provided insights into how participants tell network stories (Ryan, 2021). In a later chapter, we return to Irène's story as she reflected upon transnational ties to friends and family in France.

This chapter now picks up several of the themes raised by Irène, especially changing relationality through the life course, and considers how these were articulated and explained by participants from different backgrounds.

Making new friends in new places: students and network elasticity

Mindful of ambiguities around what is meant by 'friend' (Robertson, 2018), I want to understand how participants defined friendship ties. Most participants had many acquaintances but smaller numbers of really close friends. These "true friends" (Damien) were defined in part by their durability – "known for years" (Ewelina) – but also their proven trustworthiness – "if anything happened ... they would be there" (Magda) and "always have your best interest at heart" (Adrianna). Such enduring, trusted friendships required time and "a lot of energy" (Ewa) and hence it was impossible to maintain many such intense, relational ties. As Oliwia, who had made a "few friends" in London, explained, "I concentrate and treasure those friendships". For migrants, often separated from kinship networks, local friendship ties can become pseudo-family. As Mateusz explained, his "super friends" in London had "become like family". Similarly, Colette observed: "My best friend is English and I am godmother to her two children, so I feel like I have family".

Of course, several participants maintained close friendships in their country of origin (see Chapter 7), but, having lived in London for many years, most participants had some close friends in the city. While a few of these were pre-existing friends from the origin country who had migrated together (such as described in Chapter 4), in many cases, participants had made new friends in London.

Thus, it is interesting to consider the antecedents of dyadic ties; where and how do migrants form new relationships in new places? As noted elsewhere (Ryan, 2015a), the extent to which migrants can forge new relationships in new places depends in large part on opportunities for sociality with people who share interests, are at similar life stages and are open to making new friendships.

Irène's story about forging friendships at university echoes the narratives of many participants across the generations. Lazer's (2001) concept of 'network elasticity' describes how particular social contexts enable specific patterns of interaction and relationality. Educational settings facilitate social interaction and thus can be said to have high network elasticity.

As noted in Chapter 4, student nurses in the post-war era usually lived in nurses homes that facilitated friendship formation:

> '[T]here was a great mateship, as we were all living in the nurses home together and when we went off night duty, we all converged in one room – somebody made a pot of tea and somebody had a packet of biscuits that one of the patients had given them – that was what made us survive. I would hate to have gone to London and to have to "live out". I don't think I would have survived it.' (Emer, Ireland, 1950s)

This description of student nurses' sociality bears remarkable similarity to the experiences of more recent migrants. Laoise migrated as a student from Ireland in 2001 and found university life very sociable: "the university environment, it's quite supportive, so I moved into halls with lots of other people ... at uni everyone was in the same boat. You know everyone was new to a place and it was quite easy to mix". Similarly, Marika, from Poland, who completed a degree at a London university, remarked: "university, that was a big factor for me. It was basically just a massive part of my life, and meeting friends". Marika's university friends were "from all over the place – I've got a friend in Mauritius, I've got a friend from Greece, Italy. I've got a good friend from England". While the diversity of London universities provided opportunities to forge friendships with people from varied backgrounds, such networks could prove transient, especially if international students return home, making friendships harder to sustain.

The extent to which student friendships endured depended, in part, on subsequent geographical mobility (Bidart and Lavenu, 2005). Eithne, introduced in the previous chapter, arrived from Ireland in the 1950s to train as a nurse and thoroughly enjoyed the sociality of student life. However, she married soon after qualifying and followed her husband to Yorkshire. As discussed in Chapter 5, her husband's job meant that the family moved several times across the country, seriously impacting Eithne's ability to make and sustain friends.

Besides geographical mobility, life events can also fracture friendship networks (Greif and Deal, 2012). Catriona, introduced in Chapter 5, moved from Ireland to join her boyfriend in a university town on the south coast of England in the early 2000s. As a student, her boyfriend had a ready-made network of university friends which Catriona joined. However, when the romantic relationship broke down, Catriona realised that their shared circle of friends were primarily his friends: "the friendship group that I had was fading away all around me … I wasn't necessarily moving in those circles anymore, so I did become very isolated and that was difficult … it was a really tough time actually. I struggled".

The experiences of Catriona and Eithne suggest the fragility of friendships and the need for continued effort to make and sustain relationships over time, especially in contexts of mobility and wider relational changes.

Nonetheless, many participants seemed to sustain student friendship ties. Aoife, a teacher, qualified from a London university and, like many of her classmates, got a job in a local school. When interviewed, several years after graduation, she reflected: "I'm still friends with girls from university". The propinquity of these friends enabled frequent opportunities to socialise together. Similarly, many of the older nurses I interviewed described enduring friendship networks. Having met as students and continued to work together in the same hospital, such relationships were often described as "friends for life" (Bernadette) or as Una remarked, "We kept friends all through life". As well as propinquity and opportunities for sustained interaction over time, these enduring ties also raise a persistent question in SNA: what is the relevance of homophily for the formation and durability of friendship?

Networks and identities: beyond one-dimensional homophily

Much has been written about homophily and the extent to which people create social ties with others who are like them in some important way (Lazersfeld and Merton, 1954), as birds of a feather flock together (McPherson et al, 2001). While the dominance of the ethnic lens has been criticised (Schiller and Çağlar, 2009; Berg and Sigona, 2013; Dahinden, 2016), nonetheless, within migration research, there remains a marked tendency to conceptualise networks through ethnicity. As Leszczensky (2013: 778) argues, 'friendship networks are quite homogeneous, in terms of among other things, ethnicity'. However, other researchers found that despite strong patterns of homophily in networks, there is evidence of ethnic diversity within friendship groups (Muttarak, 2014). Although friendship networks may play a crucial role in how particular identities are expressed or reinforced (Mok et al, 2007; Robertson, 2018), identities are multidimensional and homophily should not be reduced to one particular characteristic (Block and Grund, 2014). Indeed, ethnic groups cannot be taken for granted as naturally given social units, but rather ethnicity is a construction of meanings, attitudes and practices that shift through mobility (Wimmer, 2004). By adopting an intersectional lens (Phoenix and Bauer, 2012) ethnicity can be understood in interaction with other facets of identity such as gender, age, family life stage or occupation (Ryan, 2015a).

For some migrants, ethnic associations may be sources of practical and emotional support. After arriving in London as a marriage migrant from Afghanistan, Rukhsana experienced abuse and social isolation (see Chapter 4). She eventually managed to leave the marriage with the help of an Afghan community association. Through this organisation, she became aware of other Afghan women who were isolated and in need of support. So, Rukhsana set up a women's group: "when I started this women's club there were only two or three women – I am talking about two years ago, and now I have 28 women coming every week ... I am very happy now to help these women who spend all the time at home".

There is 'solid evidence' linking social networks, social activities and participation in organisations 'with better health chances' (Cattell, 2001: 1502). While Rukhsana's club was formed of Afghans, these women were also of a similar age who shared experiences of migration and motherhood. Thus, their commonality should not be reduced simply to shared country of origin. Without wishing to discount the importance of support that can be accessed through co-ethnic ties, or the role of national and ethnic associations, it is necessary to look beyond one-dimensional homophily.

Among my data, there is evidence of homophilous tendencies, though these were often shaped and reinforced by structural contexts. For instance, due to recruitment practices in the 1940s and 1950s, many Irish student nurses found themselves on training programmes with largely Irish cohorts. Una, who was recruited in 1948, said that "the majority" of her cohort were Irish: "20 in our class and I suppose 13 or 14 were Irish". Similarly, Maura, who migrated in 1957, said: "the Whittington hospital was full of Irish girls, absolutely full of them". Thus, it is hardly surprising that many of those nurses formed close friendships with other Irish nurses.

One role of networks can be to help develop, support or reinforce a particular identity (Ripley Smith, 2013). But that is not necessarily an ethnic identity. As discussed in Chapter 2, networks can mediate between particular structural settings and the individual migrant (Bott, 1957; Boyd, 1989). For example, networks of colleagues and friends may form around a professional identity, providing support to navigate and sustain that professional environment (Ibarra and Deshpande, 2007). While nurses often described their close relationships with other nurses, I found a similar pattern among teachers.

Aoife explained the importance of her supportive network of teacher friends: "I love having my little community of friends – lots of my very close friends are from school. I see them every day and … they get everything that goes on, within school, when you're stressed, when you're happy, or when you have something to tell them".

Among the teachers I interviewed, it was remarkable how many friendship networks were composed of other teachers. Describing her friends, Sorcha remarked: "It's easier to say how many aren't teachers". Echoing a point made by Aoife, she emphasised the mutual support of teachers: "I think teachers just get it … there's camaraderie in teaching – there has to be, you know, sometimes you have a horrendous class – they are having the same issues as you".

However, unlike my nurse participants of the 1950s, who formed largely Irish friendships, teachers in 21st-century London work in multiethnic settings. This diversity was mirrored in friendship networks that usually included a range of nationalities. For example, Liadan commented: "I made one good friend … from New Zealand. So, we had a lot in common because we were both new to the system". Similarly, Blaithin included among her teaching friends "a Kiwi and an Australian girl".

While Rory agreed that "teachers hang out with teachers", the make-up of his friendship network was quite diverse. Adopting an intersectional lens offers a better understanding of how networks may connect different aspects of identity. Growing up in a remote area of rural Ireland, Rory had found it difficult to express his sexuality as a gay man. Migration can provide an opportunity to explore new ways of being and free oneself from particular expectations and constraints (King, 2002), including heteronormativity (Harris et al, 2020). Moving to London in 2006 gave Rory the opportunity to reflect on his identity. His partner, also a teacher, was a New Zealander of Chinese heritage and Rory had an ethnically diverse network made up of teacher friends of various nationalities, friends from his university course, as well as existing friends from Ireland who also migrated to London. The relationship between identity and place continues to be complex, mutually interconnected and mediated by relationality (Easthope, 2009; Butcher, 2010; Botterill, 2014; Van Riemsdijk, 2014). In other words, networks can help us navigate new places, remain connected to old places and, in the process, make sense of our identities. Rory had a complex relationship with Ireland and his Irish identity. He remained very close to his family and, as a native Gaelic speaker, had a real love of the Irish language. Nonetheless, he remarked: "in terms of who I am, the fact that I live with another man, that's something I don't feel Irish about".[2]

Like Rory, several participants discussed how migration offered opportunities to explore different aspects of their identities. Gabi, introduced in Chapter 5, was married to a man in Poland but moved to London as a way of ending the marriage and exploring new possibilities. She later came out as lesbian: "why I'm staying in London is basically my sexuality ... I want to be very independent so I can live my life ... to live my life and date who I want".

Given the opportunity to explore aspects of their identities, many participants sought to meet new people and avoid ethnic-specific networks. For example, Ewa was keen to develop diverse friendship ties beyond narrow Polish networks: "I never looked for Polish friends – it is silly to look for the same nationality. If you are moving to another country, you want to learn something – you don't want to find exactly the same what you just left".

As argued in this section, the composition of friendship networks should not be analysed through a one-dimensional lens of ethnic homophily. Instead, an intersectional lens reveals the salience of different markers of identity within webs of interpersonal relationships. However, friendship is a two-way process and forging new network ties requires not only opportunities (De Klepper et al, 2010) to meet people who share similar interests but also who are motivated to reciprocate in forming a connection (Eve, 2022). As discussed in the next section, befriending the so-called 'native' British was often perceived by participants as surprisingly difficult.

Befriending the natives: network closure?

As mentioned earlier, participants prized their strong, trustworthy, supportive friendships. However, some participants expressed disappointment at their inability to forge any new meaningful friendships in London. Despite having lived in the city for several years, Justyna, a single woman from Poland in her 50s, was saddened to have no "really close" friends in London. She craved a good friend, "someone I can trust" and who "will support me" in London. But while she had many acquaintances, especially through hobby groups, including a choir, she found it impossible to establish a close friendship. Justyna concluded that unlike friendship in Poland, British notions of friendship were superficial.

Research in the US observed that recently arrived refugees tend to regard American friendships as one-dimensional, superficial and activity-based, such as meeting for coffee (Ripley Smith, 2013). It is questionable whether British or American friendships are necessarily superficial or rather that newcomers encounter obstacles to developing deeper, meaningful and multidimensional relationships. Among my participants, some had managed to build deep, family-like friendships with British people.[3]

The extent to which people made British friends depended partly on opportunities, especially where they worked. Colette, from France, was unusual among participants in having mainly British friends. In fact, some of these friendships were so close as to be like "family" and, as mentioned earlier, she was godmother to two British children. Part of the explanation may be that Colette worked for the same bank, with a close-knit team of mainly British colleagues, for over a decade. Thus, opportunity for sustained, meaningful interaction may be a key factor in building sufficient trust to forge deep friendships.

While some workplaces facilitate network elasticity and enable migrants to forge new friendships, the transition from workplace sociality to meaningful friendship cannot be taken for granted (Ryan and Mulholland, 2014b). Irène's story, cited earlier, underlined the difficulties of making friends at work. Her experiences were echoed by other participants. Charles, a successful French businessman, lived in London for many years and built up a large web of business contacts. He observed that while London's financial sector facilitated business networking, making friends was more difficult: "I had very good relations with people that never became friends". As Wellman and Wortley (1990) note, although most people spend long hours in close proximity to work colleagues, such frequency and intensity of contact do not necessarily lead to friendship. Coleman (1990) has written about 'non-fungibility' of social connections. In other words, relations associated with one context, for example work colleagues, do not necessarily translate to other contexts, for example meaningful friendships. One challenge mentioned by several participants was the lack of opportunity to socialise with colleagues outside of work settings. As Charles noted, after work "these English" get on the train to their suburban home; a line is drawn that "a foreigner" cannot cross.

Outside of work, many participants narrated difficulties in entering British networks. As Ewa explained, "it is quite hard to actually enter the circle". Similarly, Sonia from Poland remarked: "it's very difficult to make friends with Brits". This could be perceived as an example of network closure (Coleman, 1990) as tight British networks exclude newcomers. However, this may not be deliberate exclusion but rather a reflection of non-migrant networking practices. As Damien observed, while migrants seek to make new friends, British people already had established networks and were not looking to invest in new friendships: "a lot of people from here, like everywhere else, they have their families, they've been here for years, they have their friends, so they don't really need to socialise a lot with people from other communities". Odile, also from France, echoed this point and suggested that reluctance to make new friends was not unique to the British context: "I don't think there is much difference in the way British people would behave and the way French people would behave ... I wouldn't think British people moving to France would have it easier". Indeed, research suggests that migrants, including British people, experience similar challenges making local friends in other destination countries (Beaverstock, 2005; Scott, 2006; Van Riemsdijk, 2014; Cederberg, 2015).

Hobby groups could be a way to make new British friends: "I have a feeling that if I may ever get a foothold in getting British friends would be through things like Pilates" (Chantal). Joining such groups provided a chance to meet people with shared interests: "I think the best strategy probably is to start doing what you love and you meet people who share the same interest and that's how you make friends" (Angelika). By providing a 'foothold' (Grzymala-Kazlowska, 2018), hobby groups may become a route, a first step, to embedding in local relational networks.

For some migrants, language can be a barrier to making new friends. Dominik did not speak any English at all when he arrived from Poland in the early 2000s. Hence, initial interactions with anyone outside his small Polish circle were severely limited. However, most participants, having lived in London for many years, spoke English well. Nonetheless, several highlighted communication barriers caused not by language per se but rather by cultural codes. Klaudia from Poland referred to "hidden cultural codes". Like many participants, she highlighted the British tendency towards "politeness" rather than more direct forms of speech: "I'm looking for a message, for the information they want to tell me, and not always get it". Being unable to decode subtle communications may reduce opportunities to forge meaningful relationships (Cederberg, 2015).

Of course, in some contexts, migrants may encounter active exclusion from local networks because of stigmatisation and discrimination (Behtoui, 2022). Phyllis, introduced in Chapter 4, found herself alone and socially isolated in the English Midlands in the 1950s. She sought comfort and companionship in a local church:

> 'I walked in, walked to the church and looked around – there was not another Black face … looked around and for some it must be a first time they see a Black woman. I almost turned around and fled. I felt so alone at the time, just me and all these White people staring at me.'
> (Phyllis, Barbados, 1950s)

Arriving in a new city without any pre-existing networks, church might have seemed a safe and familiar place for a young Caribbean migrant (Bauer, 2018). Hence, the hostility she encountered at church was even more disappointing for Phyllis.

While Phyllis's narrative of social exclusion from local forms of sociality took place in the 1950s, it would be wrong to assume that such experiences were confined to the distant past. Applying Elder's (1994) life course framework helps to understand how geopolitical events can frame anti-migrant hostility.

Explicit anti-Irish hostility increased around the time of the IRA bombing campaigns in Britain from the 1970s to the 1990s (Walter and Hickman, 1997; Hickman and Ryan, 2020). Cliona, a nurse, recalled: "I was on duty the night Lord Mountbatten[4] got blown up and this sister[5] nearly threw me off the ward – she said 'those bastard Irish people, how could they, the IRA … we don't want them in this country'". Grainne reported an incident around another notorious IRA bombing: "I did once have a patient at the time of the bombings in Birmingham. I had been looking after him during the night – he was very drunk I was re-hydrating him. In the morning when he became sober and realised I was Irish he refused to be cared for by me".

Wider global events can put migrants in a position where they have to carefully navigate workplace relations, as noted by Reema, originally from Pakistan, a teacher in a large London school:

'[W]hen 9/11[6] happened my colleagues who were not Muslim came to me … They expressed surprise about what had happened. I spoke to them about it, I said, "you know this is nothing to do with Islam, this is a group of fanatics, this is not Islam".' (Reema, Pakistan, 1970s)

Religion can intersect with ethnicity in ways that result in racialisation, marginalisation and exclusion from local forms of sociality (Ryan, 2011b; Meer and Modood, 2012). But, of course, religious groups can also be sources of support and sociality, as discussed later when we consider migrants in older age.

One way in which people seemed to make new connections with the 'natives' was through romantic partnerships (see also Koelet et al, 2017). Sonia, from Poland, had a British boyfriend and met several new friends through him. Similarly, Deirdre,[7] a recent Irish migrant, stated: "my boyfriend Tom is English, and all his friends are quite English, but then I introduced him my Irish friends so you know [laughs] we're mixing, it's lovely". However, simply having a British partner did not guarantee ties with the 'natives'. As noted earlier, despite having a British husband, Irène still found difficulty in forging British friendships. Moreover, for some migrants, especially people of colour, dating White British partners could carry particular risks (Webster, 2018). One of the worst racist incidents in my data was narrated by Howard. As noted in Chapter 4, Howard moved to London from Guyana when he was 19 years old. A few years later, in the 1960s, when he was in his early 20s he was dating a White girlfriend.

'I was taking her home, walking along the road, and this chap ran from behind and bumps me very hard on the shoulder and … calling me names, you know. And I said "What's the matter with you?" So,

I continued walking and went down to the station – on the platform he was waiting there for me. ... I got knocked down the steps by one punch in the face and I fell on the floor ... the guy gave me one kick in the rib and fractured two of my ribs ... Anyway, I went to the police station and reported it but nothing came of it.' (Howard, Guyana, 1950s)

Despite this terrible experience of racist violence in the 1960s, Howard expressed the view that things were much better nowadays. Indeed, mixed relationships are now more common, especially in London (Twine, 2010). Several participants were in mixed-ethnicity relationships, including Sonia, Wiktoria and Adrianna. Rory, as noted, was in a mixed-ethnicity, gay partnership and regarded London as an open society. Of course, racism has not become benign in the 21st century. In the next section, we discuss some recent experiences of racist abuse that continue to make migrants feel unwanted and excluded from local sociality.

Getting along with the neighbours: the enduring salience of propinquity

Narrating challenges in making new friendships in London, many participants commented upon the sheer scale of the city. Many were surprised by travel times across the city to meet friends: "you come to realise how huge London is" (Catriona). One way to manage the scale of this global city was to build networks within a particular locality:

'I just can't deal with thinking that I live in this huge, massive city, so I try to keep everything local, like Balham and Clapham and Brixton.[8] I'm lucky that that's where my friends live as well. I do have friends in North London, it's just so stressful to think, "okay, how am I going to get up there, how do I get home at night". It's just too far, it's too much. So, I try and keep it quite small.' (Sorcha, Ireland, 2000s)

These observations highlight the importance of propinquity and proximate forms of sociality. Within SNA, it has been noted that local ties, especially in residential neighbourhoods, continue to be important sources of practical and hands-on support for many people (Cattell, 2001). In his study of a Toronto suburb, Wellman found that while ties to neighbours were rarely intimate relationships, nonetheless, most participants valued knowing neighbours (1979: 1225).

In visualising social networks, I asked participants if they knew and got along with their neighbours. Several young, recently arrived migrants living in rented accommodation, often moving around the city for work, had no connections to neighbours. Some concluded that London lacked any sense of neighbourhood community. As Deirdre, a young Irish teacher, remarked: "you can't call around for a cup of tea ... I live in a block of flats ... you're kind of on your own".

Newly arrived migrants often described difficulties in getting to know neighbours. When interviewed, Martine, introduced in Chapter 4, had recently moved from France with her husband Florin. In Paris, they had lived on the same street for years and enjoyed good neighbourhood relations. Moreover, their children had attended a local school and their classmates also lived in the neighbourhood. Their deep embedding in that Parisian neighbourhood was reflected in trusting and mutually supportive ties. Martine narrated stories of neighbours providing emergency childcare: "I can call a friend and tell her to just pick up them and if they have no keys they will go to another house". In London, by contrast, the children travelled a great distance to school, as did most of their classmates, so there were fewer opportunities for embedding in local neighbourhood, child-based sociality.

Building new trusting local relationships can take a long time but may also require shared interests as well as opportunities to meet. Ewelina and her husband, from Poland, lived in London for over a decade and owned a house in a vibrant area of south-east London. Most of her neighbours were British, though there was an American and a New Zealander as well. Ewelina described her neighbours as a "nice circle of friends or community".

When Ewa and her husband moved to a quiet suburb in the south-west of London, she told me how she managed to get to know the neighbours. Being on maternity leave, Ewa was at home during the day and often accepted parcel deliveries for neighbours. She then had friendly chats when neighbours collected their parcels. This point was echoed by Chantal: "I know my next-door neighbours; we take each other's parcels".

Knowing neighbours was often a feature in how participants narrated their attachment and overall sense of embedding in a locality. Jennah, originally from India, when talking about her sense of belonging in London in the 1990s, spontaneously mentioned that her English neighbours had a key to her house:

Jennah: The neighbourhood where I live, there are so many English people and Irish people living there and they are so kind. Like you go off on holiday and then you come back there will be bread, butter and milk on the table waiting for you.
Louise: So they have a key?
Jennah: Oh yes, they have a key and we have their key. I can trust them. I wouldn't do that back home [laughs]. These are people

I get along with, we trust them, they trust us. We have their car keys. They say 'can you move the car around when we are away just to show that someone is there'. That is part of being in British society, getting along with everybody.

The exchange of 'small favours' (Wellman, 1979), such as accepting a parcel delivery or keeping an eye on someone's house whilst they are on holiday, requires propinquity and so can be achieved best by neighbours. However, as Jennah noted, such favours need trust and cannot be taken for granted. Jennah added that she would not do that "back home", meaning in India. As a Muslim woman who wore the hijab, she was critical of aspects of Indian society (see Chapter 7). By contrast, she found London to be more open and tolerant (see Ryan, 2011b).

However, it would be wrong to assume that London is always perceived as open and welcoming. The extent to which migrants felt accepted varied according to the socioeconomic and ethnic profile of the area but also change over time. Older migrants recounted hostility encountered upon arrival in London. During the 1950s and 1960s, looking for rental accommodation could be daunting (Webster, 2005). Hannah from the Caribbean recalled: "you couldn't get accommodation … You have doors slammed in your face". Hannah described seeing signs in windows that stipulated: "No coloured". Several older Irish participants recalled the signs about "No Blacks and No Irish" (Ryan et al, 2021). Fiona related a conversation with her Jamaican neighbour where they shared experiences:

'There is a family next door to me now, a Jamaican family, and she always said to me "if you looked for a room when I was young, 'no Irish, no Blacks, no dogs'". But she says "we all bought our own houses". That is actually why the majority of Irish people got their own houses – they bought them.' (Fiona, Ireland, 1950s)

While buying a house was protection from hostile landlords, it did not necessarily insulate from neighbourhood hostility. Lohendra, originally from Guyana and of Indian heritage, worked as a civil engineer and by the 1960s had enough money to buy a house in a largely White British suburb. He recalled that when he and his wife first moved in, the neighbours were less than welcoming: "they think they probably are going to get a curry smell every day [laughs] … So, they probably think when we moved in … 'Oh Christ, we're going to get this blast of Bombay'". However, having lived in the same house for over 40 years, relations with neighbours improved significantly: "after a time we were great friends". When I visited his house in 2019, along with my colleague Magdolna Lorinc, Lohendra narrated how he and his British neighbour share an interest in gardening and regularly exchange advice on plants.

That is not to imply that racist hostility within London neighbourhoods is a thing of the past. Maryam, introduced in Chapter 2, originally from Somalia, became an activist and campaigner. She described a campaign, from the early 2000s, to highlight racism against Somali families on a large housing estate in North London:

> 'Children were being called monkeys on the estate. The women did not want to bring their children out, and I told them that if they stopped taking the children out then they [the racists] will win ... I used to go to the estate and they would throw eggs at me and call me names but that didn't stop me.' (Maryam, Somalia, 1990s)

The materiality of place matters (Phillips and Robinson, 2015) and neighbourhood characteristics such as levels of deprivation can impact on patterns of sociality and trust (Cattell, 2001). In deprived neighbourhoods, where residents experience poverty and marginalisation, migrant newcomers may be labelled a drain on local resources (Rzepnikowska, 2019; Kay and Trevena, 2021). The extent to which newcomers are able to cope with local conditions may depend in part on how they mobilise support networks (Cattell, 2001). As noted in Chapter 2, Maryam proved adept at building networks and generating social capital across social, religious and ethnic lines. She mobilised connections with local organisations, including faith groups and statutory authorities, to arrange meetings on the estate and expose the racist abuse. Hence, she used her vertical weak ties (Ryan, 2011a; 2016) to authority figures in the local council and police as well as strong ties to Somali women on the estate, acting as a broker to span a structural hole (Burt, 2009). Her efforts were acknowledged with a national award.

Thus, neighbourhoods may be perceived as sites of sociality enabling exchange of small favours based on trust or as sites of hostility and mistrust. Moreover, embedding in local networks requires not only time but also opportunities to meet and engage with co-residents as well as mutual interest in making new connections. For many participants, having children often changed relationships in local places.

Evolving networks through the life course: the role of child-based sociality

Networks adapt and change over time and through different stages of the life course (Wellman and Wortley, 1990). This is well illustrated by Patryk. Upon arrival from Poland, he had a large circle of mainly Polish, male friends: "Polish people at the beginning when they come over here, they're not very rich. So, we share the house and sometimes even like eight people living there ... Friday there's a party and because like everybody knows someone else they invite them over". However, a year later, his wife joined him from Poland and Patryk's social life was transformed as they set up home together: "we moved out and now we live alone and because I work Monday to Friday and my wife, unfortunately, she works Tuesday to Saturday so we have only one day off together so we don't have that much time for social activities with them [former house mates] anymore".

Patryk's experience vividly illustrates patterns noted by Bidart and Lavenu (2005), as social networks can shrink when couples form and there is less time for wider friendships. Izabela, also from Poland, stated: "I haven't made many new relationships ... because I have a boyfriend and I always prefer to meet with him than any other person". This point was echoed by Owen, from Ireland, when he explained that he did not invest in making new friends partly because of his busy job but also because "I don't need emotional support apart from my fiancée. I'm lucky".

Nonetheless, as Bidart and Lavenu (2005) also noted, networks can expand again with the arrival of children. Indeed, for migrant families, child-based sociality can provide a route to embedding in local networks (Ryan, 2007a; Ryan, 2018). Of course, that is not to suggest a simple linearity of migrants arriving alone as single young people, then forming couples and later having children. My data include a wide range of patterns, including those who arrive with children as part of family reunification (Ryan and Sales, 2013), as well as those who remain single and do not have children and some who take advantage of migration to reject heteronormativity (Erel and Ryan, 2019).

As noted in Irène's story, for migrants without children, London's world of child-based sociality may be completely invisible. Indeed, several younger participants could not imagine having children in London. Patryk said he and his wife would prefer to go back to Poland when they have children because it would be difficult to raise a family in London: "when you're back home you have grandparents. It's your parents, they'll give you a hand – they tell you, 'okay, this is how you do this, this is how you do that'. In here there's nobody like that". Similarly, Sile from Ireland, who was planning to marry her Irish boyfriend, was adamant that she could not rear children in London: "the ideal, for me anyways, is that we go home like in about three years' time and that we bring up our children there ... because I need a family network around me whenever I want to have children ... I don't feel that I have that here".

While it is possible that Patryk and Sile will return to their respective countries to have children, it is also possible that they may change their minds. This change was apparent in my repeated interviews over time with Magda. When first met in 2006, Magda, then a student, was determined to return to Poland upon completing her degree, marry her Polish boyfriend and have children in her native country: "because if I want to have babies, I want to have them in Poland". However, when re-interviewed in 2014, I found that Magda's life had taken a different route. She had established her career in Britain, met a British partner and had a baby. Thus, her life was almost exactly opposite to what she had predicted during the earlier research. A clear advantage of longitudinal research is providing insights into how plans evolve over time (Thomson, 2007). Repeat interviews, as in the case of Magda, can reveal surprising migration trajectories (Ryan et al, 2016).

When I first met Ewa in 2006 she was a single woman trying to develop her career and overcome deskilling (Ryan, 2011a). When I reconnected with her eight years later, she was married and had recently had a baby. She narrated how having children had transformed her embedding in London:

> 'I think it's very different way of settling in a country if you do or don't have children. I think it's impossible to really settle without starting a family. Because if you have children you have to participate in everything what's happening in society. You have to go to the same hospitals, the same playgroups, midwives, start the same schools, parent evenings, and you really get more and more understanding of what's happening.' (Ewa, Poland, 2000s)

Nonetheless, and notwithstanding her British husband, while completing the sociograms, Ewa reflected that most of the other mothers in her network were migrants: "I much easier will connect with mums who are non-English – somehow we click ... I have massive groups of mums I met through antenatal classes and childcare centres and we visit each other and we play together with our children – they are non-English". The fact that non-English mothers 'click' may be partly about a mutual desire to make new friends, especially in the absence of wider kinship networks. However, Ewa had not yet started to engage with schools. It is possible that school may provide opportunities to access different networks (Ryan and Sales, 2013). Indeed, school did appear to become crucial for Ewa and her family, as will be discussed in the conclusion chapter where I discuss my third interview with Ewa after the Brexit referendum in 2016.

Martyna, also from Poland, lived in south-east London, in a largely British working-class neighbourhood, and had two sons in the local school. While her husband, who worked in construction, had mainly Polish friends, Martyna made lots of British friends through the school: "we go camping together, we do drinks, and went for a wedding last month – almost the whole school was there. So, it's really nice. It's a very small primary school, so people are quite close". While the school provided an opportunity to meet people, Martyna emphasised the need to be open and sociable: "Probably it depends on the personality. I'm quite open – I've got loads of friends, Polish, English, Chilean, Spanish, French. No, I can't say it's hard to find friends when you're open". One reason why Martyna had made friends with local British parents, while Ewa had not, may be partly about time and network elasticity. Schools can provide opportunities for sustained interaction (De Klepper et al, 2010). Attending the same primary school for over five years afforded opportunities for Martyna to engage in regular social encounters with other parents that carried over into shared social activities. The significance of these local friendships become apparent in the conclusion chapter when I discuss my follow up interview with Martyna after the Brexit referendum. While it was mainly female participants who described making new, local friends through schools, some men also shared this experience. For example, Odile, from France, narrated how he had made new friends in London mainly through his children's school.

Of course, we should not assume that all migrants want to make British/English friends. Neither should it be implied that there is a linear progression over time as migrants become more familiar with their local area and their social ties become more diverse. In Irène's story, presented earlier in this chapter, she described how her network became more French after the birth of her children as she actively sought out French families for child-based sociality. Her narrative suggests how networks evolve based on a mix of opportunities but also personal preferences and shifting priorities, especially at different life course stages.

However, it may not be possible for migrants to realise their personal preferences and make friends just as they choose. For instance, class barriers may be a factor, especially for migrants who experience downward social mobility (Lopez Rodriguez, 2010). Aisling, from Ireland, worked as a nurse in London in the 1970s. Her husband was wealthy and the family enjoyed considerable affluence. However, when she left the marriage, following his infidelity, Aisling was rehomed on a social housing estate in a different area, where she knew no one. Divorce and relocation prompted a rupture in support networks (Greif and Deal, 2012). Moreover, Aisling felt unsupported by her sister, who also lived in London, causing a rift in the relationship. Hence, even the support of siblings, a noted source of emotional support (Wellman and Wortley, 1990), cannot be taken for granted (Del Real, 2019). In reduced economic circumstances, Aisling described how she felt unable to forge relationships with other parents at her children's school: "I didn't mix with the school mothers much … because I was living on the estate and I didn't want them to know. I wouldn't have birthday parties or anything because I wouldn't expect the other mothers to let their children come to the council estate". Aisling became socially isolated: "that was the worst scenario ever – when I look back it was like a prison".

Similarly, Sylwia, from Poland, narrated her embarrassment about living on a run-down housing estate. Her son attended school in an affluent area. But Sylwia felt that class barriers prevented her befriending parents at that school: "I live in a post council flat, and stigma around that is still huge barrier ... his friends were very well-to-do families, huge houses in Highgate or Crouch End".[9] When other parents found out that she lived on a notorious estate, Sylwia mimicked their reactions: "'oh no, it's not there is it?' 'There? Is it rough there?' 'Oh my god'".

Merton (1957) has described how individuals judge their own situation in comparison to 'reference groups'. Aisling and Sylwia were health professionals, but following divorce, both lived with limited financial resources in social housing. They experienced stigmatisation about living in deprived housing estates, especially in comparison with their reference group of well-off parents at their children's schools. Moreover, run-down estates may not provide spaces of sociality where newcomers can forge new, local ties (Cattell, 2001; Kay and Trevena, 2021). Thus, child-based sociality does not guarantee access to networks (Lopez Rodriguez, 2010; Gilmartin and Migge, 2016) and indeed migrants may not wish to embed in particular local neighbourhoods (Ryan, 2018). This experience highlights how unexpected life events, including downward socioeconomic mobility, may not only rupture existing relationships but also create barriers to accessing new friendship networks. As further discussed later, networks are dynamic and continue to evolve and change throughout the life course.

Ageing – changing social networks through the life course

In older age, especially post-retirement, networks may shrink. Nonetheless, Oliver (2012) cautions against discourses of vulnerability and passivity in older age. Instead, it is necessary to understand how older people may 'develop strategies like creating and maintaining supportive social networks' (Spalter, 2010: 330).

My studies have included migrants who were post-retirement, including some in advanced older age, that is, over 80 years. I discuss this group in more detail in the next chapter on transnational relations and consider attitudes towards return, particularly post-retirement. For this chapter, I focus on their local networks. Barry, my oldest participant at 92 years, worked in construction all his life. Widowed for many years, Barry lived with his unmarried son in North London. He was very proud of his son's university education and professional job. However, the son's career meant that Barry was alone in the house all day. Because of his remarkable physical health, he was able to go out every day and walked the short distance to a local community association where he socialised, engaged in activities and had lunch. As Spalter notes, 'a supportive social network compensates for the loss of intimate relations in old age because it provides some of the major needs at that stage in life ... companionship, friendship and emotional and instrumental support' (2010: 333).

As noted in the literature, faith organisations may also constitute 'an important place for meeting people and for gathering, establishing and strengthening ties' (Ciobanu and Fokkema, 2017: 209). Lohendra, aged 82, originally from Guyana, is of Indian heritage. Since retiring as an engineer, he became active in a Hindu association: "[it's] important to me in two ways ... reminds me about my culture and the religion ... And, to be honest, right now, it's also almost a social thing ... you know, you come here and meet, you chat".

While many older participants had families in London, some participants had no relatives living locally. As Palmberger observes in research with older migrants in Vienna, the prevalence and availability of 'family support networks among migrants are exaggerated' (2017: 246). Lilian migrated from Antigua to London in the 1970s. At that time her three children remained with relatives in Antigua. Having worked in hospitality prior to migration, upon arrival in London she got a job as a chamber maid in a large central London hotel. She remained single throughout her life and did not have any further children in London. One of her daughters came to London to study but then returned to the Caribbean. Lilian wanted to bring her son to London but instead he chose to join a cousin in the US. Aged 82 at the time of the interview, Lilian had been retired for many years. She lived alone and, despite some health issues including diabetes, had an active social life. Lilian was involved in many local associations including faith groups: "I go to the Salvation Army on Tuesdays, and Thursdays I go to my church – they have a knitting group ... and Wednesdays I come here [day centre[10]]".

Furthermore, Lilian had several good friends living locally: "sometimes growing older, especially if you don't have a family nearby, you know, some people say they're lonely. I'm not really that lonely, but still, if I did have family here it would be much better. I have friends that we phone each other every evening".

As Ciobanu and Fokkema argue, 'only recently has there been a growing interest in the experience of loneliness among older migrants' (2017: 200). Thus, more attention is needed to the strategies used by older migrants to access support through particular social ties (Ryan et al, 2021). Lilian's three close female friends had an arrangement to phone regularly to check on each other. One woman was a lifelong friend originally from Antigua: "We're neighbours from back home". The other two women were friendships forged in London: "one is from Monserrat and one is from Granada". All four women live in close proximity in North London and met at a social club or at church. Living alone, without any relatives in London, Lilian's friendship network was fundamental to her sense of well-being.

Lilian's experience contrasts markedly with Phyllis's narrative. Phyllis, also from the Caribbean, originally worked in the Midlands but later moved to London where she retrained as a nurse and started a family. When I met Phyllis, she was aged 86 and lived alone, although she had a large extended family living around London, including her daughters, grandchildren and great-grandchildren. Her relatives phoned regularly and visited at weekends but most of the time Phyllis was in her flat alone. Unlike Lilian, Phyllis's health issues meant that she was unable to go out and about. Phyllis narrated how her loneliness and isolation were compounded by shrinking friendship networks:

'[T]here was one time there was a lot of friends coming in and out, and I would go and visit them. But, now, it's not the same. As you get older, your friends they die out or they, like myself, they are all too old to travel. So, that's part of getting older, I suppose.' (Phyllis, Barbados, 1950s)

Moreover, one of Phyllis's closest friends had moved back to the Caribbean: "she's gone home to Barbados … She's really my good friend". As well as bereavement, return migration, as discussed in the next chapter, can impact on migrants' networks, especially through the ageing process. Phyllis felt the loss of her "good friend" very strongly, especially as other friends have died. Moreover, because of her reduced mobility, Phyllis was unable to attend any social clubs and so had no opportunity to forge new social ties. Adopting a life course perspective, this section clearly shows network dynamism as social ties evolve and change through the ageing process, with consequences for migrants' support and attachments in local places.

Conclusion

This chapter contributes to growing interest in how migrants make and sustain new friends in new places (Harris et al, 2020) as well as how networks evolve in particular places over time (Lubbers et al, 2021) as part of dynamic processes of embedding (Ryan et al 2021; Mulholland and Ryan, 2022). Hence, beyond simply describing friendship ties, I draw upon network stories to understand how ties are formed (antecedents) and what they do (consequences). Drawing upon SNA concepts such as elasticity, homophily and propinquity, as well as a life course lens to analyse change over time, the chapter adds to understandings of the dynamic contexts, characteristics and constraints that influence migrant friendship formations in four key ways.

Firstly, while much research on migrants' relational ties focuses on transnationality, this chapter has focused on relationality in the local places where migrants live, study, work and socialise to understand how friendships are formed and sustained. In so doing, I have sought to understand relational embedding in new places. Furthermore, rather than generalised and vague notions of 'friends' (Ripley Smith, 2013; Robertson, 2018), I have applied qualitative SNA techniques to understand how participants narrate the meaning and roles of close, trusting and enduring friendships.

Secondly, although migrants often forge new social relationships with people who share particular characteristics, the chapter has shown how these relational ties can extend beyond narrowly defined homophily. Using an intersectional lens, I explored how factors such as professional identities, life stage, having children at the same school or being members of a social club or faith group may facilitate relationality.

Thirdly, applying the life course framework to situate individual stories within wider sociohistorical contexts, I highlighted how geopolitical events can shape attitudes towards migrants. Hostility against particular ethnic or religious groups may produce 'network closure', curtailing opportunities to access local networks.

Fourthly, the life course lens, combined with rich biographical interviews, highlight the dynamics of friendship ties over time, including in older age where bereavement and poor health may result in network shrinkage. However, as illustrated by the stories shared by participants, friends can also play a vital role in supporting older migrants and maintaining a sense of local connectedness, underlining the enduring role of propinquity for practical, hands-on support.

Having explored local connections, the next chapter considers the dynamic interplay between local and transnational ties within network stories over time and through different life course stages.

7

Transnational Ties: Narrating Relationality, Resources and Dynamics over Time

Introduction

Ever since the 1990s' 'transnational turn' in migration studies (Schiller et al, 1992), there has been a huge body of research on the salience of migrants' identification and connection with their origin countries (for example, Faist and Ozveren, 2004; Parreñas, 2005; Goulbourne et al, 2010; Bryceson and Vuorela, 2020).

However, as Dahinden notes, 'the initial euphoria' about transnationalism 'has been replaced by a certain sobriety' (2005: 192): 'While the transnational perspective brings interesting insights to the study of migration processes', she cautions that 'transnational ties and social relations must not be presumed but rather carefully analysed' (Dahinden, 2005: 191). The fact that migrants have transnational connections tells us very little about what is actually going on within those relationships (Ryan and D'Angelo, 2018; Nowicka, 2020). SNA can reveal much about the make-up, meaning and dynamism of transnational ties (Bilecen et al, 2018; Lubbers, et al, 2021). The first aim of this chapter is to apply the framework of telling network stories in order to explore the meaning of long-distance relationships and the resources flowing therein.

Of course, migrants' cross-border communications are not new. Historians have studied the importance of long-distance correspondence, especially letters, over the centuries (Skrbiš, 2008). As Nancy Foner (1997) notes, many transnational practices hailed as 'new' actually have a long history. Nonetheless, a key difference nowadays is the extent to which technology can create a sense of co-presence in real time (Madianou and Miller, 2013). So-called 'transconnectivity' can mean that migrants feel part of the everyday lives of relatives back home (King-O'Riain, 2015). However, such technological connections are not without limits (von Koppenfels et al,

2015) and rarely replace the need for proximate physical contact, especially hands-on care with children (Ryan, 2007a) or elderly relatives (Wilding and Baldassar, 2009). Hence, the chapter's second aim is to consider how migrants connect transnationally and the changing patterns of long-distance communication over generations.

Through network stories, including visualisation techniques, and longitudinal methods, I also seek to understand relational change over time (Ryan and D'Angelo, 2018). Migrants' continued embedding in transnational relationships cannot be taken for granted (Ryan et al, 2021). Despite communication technologies, ties may weaken through prolonged separation. Hence, the chapter's third aim is to analyse how transnational ties ebb and flow, with changing needs, through different life course stages (Ryan, 2018).

Furthermore, a network lens is particularly useful when considering return migration. Research suggests that networks are often a factor in motivations and opportunities to return (Christou, 2006; De Haas and Fokkema, 2011; Salaff and Greve, 2013; Bilecen et al, 2015). Of course, the existence of social ties, including family ties, in the origin country is no guarantee of return. Moreover, geographically dispersed ties, including in the destination society, may mean that migrants have competing responsibilities and affiliations in different places. Therefore, the fourth aim of this chapter is to use network stories to analyse how migrants narrate, prioritise and make sense of varied social ties in different places and the implications for potential return.

But first, we begin with Agnieszka's story, which illustrates many of the themes and approaches that will be explored throughout this chapter.

Agnieszka's story

Agnieszka was originally interviewed in 2006, soon after she was recruited from Poland to work in the care sector. When first interviewed, Agnieszka described experiences of depression and isolation in London. Although her Polish boyfriend had migrated with her, she felt that he did not understand her mental health issues. Her closest ties were back in Poland: "in such situation when I need someone close, I rather call Poland. I often speak to my mum. I have very good contacts with my cousin and with my friends". During the interview, Agnieszka spoke warmly about her friendship networks in Poland: "the friendships from secondary school are the strongest ones and I am in frequent contact with people from Poland – my friendships are there".

When I reconnected with Agnieszka, eight years later (2014), I was curious to understand how her networks may have evolved. During the interim period, she had changed jobs frequently, with each move getting closer to her dream job in psychology, while also pursuing a course in counselling. She

Figure 7.1: Agnieszka's sociogram

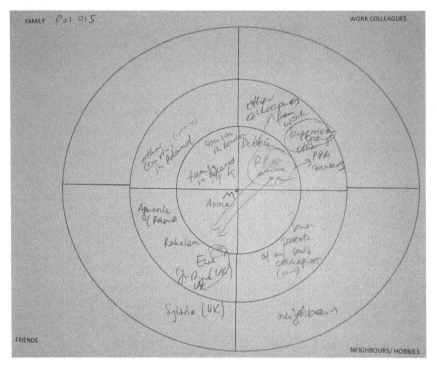

married her Polish boyfriend and had a son. Populating the sociograms (see Figure 7.1), she emphasised the closeness of family ties by putting relatives in the central circle: "my son, Michal, my partner, then my parents and my brother and sister-in-law". Apart from her son, partner and one cousin, all her relatives were in Poland. Thus, her close family ties were split transnationally between her home town in Poland and London. Agnieszka remained very close to her parents and communicated with them regularly. She described missing the physical proximity of parents, especially when she became a mother: "I was really missing family". She emphasised that "definitely with small children it is better to be close to family, grandmothers".

As Agnieszka completed her sociogram, I observed that no friends in Poland were added. I asked what had happened to friends from secondary school, mentioned in the first interview. She replied: "I'm not in good contact with them anymore". She added that although she missed "old good friends" in Poland, it proved difficult to sustain relationships and over time these ties had "gradually weakened". But that is not to suggest that such deep friendships had been replaced by new friends in London. Indeed, while Agnieszka populated her sociogram with many acquaintances, friends and work colleagues, she remarked that: "I have many friends. But maybe, I'll be honest, I don't have very, very good friends, in here, just friends". Her story suggests that while old friendship ties in the origin country may fade or weaken, it can take a long time to form new, meaningful friends in the destination country, as discussed in the previous chapter. Hence, we should not assume that old friends are simply swapped for new friends.

Although sociograms may be criticised as static images (Conway, 2014), as discussed in Chapter 3, they can be used to prompt narratives (Hollstein, 2011) and, when combined with follow-up interviews, can reveal relational dynamics (Ryan, 2021). Agnieszka's repeated interviews and sociogram suggest dynamic transnational relations over time. While family ties remained strong, friendship ties weakened, a pattern noted elsewhere in the literature (Eve, 2002). Moreover, despite regular visits, Agnieszka's sense of connectedness to Poland changed: "Even I'm going there so often, I feel like I'm, I don't really mesh as good as before. I don't know anymore the situation in Poland ... but I still feel very, strongly patriot". As Fortier (2000) observed, over time, despite enduring family ties, and a strong sense of national identity, migrants' involvement in and knowledge of their origin country may weaken. This suggests not only the dynamism but also the multi-dimensionality of transnational embedding (Ryan and Mulholland, 2015). Many of the themes raised by Agnieszka's story will be revisited throughout this chapter.

The strength and intensity of family ties

Like Agnieszka in her initial interview, many recently arrived migrants stated that their strongest ties were in the origin country. Ciara, who migrated to London two years before our interview, maintained daily contact with family in Ireland: "Oh, yeah, all the time ... daily I would say ... I do miss family a lot". It was not unusual for participants to contact parents several times per week. Desmond phoned his parents "maybe three times a week", while Sile stated: "I probably ring mummy like every other day". Similarly, Sorcha noted that although she had friends in London, her primary source of emotional support was her family in Ireland. So, in stressful situations, "I still have to call home in those kind of situations ... I'm really lucky that I have friends very close by ... But I probably would be more likely to call home". Thus, even in cases where migrants have social ties in London, family "back home" may continue to be a particular source of emotional support.

Darek, a man in his 50s, migrated to London soon after EU enlargement in 2004. His business in Poland collapsed and he needed money to clear debts. When interviewed[1] two years later, he had found a well-paid job and established a local network through his adult daughters who both lived in London. However, his wife had stayed in Poland to look after her ailing mother. It was clear that his wife was Darek's main source of emotional support as the couple phoned daily and at weekends chatted for hours: "Friday, Saturdays and Sundays sometimes we can talk for three hours … really it is nearly as if we were next to each other". Through these long and regular phone calls, Darek and his wife may spend more time conversing than couples who actually live together. Darek's experiences raise issues that will be explored throughout this chapter, including the emotional aspects of transnational relationships, the role of new technology in creating a sense of co-presence ("as if we were next to each other") but also care and the gendering of caregiving, especially through the ageing process.

Intense emotional connections to relatives back home are not only associated with recently arrived migrants. Colette, from France, lived in London for over a decade at the point of our interview:

> 'I speak to my parents every day. … I have a very close family and I go to France about four times a year, usually Christmas, Easter, I'm from a Christian family so religious holidays. Every year we try and do a family reunion in the summer. We hire a villa and we all go there and spend a week together.' (Colette, France, 2000)

Damien, originally from France but who had previously worked in Luxembourg, had lived in London for more than five years, when interviewed, and still called his mother regularly and visited several times per year: "I am very close to my family, generally speaking, sisters, I have got two sisters, mother, nephews, grandparents, cousins". It is noteworthy that Damien included his grandparents but also extended family such as cousins. This was not unusual among participants. For instance, Chantal described her family in France as a wide and enduring kinship network: "When I am with my cousins and my parents and aunts and uncles it's just like it's a family thing, it's just not changed. We always gel".

Migrants from within Europe tended to visit home frequently. For example, Damien visited his family "four or five times a year because with Ryanair it's very easy". Izabela returned to Poland regularly: "I prefer real relationships to virtual ones. I mean I can upload a picture or something like that but it will never be the same really as coffee with somebody". Similarly, Blaithin stated: "I need to personally go and make sure I see them and spend time – the phone and Skype can only do so much so you gotta go home, spend some time".

Maintaining transnational kinship ties is often motivated by promoting intergenerational relationships (Richter and Nollert, 2014; Koelet et al, 2017). For example, Irène, who had been in London for two decades, brought her children to France every year to share her family's traditional summer holiday, "because my family is still in France and my mother's got a summer house and that's where I would go when I was little".

It should not be assumed, however, that participants were simply negotiating family relationships across two countries. Participants often had relatives in several countries. Because of migratory links between the Caribbean and North America (Duval, 2004; Sutton, 2004), many participants had close relatives in the US and Canada. Howard, introduced in Chapter 4, explained that his whole family "are living in Canada". As a result, he had not visited the Caribbean for 30 years because "my mum and dad also moved to Canada". Similarly, Lalima, originally from Guyana, had lived in London since the 1960s; her sister also moved to London. Meanwhile, her brother moved to Canada where he worked as a doctor. After her parents died, Lalima had no close family left in Guyana. Thus, patterns of family migration shifted the site of Lalima's kinship networks from Guyana to North America. Furthermore, Lalima's only daughter moved to the US. As noted in the literature (Sutton, 2004), because of international connections, family reunions may take place in locations other than the origin country. Indeed, just before our interview, in 2019, Lalima had recently returned from a family reunion in Canada where her brother celebrated his 90th birthday.

A similar experience was described by Aoife, a young Irish migrant. Apart from Christmas, Aoife stated, she no longer visited Ireland frequently. As a child, her family visited the US often for business reasons. Her sister had migrated to the US and so the family reunited every summer in Florida. Using her long holidays as a teacher, Aoife stated: "I go to Florida for the entire summer".

Cliona, also a teacher from Ireland, had to negotiate close family ties across multiple sites, including a parent who retired to sunnier climes: "my dad lives in Tenerife – I feel this compulsion to make the effort to see him and then my twin sister has just moved to France so I have to make the effort to see her". Cliona also had relatives, including parents-in-law, in Ireland. So, negotiating family visits across several countries could be complicated: "you feel a bit torn". A strategy to manage these scattered connections was to invite relatives to visit London: "My in-laws are over quite a lot, my mom's over quite a lot, yeah, it's nice … my family comes over here quite a lot".

Indeed, several participants, especially those with young children, found the logistics and costs of regular visits to dispersed relatives expensive and exhausting. As Martyna from Poland observed, it was easier to invite visitors to London: "we prefer when people come here – it's less expensive".

Of course, that is not to imply that all transnational families are closely connected. Oliwia visited family in Poland "just once a year actually … it's turning into more, into a duty, than like holiday". Return visits to family can be emotionally intense experiences (Skrbiš, 2008; von Koppenfels et al,

2015; Pustułka and Ślusarczyk, 2016; Wojtyńska and Skaptadóttir, 2020) and, as discussed in the next section, are not necessarily restful holidays.

Family tensions and fractured transnational kinship ties

Migration can be associated with a reconfiguration and renegotiation of family relationships (Skrbiš, 2008; Botterill, 2014). Migration may be used to avoid family pressures and tensions, what Heering et al (2004) refer to as 'escape motivation'. Odile, from France, had married a woman of Asian heritage. Neither his family nor his wife's family approved of the marriage. Moving to London allowed the couple to be together without family interference. But migrants' decisions and life choices may continue to incur the disapproval of relatives in the origin country, with implications for the availability of support in times of need.

Two participants narrated accounts of how marital breakdown impacted upon already tense transnational family relationships. As mentioned in Chapter 6, Aisling left her husband after his infidelity and was rehoused in a run-down estate in the 1980s. She described being disappointed by the lack of transnational support offered by family in Ireland: "I didn't have any [support] because my family didn't want to know – they didn't want the neighbours to know my marriage broke up'.

A similar experience was narrated by Fidelma:

'I remember going home one year, the children were about 7 and 8 years, and I said to my mother "I am going to get divorced". I didn't tell her that he punched me, it was the embarrassment of it all, you know, but she said to me "oh we don't have divorces[2] in this family". You know this religious thing.' (Fidelma, Ireland, 1970s)

Return visits can bring to the surface clashing expectations and obligations (Skrbiš, 2008; Von Koppenfels et al, 2015). For Fidelma, visits to Ireland brought to a head the tensions between her family's religious values and her own life experiences in London (Ryan, 2008a). Return visits will be discussed again later in this chapter.

Of course, families are not single homogenous units. Migrants may feel close to some relatives but not others. Using a qualitative approach to networks, including sociograms to visualise ties, revealed the range and diversity of relationships within families. Karina had lived in London for over ten years and remained close to her mother in Poland but had gradually lost contact with other relatives: "I'm not very family oriented ... We had a massive fall out". Moreover, in completing the sociograms, it was apparent that Karina regarded some friends as closer to her than relatives: "they are the closest, emotionally". Thus, rather than treating kinship and friendship ties as two separate groups, as mentioned in Chapter 6, the distinction between family and friends may be blurry (Robertson, 2018). The next section explores the salience but also dynamism of transnational friendships.

"It's like a different friendship": the dynamics of transnational friendship ties

Findings from social network research suggest that strong friendship ties may endure physical separation (Wellman and Wortley, 1990). Most of my recently arrived participants said their closest friendships were in the home country. Izabela, recently arrived from Poland, stated: "my old friends are in Poland". These long-established friendships from childhood and school days were "real friends … what I call friends". This point was echoed by Clodagh from Ireland: "I mean they're my friends from all through school … we know each other very well". Long-established friendships may represent a connection with the place of origin, offering some stability and reassurance for migrants as they enter new and unfamiliar contexts. As Laura Morosanu (2013) notes, long-established friends in the country of origin may be considered 'soul friends' and have deeper meaning for migrants than newly established and potentially fleeting friendships in the destination society.

After more than a decade in London, Sylwia stated: "my friend lives in Poland, although I'm not seeing her physically, that's my friend from school, that's the kind of friend that if something really horrible happens, or something great happens you know, I kind of have her in my mind".

Nonetheless, as noted earlier in Agnieszka's story, it cannot be assumed that these ties endure or remain static over many years of separation and through life course changes. Continued relational embedding, especially in geographically dispersed friendship networks, requires ongoing investment of time and effort, as Liadan, from Ireland, succinctly explained: "I don't see them as often as I'd like because everybody's busy and, you know, it is more of an effort". Having interviewed participants of all ages and stages of migration, my data reveal the dynamics of transnational ties over time. Even Izabela, cited previously, was aware that some of her established friendships in Poland may not survive sustained separation: "I understand that some of the friends will go away [fade away] … well I'm sad about it but it will happen".

I am curious to understand why some transnational friendships appear to endure while others fade. Analysing network stories, especially combining narratives and pictures by using a sociogram, provides valuable insight into how participants perceive and present their networks (D'Angelo and Ryan,

2021). Moreover, as illustrated by Agnieszka's story at the start of this chapter, conducting longitudinal research through follow-up interviews over several years enables participants to narrate the ebb and flow of ties, including transnational relationships (Lubbers et al, 2021; Ryan, 2021).

Over time, living in a different country, migrants' lifestyles may appear out of step with old friends in the origin country. Return visits can bring these different lifestyles into sharp relief (Bell and Bivand Erdal, 2015; Grabowska and Garapich, 2016). In describing friendships in Poland, Gabi revealed the effort required to sustain transnational ties: "it's like a different friendship but it is still very close and very important ... But we live in two different countries so I try not to talk too much about UK. I do talk but not in details". So, in order to maintain these friendships, ongoing effort and emotional labour are required. Migrants have to be careful about how they discuss their new lives so that commonalities can be sustained, despite different lifestyles.

Some participants described how divergent lifestyles made it impossible to sustain old friendships. Initially, Oliwia tried to sustain transnational friendships: "When I was going back first, it was always easy". But eventually she and her friends had less in common: "my life changed so dramatically, and so did theirs, they've got families and children ... we didn't understand each other anymore". Unlike friends in Poland, Oliwia did not marry or have children. She spent her free time travelling extensively, including Asia and Australia, and described how her old friends disapproved of her lifestyle and judged her for not settling down to marriage and motherhood (see also Botterill, 2014; White et al, 2018). She found herself dis-embedding from these networks as the friendship ties "dissolved": "I actually felt that it was becoming artificial, you know, trying to be friends – it was not really natural anymore".

While friendship groups seem to weaken over time, some participants prioritised sustaining their "best friend". Klaudia explained: 'I've got my best friend, of course we are, you know, in touch all the time, but the rest are, you know, an email every now and then". Colette pointed to time constraints as a reason why she prioritised her best friend:

> 'I have three good friends in France, and I don't see them often – we probably speak about once a month ... I have my best friend in France – we went on holiday in February together ... I only get five weeks' holiday and I like to go and see my family every two or three months. So, it's difficult for me to allocate time for friends in terms of, you know, paid holidays.' (Colette, France, 2000)

Colette's narrative indicates how migrants appear to balance their time between different transnational ties, including family, best friends and other friends. This point was echoed by several participants and underlines the importance of not focusing on one type of transnational tie in isolation but, instead, adopting a networks lens to consider how particular ties may be evaluated and prioritised over others.

Of course, migrants cannot simply decide which relationships to sustain and which to 'dissolve'. As mentioned in the previous chapter, friendship is a two-way process based on reciprocity, shared interests and affinity. Friendship networks in the origin country are also dynamic:

> '[O]bviously, I recognised that we don't have much in common any longer. Because I am a different person than left 11 years ago from Poland, and they are different people than I'd known 11 years ago … now they've got their families, they've got their kids … and they've got their new friends.' (Dominik, Poland, 2000s)

Dominik's observation that friends back home make "new friends" suggests that migrants may feel they have been replaced in their former friendship networks.

So far, the focus has been on cross-national friendship ties between the origin and destination country, but as already noted, coming from societies with high outward migration, many participants had networks that spanned numerous countries. Among 21st-century Irish migrants, in particular, the geographical dispersal of their network ties was remarkable: "Lots in London, Australia, my fiancé's friends in Canada as well, but everybody has just kind of scattered" (Laidan). Interestingly, the word 'scattered' was repeated by many Irish participants to describe their networks: "a lot of my friends are scattered … one friend went to Glasgow, another is in Liverpool, another one is in Birmingham, another one is now in Australia so there's not really anyone in my home town" (Clodagh). Clodagh's observation that few of her friends had remained in Ireland was echoed by other participants. Owen explained that he had no friends left in his home town in the west of Ireland: "they've gone to New Zealand, Australia, Canada, the United States, Korea, Japan, China, Qatar". Humorously, he added that if you "threw a dart at a map of the world, hit any country, I have a friend there, unless you hit Ireland [laughing]".

Using a life course framework (Elder et al, 2003), these narratives need to be understood within specific historical conditions, especially the economic recession of 2008 when Ireland experienced a rapid increase in outward migration (Glynn et al, 2013). Moreover, that generation of migrants also tended to be highly engaged with social media. The ways in which technology enabled participants to maintain contact with their spatially dispersed networks was a recurring theme in the data.

Transnational communication over time: from writing letters to reading Facebook

Technology enabled some participants to create a sense of co-presence across geographical distance. Adrianna described how her family in Poland had arranged a birthday party on Skype: "we put Skype on and they were actually singing happy birthday and they had a cake, which they were eating and you imagine we were sharing it". Similarly, Deirdre, a recent migrant, described her family in Ireland connecting on Sundays over a meal: "in my family we're quite close – there's five of us. So, they'd have Sunday dinners and they'd always call me". In this way, technology allowed migrants to share a meal or celebration with families at a distance.

Younger participants often opined that technology had transformed their experience of migration. Owen, an Irish man in his late 20s, remarked: "look, we've got Skype. I can see my mummy's face any time I want, you know – it's different now". Similarly, Sile, another young Irish migrant, observed: "my friend just had a baby so she can send me photos of her baby". In this way, many participants felt a sense of shared lives and emotional closeness with geographically distant friends and relatives. As noted in the literature, communication technologies allow migrants to be 'peripherally, yet constantly aware of the actions and daily rhythms of their peers' (Madianou, 2016: 183).

However, this 'always-on' lifestyle, as discussed by Danah Boyd (2012), can reinforce a fear of missing out on events in the origin country. Deirdre remarked: "I hate missing out on stuff at home". For some migrants, especially the more recently arrived, this can have an unsettling effect:

> '[M]y home friends are a great circle of friends and I hate that I'm not there, missing things. Like one of my friends is getting married in September, I'll go home for the hen party but yeah, there's little things I see on Facebook that I wish I was there for them. But I have to remember, you know, that I'm having a great time over here.' (Sorcha, Ireland, 2000s)

Social media sites like Facebook allow for particular presentations of self (Hogan, 2010) in ways that can appear to amplify fun and excitement. Those viewing the depicted events, from a distance, may feel envious or even sad about what they are missing (Oberst et al, 2017). As Sorcha narrated previously, reading the Facebook pages of friends in Ireland reinforced a sense of 'missing out' which she sought to assuage by reminding herself that living in London was also fun. Thus, while social media could be viewed as a tool in maintaining transnational networks, the emotional impact on migrants of 'missing out' should not be overlooked.

Moreover, some participants were mindful of the limits of technology in building intergenerational relationships. Ewelina used Skype to connect her children to their grandparents in Poland at least once per week. But this was not necessarily an easy process with young children:

'It's not a natural conversation – kids are sitting there, staring at the screen and the grandparents are asking what's the school like, how is this and how is that and they answer but it never turns into a conversation … So both kids stay in front of it for a little while and get bored really quickly.' (Ewelina, Poland, 2000s)

While technology creates the capacity to connect across geographical distance, the experience can be frustrating and lacking in intimacy, especially when bridging generational divides (von Koppenfels, Mulholland, and Ryan, 2015). Interestingly, there were notable generational patterns in how technology was used. For example, Deirdre noted: "I have an iPhone, I WhatsApp my brothers and sister, mom. Dad's completely behind with technology so he'll call me every week". Many participants described phoning parents but using different platforms to connect with siblings and friends. As Izabela noted, "Facebook, Instagram and Twitter, everything … with my parents it's only about phone calls". Angelika's parents were elderly and lived in a remote part of Poland with unstable internet connections. She had considered buying them a laptop and connecting Wi-Fi but decided it would be too stressful for them, so she continued to phone instead.

Lalima, aged 76, and originally from Guyana, did not own a computer or tablet or use any social media, yet through cheap telephone deals she remained connected transnationally to her daughter in the US and her brother in Canada. Indeed, many of my older interviewees described using the telephone to engage in regular communication with transnational relatives, especially siblings who were also getting older and experiencing poor health.[3]

But that is not to suggest that such regular, long-distance communication is a new phenomenon. Interviewing older people about their migration histories revealed the importance of transnational networks through the life course. Maura left Ireland in the 1950s and described regular communication with her parents: "we used to write letters home and my parents would ring me up … we didn't have a phone at home that time – they used to phone me from a phone box".

Writing letters home was a common theme in interviews with earlier waves of migrants. For researchers, this tangible form of transnational communication is an invaluable resource. In *The Polish Peasant in Europe and America*, described as the 'first systematic study of transnational family life' (Skrbiš, 2008: 232), Thomas and Znaniecki (1919) used letters between migrants in the US and families in Poland to study long-distance relationships over one hundred years ago. Those early 20th-century letters shared gossip and local news, and revealed emotional connections between migrants and relatives, including some family tensions and disagreements.

When I interviewed Fiona, a retired nurse, she showed me a letter written by her father in Ireland during the 1950s. I felt honoured to see that old, faded but treasured letter. Interestingly, her father was thanking Fiona for sending money home. This historical record of remittances between migrants and their parents offered an insight into one aspect of transnational relationships. Beyond simply noting the medium and extent of transnational communication (Nowicka, 2020), using the framework of network stories provides insight into resources flowing between these ties (Ryan, 2011a). As discussed later, these insights offer deeper understanding of the expectations and motivations of these connections and the consequences for real or expected resource exchanges.

Remittances: the flow of financial resources through transnational networks

For many migrants, moving abroad to find work and earn money was motivated, at least in part, by the need to support families in origin countries. Among older Irish participants in particular, there was a common theme of sending money regularly to parents. Eileen described sending "back two pounds" every month. Remittances were often expected, especially by poorer families. This seemed to be especially prevalent when migrants were young, single and without family responsibilities of their own in the destination country. However, once participants started their own families in London, the pattern of sending money to parents seemed to decrease. Nonetheless, some narratives revealed how expectations to support relatives in the origin country could clash with migrants' own aspirations in the destination context.

Mairead, an Irish nurse, recalled how plans to buy a house in London in the 1950s were postponed because her husband had to remit money so his parents could build a house in the west of Ireland: "for four year he sent home the money to build the house". Only after that project was completed could Mairead and her husband start to save for a house in London. Given the hostilities that Irish migrants could face in renting accommodation (Ryan et al, 2021), postponing plans for their own home was a considerable sacrifice for the couple.

Mairead's story was not an isolated example. Barry, my oldest participant, aged 92, told a similar story. Working in construction, Barry remitted considerable amounts of money and made many sacrifices to support his parents and younger siblings back in Ireland. He recalled sending money to his parents every month: "Ireland was very poor in the 50s. I used to send £1 home every month to my father and mother". Nonetheless, through hard work and regular saving, he managed to accrue enough money for a deposit on a house in London. However, once again it is apparent that the personal project of a migrant might clash with the needs of the wider family. Barry was asked to help his sister: "Molly was going to Australia; she had no money … I could have bought a house but instead I helped my sister and brother-in-law to go to Australia".

After supporting his relatives, Barry had to start saving again to buy a house in London. During our interview, Barry was accompanied by a younger sister, Annie, who was visiting London. When he related the story about helping Molly to migrate to Australia, Annie suddenly interrupted and expressed surprise as she had never heard that story. She seemed genuinely shocked that Barry had given a substantial amount of money to Molly. This incident underlines the point that 'family' is not a homogenous unit and instead we need to look at relationships and resources between specific ties within kinship networks.

Not all migrants sent remittances. Some participants came from well-off families and did not need to send money to parents. Nonetheless, they usually sent gifts. Howard, for example, came from an affluent family in the Caribbean and did not send remittances. But he remembered sending a big parcel at Christmas: "I had two younger brothers and two younger sisters and Christmas time I used to send them gifts, you know … I used make a parcel and send it recorded mail".

Most of the younger participants, from recent waves of migration, did not send regular remittances. The Irish, Polish and French younger migrants were not expected to send money to their parents. Nevertheless, as discussed later, non-financial resources, especially care, often flowed through these kinship ties. However, for some migrants, especially those from poorer countries, sending money to support family projects or emergency expenses continued to be important.

Rukhsana, from Afghanistan, introduced in a previous chapter, separated from her husband and lived in modest circumstances relying upon social security benefits. However, when her niece was attacked with acid in Afghanistan and needed emergency medical treatment, Rukhsana, together with her brother in Germany, managed to pay for the girl to go to India for surgery. This transnational network across four countries, and two continents, was quickly mobilised to ensure that the niece received the best treatment available: "last year she went to India and had two or three operations on her face – they took skin from her leg". The traumatic impact of this attack upon Rukhsana will be discussed later in the chapter.

While so far we have focused on financial remittances, it is apparent that many resources flowing through transnational kinship networks were non-monetary (Bilecen et al, 2015; 2020). Care was a recurring theme in narratives and, despite advances in communication technology, highlighted the enduring need for propinquity, especially for hands-on care (Ryan, 2007a).

Transnational care networks through the life course: the need for propinquity

Childcare may be a practical resource that migrants attempt to access through their social networks (Bojarczuk and Mühlau, 2018). Especially in cases where private childcare is expensive or in emergencies when additional childcare is required, migrants may turn to close relatives or trusted friends (Ryan, 2007a). But childcare highlights the enduring salience of propinquity (von Koppenfels, Mulholland and Ryan, 2015). This point was humorously noted by Martyna who used Skype to connect her children with their grandparents in Poland: "it's a shame they can't babysit on a Saturday night … not over skype, no". Thus, while many forms of care and support can be provided via technology at a distance, childminding requires physical co-presence (Wilding and Baldassar, 2009; Kloc-Nowak and Ryan, 2022).

Among my participants, some had left children back in the origin country with the expectation that the family would be reunited in due course. As noted in Chapter 6, when Lilian migrated to London in the 1970s, her three children remained in Antigua with their grandmother. Lilian sent back regular remittances to support her family. One daughter moved to London to study, but later returned to the Caribbean. Lilian hoped that her son would follow her to London but instead he chose to join a cousin in the US. Lilian's story indicates how transnational care arrangements may become extended and family reunion plans may not work out as anticipated (see also Phoenix and Bauer, 2012).

Among other participants, transnational support with childcare was associated with holiday visits. As discussed in Chapter 4, Chantal and her young son migrated from Paris to London in 1996 to join her husband who was working in the financial sector. Soon after arriving in London, Chantal gave birth to a daughter who had a serious, life-limiting illness. As a newly arrived migrant without support networks in London, apart from her husband, who worked long hours, Chantal turned to her transnational network for emotional but also practical support:

> '[A]s soon as my son was on school breaks, I would fly off to stay with my parents and stay there for all the holiday breaks. Especially for my son, it didn't feel completely fair because his sister was a full-time job. At least when I was with my parents, there were three people to look after the two of them.' (Chantal, France, 1990s)

Reflecting on those difficult years, Chantal stated: "There is nobody as close as family". She explained that, in situations where intensive support is required, such as care for a disabled child, the bonds of trust and obligation within families, especially with grandparents, are of primary importance. In such situations, it is difficult to ask friends or neighbours to commit to protracted, hands-on care. Moreover, because all her time was absorbed with her daughter, Chantal had no energy to invest in maintaining reciprocal friendship networks. She remarked that having a severely disabled child "tends to kill all your networks, except family". In analysing sources of support within social networks, Wellman and Wortley (1990) note that in times of crisis, people usually turn to family. This is motivated at least in part by mutual expectations and obligations underpinned by social norms: 'the densely knit structure of most kinship ties intersects with the norm that "blood is thicker than water" to encourage supportive relations among kin' (Wellman and Wortley, 1990: 572).

Chantal had the resources to travel to France during every school holiday; moreover, as a full-time mother she was able to spend these long periods of time away from London. For other migrants, transnational networks may be utilised to provide childcare so that parents can work through the school holidays. Cliona, an Irish nurse, recalled that, in the 1980s, her younger sister, who was a student in Ireland, would help out with childcare: "my sister would come over for a month in the summer". As noted in Chapter 4, siblings often featured in narratives as facilitators of migration processes. Social network analysts have noted that, while siblings are similar to friends as key sources of emotional support, they are more likely than friends to provide important resources such as care (Wellman and Wortley, 1990: 574).

As well as sisters, mothers also featured strongly in care narratives. In the 1960s Fiona's mother came from Ireland for extended visits to help with a new baby. Similarly, Ewa, from Poland, described her ongoing reliance on transnational networks. Despite living in London for over a decade, and having a British husband, Ewa found that in times of need it was her mother and sibling who were the most reliable sources of care: "my Polish family is at the heart of my social links. … in any troubles I reach back for Poland". Indeed, on the day of our follow-up interview in 2014, I met Ewa's mother who had arrived for an extended stay to help with childcare. As Wellman noted in his analysis of interpersonal networks in Canada, 'regardless of where they live' parents are 'more apt than other intimates' to help in emergencies (1979: 1219).

Another notable trend in the data, particularly among European migrants, was to send children to grandparents in the origin country during summer holidays. For example, Ewelina from Poland explained: "they spend one and a half weeks with one set of grandparents and one and a half weeks with the other, so three weeks in total … one of us goes with them for the first few days and then one of us picks them up". Half a century earlier, in the 1950s and the 1960s, Mairead sent her two daughters "to Ireland for the six weeks of the summer".

Mairead's experiences reveal patterns of reciprocity as care exchanges within transnational family networks operate in both directions. Mairead told me the story of Lily, her disabled sister. Lily lived in Ireland with their mother but following the mother's death, Lily needed a new care arrangement, so Mairead brought her to London. In exchange, another sister in Ireland looked after Mairead's two daughters during the summer holidays "to give me a rest here". While 'reciprocity' permeates social relations 'in fundamental ways' (Bernhard, 2020: 4), reciprocal exchanges are not necessarily of equal value (Bilecen, 2020). Her two children spent summers in Ireland, but Mairead cared for Lily for 36 years. Mairead narrated this story in a matter-of-fact tone without revealing any clues to how she felt about this protracted care provision. Nonetheless, when discussing her nursing career, Mairead commented that she was only able to work part-time night shifts, even after her children grew up, because of caring for Lily. Consequently, her nursing career never progressed: "I think I would have become a sister tutor.[4] I would never have stayed on night duty but … I couldn't advance from that because Lily was priority". As noted in a study of migrants in Australia, care obligations can result in women compromising their careers in order to look after sick and elderly relatives (Wilding and Baldassar, 2009).

It was remarkable among my data how many migrants brought relatives from origin countries, especially ageing or sick parents, to live with them in London. Fiona, mentioned earlier, benefited from the regular visits of her mother when her children were young. Later, Fiona brought her widowed mother to live with her in London. Noreen was an only child and somewhat unusually, both of her parents, after retiring, moved from Ireland to be near her in London. However, this placed significant caring responsibility on Noreen for many years: "I helped to look after my father and he died and then my mother … I looked after her until she died".

Hannah, originally from the Caribbean, also brought her mother to London in later life and provided care until her death. Hannah ran her own business and could not take time off so she needed to draw upon formal care provision to help look after her mother:

> 'I had my mother over here. She was an elderly person and she had a fracture so she couldn't move – she was in bed all the time. I would say I had good care because they used to come in the morning. I was working – they used to come in the morning and clean her and get her ready for breakfast. We used to do the rest of it. … She came here in 1991 or 1992, and she died in 1996.' (Hannah, Guyana, 1960s)

As a British citizen, Hannah was able to bring her mother to London. Needless to say, immigration restrictions can limit how migrants provide hands-on care (Kofman et al, 2005; Madziva and Zontini, 2012). As discussed in the conclusion chapter, changing immigration rules associated with Brexit raise concerns for future care arrangements. Cost and fitness to travel also impact on migrants' ability to exchange care resources transnationally (Kloc-Nowak and Ryan, 2022). Although in her 80s, Deirdre visited Ireland regularly to see her older sister: "My sister was 90 earlier this year and she can't walk very well or hear or see very well and it is a big strain to talk to her. But because of that we go over every three or four months to visit". When I interviewed Phyllis, aged 86, in 2018, she had recently returned from her brother's funeral in Barbados. Despite her own health issues, Phyllis was planning another visit in the near future to sell her brother's property. Thus, so long as they were able to travel, older migrants could actively participate in transnational visits and care.

For younger participants, providing hands-on care to ageing relatives was not yet a reality. Nonetheless, several anticipated that it might occur in the future and could shape their future migration plans. Colette, from France, reflected on the future needs of her parents: "because my parents are getting older and there will be a time when I will go back just to look after them ... because my brothers are useless, useless". This quote again suggests gendered expectations of care whereby female migrants are more likely than their male counterparts to return to provide hands-on care (Wilding and Baldassar, 2009; Kraler et al, 2011). Colette had several brothers in France but as the only daughter, she felt a moral obligation to be the primary source of care. Although this eventuality had not yet arisen, she explained: "in the back of my mind, there is always that, if something was going to happen to one of them, or they were critically ill, I would definitely move back home, because they couldn't cope".

Justyna visited Poland often to see her widowed mother and take her to hospital appointments. However, as her mother got older, and could no longer live alone, Justyna was committed to returning permanently to Poland to provide ongoing, hands-on care (see also Kordasiewicz, Radziwinowiczówna and Kloc-Nowak, 2018). Similarly, Blaithin, a young Irish woman, emphasised that she would want to go home to help a seriously ill relative: "And God forbid, if anyone got sick in my family or anything, you know, seriously ill, I'd have to go home – it's always in my mind".

So far, using a life course lens, this chapter has focused on the dynamic composition of transnational networks over time and the associated ebb and flow of resources between long-distance ties, including hands-on care. Transnational networks may also be a factor in migrants' plans for return to the origin country.

Transnational networks and questions of return

Following the mobility and transnational turns in migration studies, there is increasing interest in return migration (King and Christou, 2011). However, while the possibility of return is often a common theme within migrant narratives, it is not necessarily easy or straightforward (Reynolds, 2010; White, 2014; Ni Laoire, 2014). As discussed later, adopting the framework of network stories helps to illuminate the complex and dynamic interplay between social ties 'here' and 'there' over time, through key life course transitions, with implications for potential or planned return.

As noted in Chapter 4, while many participants arrived with short-term migration plans, over time these gradually became extended (Ryan et al, 2009; Ryan, 2019). A common theme was the way in which children's education can shape decisions to stay in the destination society (Ryan et al, 2009; Ryan and Sales, 2013; Moskal and Tyrrell, 2016; Sime, 2018). A participant from the 1950s wave of migrants told me how relatives in Ireland wanted her and her husband to return and manage the family farm: "my family wanted me to come back to the farm, but no I wouldn't ... well, Cathy had just started school and really it wasn't practical" (Eileen). Of course, it is also possible that children's schooling gave migrant families a justification for staying put in the face of transnational family pressures to return. This story suggests some of the complex negotiations and decision making between local and transnational family ties.

While relationality, including children and partners, may reflect but also reinforce migrants' embedding in the destination society, over time, depleting transnational ties may become a factor in decisions about whether or not to return (Buffel, 2017). Niamh, a retired nurse, was recently widowed when I interviewed her but she had decided to remain in London:

> 'I've lost my husband now but my children are here, and my grandchildren, and I couldn't see myself, at my age, going back to live in Dublin. I have a sister in Dublin, but I couldn't see myself going back even to retire there.'

Phyllis gave similar reasons why she did not return to Barbados after retiring from nursing:

> 'I would have had to start all over again. Build a home, because I didn't have a partner, husband or anything. It was me on my own. I could go to live with my brother. I wouldn't want to do that. So, the children and grandchildren were all here – why go to live a lonely life in Barbados?' (Phyllis, Barbados, 1950s)

The narratives of Phyllis, from Barbados, and Niamh, from Ireland, are remarkably similar and illustrate the importance of differentiating between particular kinship ties. Phyllis had a brother in Barbados (he had since died, as mentioned earlier), while Niamh had a sister in Ireland. But dyadic ties to a sibling did not compensate for separation from children and grandchildren. Moreover, after 50 years spent in London, moving back 'home' would mean starting all over again. As Phyllis added, "I came here a young person. To go back to live there, I don't feel myself fitting in … pick up roots and go to live there, no".

Concerns about no longer fitting in were recurring themes in the data. As Tracey Reynolds (2010) found in researching Caribbean return migration, fitting back into or re-embedding in a society, no matter how strong the cultural affinity, is far from guaranteed. Like many other migrants from the Caribbean, Lohendra observed that his family had scattered and "very few" were left in Guyana: "most of them now are in North America". Those relatives who had remained in Guyana had now passed away: "I used to have a reason to go to see relatives, uncles, aunts … they've all died out … I have nephews and things like that. But it's not the same – they don't know you, you're like a foreigner". These narratives suggest how, with passing years, migrants may experience dis-embedding from origin societies (Ryan and Mulholland, 2015; Mulholland and Ryan, 2022).

It might be tempting to think that this phenomenon of feeling "like a foreigner" mainly impacted on long-distance migrants like those from the Caribbean, because expensive travel and visa restrictions may have impeded regular family visits over the decades (Duval, 2004). However, it should be noted that many European participants, despite regular visits, made similar observations about no longer fitting into the origin country.

Dominik, as noted earlier, remarked that he was not the same person who had left Poland 11 years previously. Similarly, Colette, despite regular visits, described dis-embedding from French daily life: "I feel a bit detached because there are things that I cannot relate to". Several participants echoed these sentiments. Sylwia, for example, noted how her attitudes had changed over time and she found aspects of Polish society "rigid in terms of acceptance of any minorities or homosexuality or any different nations and any kind of alternative lifestyles". This point chimes with Oliwia's earlier observation about growing apart from former friends in Poland because of divergent lifestyles and values.

Among my data, it was striking how often the difficulties of return migration were narrated through the trope of a friend or relative who tried but failed to successfully re-settle in the origin country. As Lilian remarked about Caribbean returnees, "a lot of people that go home they have to come back here". Similarly, Eileen, from Ireland, told me: "A brother of mine went back and he came back again and I know other people that have come back again". Eileen explained why people returned but were unable to settle: "I think it is difficult to get into the routine there now ... You see, we are expecting it to be the same and it's not. It is not the same at all". As Una, another Irish woman, put it, "we can't go back to the good old days". Migrants have changed but the home country has also changed.

Hannah was critical of how the Caribbean had Americanised and bore little resemblance to childhood memories:

> 'So, it is not like what we left ... now you go back, it's more modern ... when you go back, you think you are in New York, everybody having different clothes ... I think it's not the same. So, if I should go back there to live, it wouldn't be the same.' (Hannah, Guyana, 1960s)

Several participants stated that return migrants were not welcome. Martyna from Poland explained: "they don't really appreciate people coming back from England ... Well, it's just that they don't like us, because we've got more money". Eileen, from Ireland, noted: "we're not quite accepted ... a lot of people who have gone back, they tell us that".

Of course, my data are skewed towards those who did not return, or who tried to return but remigrated again. I have not interviewed people who successfully returned to their origin country. Nevertheless, it is still important to consider the role of networks in stories of non-return or 'failed' return. The complex dynamics of social ties are clear in the stories of two women, both from Ireland, who had actually returned.

Roisin had retired back to Ireland with her husband a few years prior to our interview: "Our plan was that we were going to have a great time – we were going to play golf and all that". But the reality of moving back was very different from visiting Ireland for summer holidays: "when you go on holiday, people put themselves out to entertain you but it is different when you go to live there". Roisin found being back in Ireland "a culture shock". Unable to readjust, she and her husband returned to London. An interesting feature of Roisin's story is the sense of disappointment about her networks in Ireland. When on holiday, friends and relatives make time for visitors but when one returns permanently, local people resume their busy lives and have less time for socialising with returnees.

Emer narrated a similar story which was all the more poignant because I interviewed her in Ireland as she was packing up to remigrate. Having completed nurse training in London (see Chapter 4), she and her sisters migrated to Australia. Emer married, had a son and enjoyed a successful career in nurse education in Australia. She retired to Ireland but after two years could not settle and, when we met in a hotel in Cork, was about to return to Australia. Emer explained why it was hard to resettle in Ireland:

> 'I think it is the isolation. You see, my age group, they have their own families, grandchildren, that is their whole lives, and they are very nice to me, but they have their own … and even my very good friend, she has three children and two grandchildren and she lives their lives for them.' (Emer, Ireland, 1950s)

As Emer's sisters had also migrated, she had no close relatives in Ireland. Although she had a very good friend in Ireland, the sense of disappointment is palpable in Emer's narrative. This very good, childhood friend was preoccupied with her own family. There was little space for Emer in her friend's densely packed kinship network. Thus, having long-established ties in the origin country does not mean these networks can be reaccessed after a long absence. Hence, relational re-embedding may be harder than expected. By contrast, Emer had a strong network in Australia and that motivated her decision to return:

> 'I have got two sisters in Australia, I've got my husband, who I am separated from but who is a great friend, and I have got my son. I am 68 now – let's face it, I am hitting old age and I think it [Ireland] is no place to be by yourself.' (Emer)

Of course, not all migrants entertained ideas of return. For some, return was impossible for reasons of safety. Rukhsana spoke about her complex relationship with Afghanistan:

> 'Well, everyone misses their country – I was born there, I lived there for 22 years. I miss it – my family lives there. When I went there three years ago, I saw so many changes. Before I went there I thought "I love Afghanistan – I want to live there" but after all that time things had changed, people had changed, their minds had changed.' (Rukhsana, Afghanistan, 1990s)

As noted earlier, Rukhsana's niece suffered an acid attack in Afghanistan. This seriously impacted on Rukhsana's views about future return: "When I heard this news I cried and cried … All this makes me hate Afghan men. They just think about themselves. They treat women like slaves. When I saw my niece, I thought no way am I living in Afghanistan".

Jennah was born in India but her family lived for many years in Kuwait, before her parents returned to India and she moved to London with her husband. As a visible Muslim, who wears a hijab and jilbab, Jennah told me she felt unsafe in India. She described "blatant racism and Islamophobia there":

'I have been to India a lot recently because my dad was ill and then he passed away. Every time you go there you feel you don't belong, it is a Hindu majority country, you feel like an outsider there ... India is my country, but I don't feel safe there – I feel safe here. It is very sad. I don't feel a part of it, I feel an alien. I don't fit in there. But here I feel safe – I can go out here at night to the shop if I need something – you can't do that in India. Back home you need to think twice. If you have to go out in the dark, you don't know what is going to happen.' (Jennah, India, 1990s)

Despite maintaining strong ties to family in India, Jennah felt no desire to return permanently. Thus, while networks are important in migrants' aspirations to return, social ties need to be understood within the wider sociopolitical contexts that also frame migration decision making.

Conclusion

This chapter has explored migrants' transnational relationships, including the role of new technologies in how long-distance communication has changed over time. In so doing, the chapter contributes to the literature in four key ways.

Firstly, by analysing network stories, this chapter has considered the meaning of transnational social ties. It has been argued that migrants' transnational practices cannot be simply reduced to connectivity (Nowicka, 2020). In other words, the fact of regular communication tells us little about the meaning of particular relationships and the flow of resources between them. By presenting nuanced and at times emotional network stories, this chapter suggests the support and care but also the tensions and pressures that can exist between transnational connections.

Secondly, this chapter contributes to understanding how transnational relations change over time. Using longitudinal network analysis can reveal considerable change in the extent, durability and meaning of spatially dispersed relationships (Ryan and D'Angelo, 2018; Lubbers et al, 2021). Moreover, adopting qualitative longitudinal methods, including repeated interviews, to explore the meaning and perception of change over time suggests the dynamism of relationships to friends, close family and extended kin. My analysis reveals that embedding in long-distance ties cannot be taken for granted but requires ongoing effort. Even connections that initially appeared strong, may fade as priorities and lifestyles diverge and there is less time, or mutual inclination, to invest in maintaining dispersed ties.

Thirdly, using a life course perspective, this chapter contributes to understanding the enduring salience of propinquity, especially for hands-on care, despite advances in new technology. The types of care flowing through networks may alter at key life stages. In younger age, migrants may be recipients of childcare from transnational relatives, but with passing time, they may become the carers of ageing relatives. As discussed in this chapter, the extent to which migrants can engage in hands-on care depends in part on financial resources, fitness to travel, but also the immigration regimes that frame transnational mobility and access to care services (Bilecen, 2020; Kloc-Nowak and Ryan, 2022). Thus, while these life events and support needs also apply to non-migrants (Wellman, 1979; Bidart and Lavenu, 2005), the particularities of migrant experiences create specific challenges.

Finally, this chapter illustrates that, rather than focusing on transnational relationships as a separate and distinct category of ties, adopting a network lens allows us to see how local and transnational ties to kin and friends may interact in complex ways. As migrants age, for example, their strongest ties may be to children and grandchildren in the destination society, while networks of family and friends shrink in the origin country, associated with a sense of dis-embedding, and with implications for possible return or retirement migration. Moreover, patterns of migration may mean that interpersonal ties are 'scattered' over many countries beyond any simple binational focus on origin and destination societies.

8

Conclusion: Thoughts and Future Directions

Introduction

Migration poses particular opportunities for network researchers. Migration changes social relationships as migrants navigate new ties in new places as well as negotiating existing long-distance ties. However, that is not to suggest migrant exceptionalism (Eve, 2022). While acknowledging the specificities of international migration, I have argued that we can also draw upon the concepts and tools of network researchers who have worked with non-migrants.

This book has sought to contribute to migration studies by applying qualitative SNA to gain nuanced understandings of dynamic relationships, the resources flowing between particular social ties and the relative social location of the actors within specific spatio-temporal contexts. In so doing, I have also sought to advance the field of qualitative SNA by developing my approach of telling network stories.

While presenting the many advantages of this approach, it is important to acknowledge that doing qualitative network analysis and applying the framework of telling network stories is relatively intensive and time-consuming. It is necessary to invest time in building rapport with participants, especially when seeking to remain in contact with them over a lengthy period of time. Beyond the data generation phase, the analysis of such rich data, especially including visual as well as oral data, can be quite labour-intensive. Nonetheless, as I hope to have demonstrated in this book, such an investment of time and effort is undoubtedly worthwhile.

In this concluding chapter, I begin by summarising the contribution of my epistemological, methodological and empirical approaches. I then briefly consider the implications of recent, 'unsettling events' (Kilkey and Ryan, 2021), including Brexit, drawing upon follow-up communication with some my participants. Finally, I reflect upon possible future directions for my work and the application of my framework.

The contribution of 'telling network stories'

Throughout this book, I have argued that migration stories are, at heart, relational stories. People narrate their migration experiences through accounts of dynamic and intricate networks of interpersonal relationships. Network stories are interesting and engaging for readers by presenting particular situations and experiences through vivid and evocative narratives. Moreover, the epistemological and methodological approach of telling network stories, I argue, has the potential to offer new and important insights into how we understand relationality in contexts of migration.

As discussed in Chapter 2, the framework of telling network stories can help to address several persistent questions in migration studies. Using this framework to analyse rich relational stories allows us to overcome the enduring challenge of going beyond the metaphorical use of 'network' (Knox et al, 2006). Migration researchers have been criticised for using network as a generalised, metaphorical term that lacks detail and precision (Bilecen et al, 2018; Ryan and Dahinden, 2021). Beyond a vague notion of 'a migrant's network', exploring stories offers insights into the complexity and dynamism of entangled relationality. In so doing, we can gain deeper understanding of particular ties to kin, friends, neighbours, work colleagues, including negative ties, fleeting acquaintances and weak ties.

Furthermore, telling network stories, informed by an interpretivist approach and narrative analysis, offers an alternative to the dominance of computation and big data in social network research. Rather than quantifying network ties to calculate measurements of centrality and density in order to test hypotheses of causality, my qualitative approach analyses network stories as dynamic discursive devices to explore meaning making, interpretation and presentation of self. As clearly shown by Emer's story of migrating to study nursing in the 1950s, the mere existence of a kinship tie to an aunt, also a nurse in London, tells us little about the meaning of that relationship. Far from assuming a causal link between these two alters, Emer's narrative reveals relational tensions as she disliked the aunt and rejected her advice. Therefore, I suggest that analysing these stories offers insights into what these networks of relationships do, that is, their influence on motivations for mobility, the sources of support that enabled migration processes, the ways in which jobs and accommodation were accessed, how friendships were sought and sustained, how intersectional identities were experienced and enacted, how embedding in local places was navigated, as well as the salience of long-distance ties in places of origin and elsewhere.

In addition, as also noted in Chapter 2, this rich, in-depth, qualitative approach helps to advance comprehensions of the thorny associations between networks and social capital. Far from simply assuming that social ties provide access to particular forms of capital, these intricate network stories recount the challenges of converting, accessing and forging capital in specific socio-temporal contexts through different relational ties. Beyond static and simplistic binaries of bonding and bridging capital, my analysis complicates the assumed association between tie content, direction and strength. Thus, I argue that adopting the framework of network stories offers insights into not only the obstacles and barriers that migrants encounter but also the varied strategies and sources of capital mobilised to negotiate those impediments.

Of course, that is not to suggest that networks of relationships tell us everything we need to know about migration. Social structures, including labour markets and immigration regimes, form the framing societal contexts for migrants. Indeed, drawing upon the stories of participants who migrated from different countries, during different decades, reveals how structural dynamism over time, such as, for example, shifting immigration regulations and institutionalised gendered and racialised practices, have shaped migrant experiences, opportunities and trajectories.

Nevertheless, in attempting to avoid a structure versus agency dichotomy, I have applied classic network scholarship (Bott, 1957) to show how networks may play a vital mediating role, on the meso level, between the micro experiences of the individual actor and macro-structural contexts. As shown through many examples in this book, migrants may draw upon webs of interpersonal relationships to help navigate and negotiate sociostructural settings in particular places at particular moments in time. However, it should be noted that not all relationships are positive and supportive. Some relationships can be abusive and discriminatory (negative ties), thus exacerbating the challenges that migrants may encounter.

Obviously, as noted in previous chapters, these narratives are told from the perspective of the migrants and so are shaped by their perception of relationships. As explained in Chapter 3, I am interested in the meaning making of network stories as dynamic discursive devices co-constructed by interviewer and interviewee within specific research contexts.

To apply a dramaturgical approach, following Goffman (1978), stories of migration usually involve intriguing plots and a complex cast of characters, as shown throughout this book. Centre stage, playing a leading role, may be a close friend or relative who appears to act as a strong, alluring tie, encouraging the migration project. Sometimes this central character is a romantic partner and the plot becomes a love story. In other plot lines, it may be a firm, an organisational tie, which instigates the relocation. Some migrants initially appear alone on the stage, as a single actor in a one-man/woman show, seemingly without any ties in the destination country.

But migration stories are rarely one-dimensional or follow a simple linear narrative. There is often a plot twist, indecision, uncertainty, back-and-forth movement, as the migrant tries to reconcile competing influences. The initial strong tie may prove untrustworthy or romantic relationships may break down. Other characters, such as parents or children, may complicate migration decision making, tying migrants to the origin country. Moreover, playing minor but nonetheless pivotal roles, may be a 'weak tie' to a character who provides crucial social capital to support the migrant. But although these may appear to be isolated dyadic ties, such weak ties are more likely to be trusted when they are connected to other characters, however loosely.

On occasion, there are shadowy, even villainous characters, negative ties, operating off stage, whose precise role may be hard to detect, but who seem to be influential as the plot unfolds. In addition, there may be numerous incidental characters with nameless, 'walk on' roles, fleeting ties, acquaintances who, in happenchance encounters, may provide the migrant with relevant information or support.

Of course, to push the analogy further, narratives are framed by staging, the sociostructural contexts in which the story is set (Somers, 1994; Plummer, 2002). The researcher can be seen as the audience who watches the performance. However, far from being a passive observer, her/his active participation, through questions, reactions and responses, also shapes how the story is presented. Moreover, the researcher then plays a further role in interpreting and retelling the story to others, as I have done in this book. Hence, the narratives become filtered through layers of meaning as you now, the reader, add your own interpretation to the stories.

Revisiting large, longitudinal qualitative data sets

A key aspect of my approach, therefore, is to be mindful of how network data are presented, generated and crafted in research encounters (White and Drew, 2011; D'Angelo and Ryan, 2021). As explained in Chapter 3, I did not collect any new data for this book. Instead, writing the book provided an opportunity to revisit and reanalyse qualitative data generated over 20 years of my migration research in London. In this way, I brought together, for the first time, data from separate projects. Working across this combined data set allowed me to develop new insights that were not possible within the constraints of each individual, time-limited project. By describing, in some detail, the process of reanalysing that combined data set and the challenge of how to present the data in meaningful and digestible ways to readers, using thick descriptions (see Chapter 3), I have sought to contribute to empirical, methodological and analytical techniques associated with revisiting existing data sets. As it is increasingly difficult to obtain research funding to generate new data, there may be advantages to revisiting existing data sets, either on one's own or in collaborative teams (Von Koppenfels, Mulholland and Ryan, 2015; Erel and Ryan, 2019; Kilkey and Ryan, 2021), applying different lenses to gain new insights.

In working across a large data set of interviews with diverse migrants from different countries who migrated at different times, I did not seek to conduct a comparative analysis. Instead, applying an intersectional lens, I considered how gender, class, age, religion, ethnicity, immigration status, family status and so on interacted at particular moments in time and in particular sociostructural contexts (Phoenix and Bauer, 2012) and the crucial role played by networks of interpersonal relationships, as clearly illustrated in Maryam's story of tackling deskilling and discrimination.

Moreover, an intersectional lens was also helpful in addressing multipositionalities and the ethics of reflexivity in the research process (Ryan, 2008a). There is growing interest in the ethical dimensions of social network research (Tubaro et al, 2021). However, rather than reflexivity as a form of self-indulgent narcissism on the part of the researcher (Pillow, 2003), I argue that considering how data were generated, including the complexities, confusions and messiness, is an important aspect of the research process.

This book also engaged with the methodological challenge of researching change over time (Lubbers et al, 2021). Drawing on Elder's life course framework, but mindful of avoiding simple linearity, I have adopted two related techniques. Engaging with participants who migrated in different periods, from the 1940s through to the 2010s, I sought to understand the salience of historical time. Furthermore, using a longitudinal approach, reinterviewing particular participants repeatedly over many years, I aimed to understand changes through biographical time. Far from a simple linear narrative, these repeat interviews illustrated the complexity of how migrants' experiences unfold over time and, as illustrated by Magda, whose plans had dramatically changed over eight years, sometimes in most unanticipated ways (Ryan et al, 2016).

Challenging the strong tie versus weak tie dichotomy

In Chapter 4, using a narrative approach to explore migration decision making and experiences of arrival in London, I contributed to more nuanced understandings of the role of social networks. Beyond any simple causality associated with the lure of strong ties, especially kinship ties, analysing migrants' stories showed the complex role of varied network actors. Kinship ties and friendship ties often interacted to encourage or support migration; however, as shown in Kathleen's story, as her older sister tried to persuade her to stay in Ireland, close interpersonal connections might also be a factor in discouraging migration. Thus, networks do not operate in unison to support one form of action but may involve tensions and contradictory influences that migrants need to carefully navigate. Moreover, it should not be assumed that seemingly strong ties to friends and even family can be taken for granted as trusted relationships and reliable sources of support. Indeed, the rich narratives in this book suggest that 'strong' ties can prove unreliable and disappointing, as seen in the story of Howard's uncle. Hence, while stories of migration decision making initially seemed to emphasise the role of a sister, aunt, uncle or best friend, as the narrative unfolded it often became apparent that an array of actors influenced and enabled the migration process in varied ways. Moreover, it is apparent that decisions to migrate were framed by wider cultures of migration and immigration regulations that enabled or indeed hindered mobility, as illustrated by Mateusz's story of crossing borders. Thus, as noted earlier, one should not focus on networks in isolation from the wider structural factors in which they are located.

Furthermore, weak ties to influential actors were also apparent in many narratives, such as Phyllis's story of recruitment from Barbados. As argued throughout this book (see Chapters 4 and 5), these weak ties should not be defined ethnically. Instead of defining social ties by their ethnic composition, it is far more useful to consider the nature of the relationship, the flow of resources and their relative social position (Ryan, 2011a). While horizontal weak ties share a similar social position, vertical weak ties link to people in higher social positions (such as a manager in a company) who may be able to share valuable resources including information and advice. Thus, as well as direct job offers, these vertical weak ties may also be able to provide indirect sources of support, such as sharing valuable know-how, as clearly evident in Colette's story of providing job advice to a friend of a friend.

However, as shown repeatedly throughout this book, the weakness of weak ties should not be exaggerated. Ties that are too weak may lack sufficient trust and motivation to share valuable resources. Moreover, these ties are rarely isolated dyads. Many of the stories discussed in this book show that weak ties were often nested in wider interconnections of close ties to relatives and friends. Thus, as argued in Chapter 5, someone to whom one is only weakly connected may offer help because of the brokering role of a mutual contact, as illustrated again by Colette. Furthermore, using longitudinal methods, it is apparent that ties evolve over time. Some weak ties fade, while some others strengthen and may even become friends, as indicated in Adrianna's story of a weak tie to her Cypriot manager that grew into a close friendship. Through this analysis, I advance understanding of weak and strong ties, not as polar opposites but as points along a dynamic 'continuum' (Bagchi, 2001: 37) as characters weave in and out of relational narratives over time (Ryan, 2021; 2022).

Exploring the role of networks across different labour market sectors

This book has not only brought together interviews with participants from different countries but also across many sectors of the labour market. Looking across a wide range of employment, from finance to teaching and health care to construction, has enabled me to consider how networks may operate differently across these sectors. As shown in Daragh's story of working across diverse areas of employment (from construction to media to teaching), networks may lead directly to job offers in some sectors, while in other sectors, especially those with formal and transparent recruitment practices (Lang et al, 2022), networks may play indirect but nonetheless important roles. In this way, I complicate the notion of network consequences by going beyond assumptions of direct causality to explore stories of how social ties may operate indirectly to support employment strategies.

Adopting a temporal lens, including longitudinal methods, also reveals the dynamism of employment trajectories over time. While some participants clearly experienced deskilling, at least initially, these are not necessarily permanent situations and could be overcome with time, as shown in Adrianna's story of moving from being a cleaner to a senior administrator. Hence, I caution against 'unskilled', 'skilled' and 'highly skilled' as fixed categories. The narratives throughout this book suggest the role of particular social ties in helping migrants to transfer, translate and reactivate cultural capital and improve employment opportunities. However, that is not to assume that all social ties are supportive and, indeed, some work-based relations may be obstructive, as illustrated in Hannah's story of racist abuse in a factory setting.

Utilising a life course perspective, and interviewing migrants from different ages and life stages, also shows that accessing the labour market is not a once-off event. The rich narratives presented in this book (see Chapter 5) illustrate that employment trajectories, far from being linear, may involve breaks and re-entries, especially for women. As shown here, social ties may play key roles at different points in employment stories. The role of local networks, especially as sources of help with childcare for working mothers, calls attention to the enduring salience of propinquity, despite advances in new communication technology.

Analysing the dynamism of friendship ties over time

A key focus of this book has been stories of dynamic interpersonal relationships over time. The networks that migrants may rely upon when they first arrive in a new location are not necessarily static. Network stories describe how existing ties may fade and new relationships may be formed.

I have long been interested in how migrants maintain long-distance ties in the origin country, while also making new ties in the destination country as part of dynamic, multi-sited processes of embedding (Ryan and Mulholland, 2015; Ryan, 2018; Mulholland and Ryan, 2022). Although migration studies have long focused on kinship ties, in the last decade or so there has been increasing interest in friendship (Conradson and Latham, 2005; Ripley Smith, 2013; Robertson, 2018; Harris et al, 2020). However, that is not to suggest that friends and kin should be seen as completely separate. In fact, my research suggests that the distinctions could be blurry, with some sisters being described as 'best friends', and some very close friends being regarded as 'like family'.

In my efforts to go beyond the metaphorical use of networks, I have drawn on SNA to avoid simply describing friendship ties. Instead, I used rich narratives to understand how such ties are formed (antecedents) and what they do (consequences). Using concepts such as network elasticity, homophily and propinquity, as well as a life course lens, I aimed to understand the dynamic contexts, characteristics and constraints that influence migrant friendship formations and maintenance over time, as shown in Irène's story of forging new connections at different life stages, especially motherhood.

In so doing, I have critically interrogated assumptions about migrant friendships as ethnically homophilous. Rather than a narrowly defined homophily, I have sought to understand how, when, where and with whom people make friends. As Michael Eve (2022) has argued, friendships do not form in a vacuum. It is important to understand the particular ambience in which people meet and get to know each other. Using an intersectional lens, I have analysed migrants' narratives to show how factors such as attending the same university, sharing a professional identity, being of similar age and life stage, attending a parent and baby group, having a particular hobby, such as being a member of sports club, or being active in a faith group may facilitate friendship formation. As well as sharing interests in common, this is also about opportunities for sustained interaction, over time, as a way of building trust, mutuality and likeability.

Drawing upon the work of Barry Wellman (1979), this book has added insights into the extent to which participants got to know their neighbours and if these might blossom into friendships. Propinquitous ties to neighbours may be invaluable sources of practical, hands-on support, ranging from receiving parcel deliveries or borrowing a household appliance, to childminding or looking after one's house during a holiday. Moreover, getting along with one's neighbours may help to create a sense of embedding in a local place (Ryan and Mulholland, 2015). Of course, that is not to suggest that neighbours necessarily become friends (Gilmartin and Migge, 2015). Some neighbourhoods are marked by tensions and hostilities, as powerfully described in Maryam's story of a North London housing estate.

As the stories in Chapter 6 clearly show, migrants cannot simply arrive in a new place and make friends just as they please. Drawing on the life course framework to situate individual stories within wider sociohistorical contexts, I highlighted how geopolitical events can shape attitudes towards migrants. Hostility against particular ethnic or religious groups may produce 'network closure', curtailing opportunities to access local sociality. Class is also an important factor to consider. Because of downward social mobility, some participants found themselves living in deprived areas with limited opportunities to socialise with the kinds of people they wished to befriend. Intersecting class and ethnic stereotypes led several participants to describe feeling stigmatised. Their cultural capital was not recognised and the lifestyle they had enjoyed in their origin country did not translate to their new environment in London. As Parisa explained, moving from a large house and spacious garden in Tehran to a small flat in London felt like "miniaturising" her life. These experiences could limit migrants' opportunities to access particular kinds of social networks. Being unable to befriend "the English" was a common motif across the interviews. As a result, although not their original intention, some participants ended up with largely migrant friendship groups, often based on shared experiences and living in the same neighbourhoods.

Exploring transnational relations

As discussed in Chapter 7, this book has also sought to contribute to discussions around transnational practices and the extent to which migrants can maintain active social ties across various countries, over long periods of time. Far from taking transnational relationships for granted, I have applied the framework of network stories to analyse the meaning of long-distance social ties. It has been argued that migrants' transnational practices cannot be reduced simply to connectivity (Nowicka, 2020). In other words, notwithstanding advances in new technology, the potential for regular communication tells us little about the meaning of particular relationships and the flow of resources between them (Von Koppenfels et al, 2015). Hence, in analysing the enduring meaning and intensity of transnational ties, it is important to understand what happens within these ties; what kinds of support and resources are accessed and shared? Exploring migrants' network stories has provided insights into emotional, loving, caring but also sometimes tense and fractured relationships between transnational connections.

Moreover, using longitudinal network analysis has helped to understand considerable change in the extent, durability and meaning of spatially dispersed relationships, as shown in Agnieszka's story of fading friendship ties. Repeated interviews, over many years, suggest the dynamism of long-distance relationships to friends, close family and extended kin. Ties that were initially described as very strong, such as 'best friends' in the origin country, in follow-up interviews appeared to be far more dynamic than had been anticipated by participants. It is apparent that embedding in long-distance ties requires not only ongoing effort on the part of the migrant but also reciprocity and a mutual inclination to invest in maintaining the relationship. As Dominik observed, after a prolonged absence, migrants may be replaced in their former friendship networks. While it is apparent that some transnational friendship ties weaken over time, kinship ties are often bound by mutual obligations and expectations of care and support (Bilecen, 2020). That is not to suggest that all kinship relationships will endure; as shown in this book, migration may provide a chance to escape from some familial ties. Indeed, as noted, some migrants may prioritise relationships with close friends over distant relatives. Nonetheless, as Wellman and Wortley remind us, when it comes to networks, blood is still considered thicker than water (1990: 572). Several stories in this book illustrate that, in times of need, transnational kinship ties may be activated in ways that can support but also pressurise migrants to fulfil expected obligations, as vividly recounted in Mairead's story of caring for her sister.

Furthermore, I suggest that network stories present important perceptions of the interconnections of ties 'here' and 'there'. Rather than looking at transnational relations in isolation, taking a network approach illustrates how local and long-distance ties to kin and friends may interact in complex ways. As the stories of older participants such as Phyllis, in Chapters 6 and 7, have shown, as migrants age, their strongest ties may be to children, grandchildren and friends in the destination society, while, by contrast, networks of family and friends in the origin country may shrink due to bereavement or wider migration patterns. This may create a sense of dis-embedding from the origin society, with implications for possible return or retirement migration, as recounted by Emer who was leaving Ireland to return to Australia.

Of course, the ability of migrants, their relatives and friends to sustain relationships by engaging in back-and-forth visits depends on a number of factors, including finance, fitness to travel and immigration regulations. As illustrated by the COVID-19 global pandemic, international travel is contingent upon a range of factors, beyond the control of individual migrants, with significant consequences for access to care and support. While such events also apply to non-migrants, the particularities of migrant experiences create specific challenges (Hari et al, 2021; Kloc-Nowak and Ryan, 2022).

Unsettling events

As discussed throughout this book, while macro-structural events can shape individual migration trajectories, networks of interpersonal relationships, on the meso level, can play a key mediating role. The years in which I have been writing this book, 2020–22, have been defined by the impact of the COVID-19 pandemic and, of course, after years of heated debate, Brexit came into effect in January 2021.[1] Associated with Brexit, the new points-based immigration system in the UK has changed significantly the rules of entry, the terms of employment and the opportunities to settle (King, 2021). However, severe shortages of workers in many sectors, attributed to both Brexit and the pandemic, have meant that flaws in the new immigration regulations were soon apparent and many 'temporary' work visas had to be introduced to address staffing issues across the UK economy.[2] Alongside Brexit, other events such as the Windrush scandal[3] (Ryan et al, 2021) and the pandemic illustrate the power of geopolitical and wider societal events to reshape migration plans and decision making (Kloc-Nowak and Ryan, 2022). In the summer of 2021, the collapse of the Afghan government and the Taliban return to power caused yet another wave of refugees out the country.[4] In 2022 the Russian invasion of Ukraine sparked a massive flight of refugees across European national borders. Meanwhile, in the background, the climate emergency has often appeared lower down the list of priorities in the face of other seemingly more immediate social problems. But it is likely that global warming will impact migration trends across the world in unprecedented ways that are not yet fully understood (Kaczan and Orgill-Meyer, 2020).

Using longitudinal methods and following participants over time has enabled me to gauge reactions to macro changes such as Brexit. In 2016 and in 2018,[5] using asynchronous methods, I recontacted participants, including several who had been interviewed on many previous occasions. Hence, I was able to understand participants' reactions to Brexit in the light of their previous interviews conducted years earlier before the prospect of Britain's departure from the EU.

Participants expressed their shock at the outcome of the Brexit referendum: "we were in shock, even scared about the future. I couldn't believe what had happened" (Klaudia, Poland). As argued in other publications with colleagues, Brexit has had a profoundly unsettling effect on migrants who had appeared to be embedding over many years, sometimes decades, in London (Erel and Ryan, 2019; Kilkey and Ryan, 2021; Ryan et al, 2021; Mulholland and Ryan, 2022).

Many participants expressed concern about how their rights would be effected: "I still remember when I heard the result … I had this feeling of being unwelcome … The UK had become a foreign land where I would be treated as a 'alien' with second-class rights" (Damien, France).

Several participants expressed anger about the aggression of the Brexit campaign and the negative ways in which politicians had portrayed migrants: "I was very hurt and depressed reading about xenophobic attacks – I am aware that Polish community is particularly targeted" (Ewa, Poland).

Having lived in London since the early 2000s, building her career and marrying a British man, Ewa had seemed to be deeply embedding in London during our previous interviews but now appeared very unsettled: "On a day after the vote I actually couldn't stop crying ... I feel very unwelcomed in this country". The profoundly unsettling effects of the Brexit referendum were powerfully described by Mateusz: "I quite literary found myself far away from home all of the sudden, as if in a different country as compared to that I have settled in" (Mateusz, Poland).

Of course, participants did not experience such feelings in isolation but once again, narratives of relationality framed their responses. Irène, who had migrated from Paris to London in the 1990s as a student, and married an Englishman, had previously hinted at an uneasy relationship with her in-laws. She described how the referendum had brought family tensions to the surface: "The Brexit vote had a huge effect at the time as it divided my English family-in-law right through ... I simply cannot get it out of my head who voted remain or leave and I think it will take a very long time for the feeling to go away" (Irène, France[6]).

For other participants, networks of British friends helped to mediate their fears about Brexit. As noted in earlier chapters, Martyna lived in a suburb of South London with a strong friendship network formed around her sons' primary school. This network provided vital support and reassurance in the immediate aftermath of the referendum: "seeing the results on Friday morning, I felt unwanted at that point but have lots of British friends who actually came to me to say that they were ashamed of what happened" (Martyna, Poland). Once again, it is apparent that macro sociostructural forces may be mediated through social networks as Martyna's British friends helped to counter her fears about being rejected and unwelcome in Brexit Britain.

In some cases, participants were considering leaving the country. Chantal's husband worked for an international bank and was likely to be moved to another European city. As mentioned in earlier chapters, Chantal's migration trajectory had been shaped in part by her husband's career mobility and now as she entered middle age, she was concerned about yet another family relocation which seemed somewhat beyond her control: "I'm not too keen on this particular move" (Chantal, France).

However, notwithstanding the unsettling impact of Brexit, most of the respondents stated their intention to remain in London, at least for the foreseeable future. This intention to stay was often informed by employment factors, but also by networks of relationships with significant others. Despite feeling like a foreigner, Mateusz planned to remain. He stated simply: "my home, family, work are all here". For many participants, partners and children were often a key motivation to stay in London, despite Brexit. Ewa explained that her son had special educational needs and keeping him in the right school setting was a key part of the family's decision to stay in London: "We will not move any time soon as we have arranged a brilliant schooling at primary level." Irène, although still feeling upset and angry about Brexit, explained: "My life is in the UK and has been for nearly 30 years; I have lived here more than in France, have got three bilingual children who go to very British schools and my husband is British; we are not moving anywhere".

Thus, as argued elsewhere (Mulholland and Ryan, 2022), migrants' responses to Brexit and its likely impact on their future migration trajectories are shaped in large part by networks of relationships with significant others, including partners, children, wider kinship ties and friends. Of course, factors such as employment and immigration rights are also key concerns, but motivations to leave or stay are often narrated through relationality. Hence, as noted by the classic work of Elizabeth Bott in the 1950s (see Chapter 2), the relationship between the individual and the wider social structure is mediated through a meso level of interpersonal networks.

Future directions

Having presented my epistemological, empirical and methodological approach to qualitative SNA with a particular focus on migration studies, I can see several ways in which this work could be developed in the future.

My book has focused on London which, as a global city, defined by waves of migration over centuries, has a large, diverse population. Therefore, in London there are opportunities to forge links with multiple formal and informal networks of migrants from a plethora of backgrounds. Applying my framework to other geographical contexts, with different sociocultural profiles, may help bring to the fore other kinds of experiences, perceptions and positionalities.

In this book, I have highlighted the importance of applying an intersectional lens to understand how class, nationality, ethnicity, age, family circumstances, religion and gender may interact to shape relationality in specific spatio-temporal contexts. But there is abundant potential to develop this analysis much further by addressing other intersectional identities and hierarchies of inequalities that were beyond my data set and the scope of this book. My new research, along with my colleague Maria Lopez and PhD student Alessia Dalceggio, at London Metropolitan University, focuses on Afghans who were evacuated from Kabul airport in the summer of 2021. Building on my earlier work with Afghans (including Rukhsana, cited in this book), I am keen to understand how networks are ruptured and re-established following the rapid relocation of refugees to new and unfamiliar settings.

In advancing the field of qualitative SNA through my framework of telling network stories, it would also be interesting to see this approach applied beyond migration studies. As noted throughout this book, while recognising the specificities of international migration, one should not fall back upon migrant exceptionalism. Much of my work has been informed by social network scholars who do not focus on migrants. Thus, I would be curious to see how the approach of 'telling network stories' could be applied with non-migrants.

APPENDIX

Details of the Various Research Projects Underpinning This Book

Irish nurses in Britain in the post-war era (2004–2005)

Having read in the literature (Walter, 1989) that Irish women made up a significant proportion of migrant workers recruited to work in Britain's newly established NHS in the 1940s and 1950s, I decided to find out more by undertaking a qualitative, oral history study with Irish nurses from the post-war era. I recruited the participants through advertisements in Irish newspapers in Britain, the *Irish Post* and *Irish World*, through Irish organisations such as the Federation of Irish Societies and snowballing. 26 semi-structured interviews, informed by oral history techniques, were carried out between October 2004 and August 2005. Most women had arrived in Britain in the 1940s and 1950s, with a few in the 1960s and 1970s. Clearly, those who arrived earlier were in advanced old age by the time of the interviews, with several aged over 80 years. All the women had arrived young and single; most migrated as student nurses aged 18 years or so. All bar one had subsequently married and had children (for more details see Ryan, 2007a; 2007b; 2008b).

Post-accession Polish migration to London

In 2006, as explained in the Introduction, my research embarked in a new direction when I began a study on post-EU accession Polish migration. Along with Rosemary Sales and Mary Tilki, I received ESRC funding (RES-000-22-1552) for the study entitled: Recent Polish Migrants in London: Social Networks, Transience and Settlement. Bernadetta Siara was the research fellow on the project. We conducted three focus groups and 30 individual interviews, with a combined total of 46 participants. The majority were aged between 21 and 39 years old, with approximately 20 per cent aged between 40 and 59. Just over half had children, with a majority of those living with them in London, but almost one quarter of those who were parents had children living in Poland. A number of stakeholder interviews were also conducted with people from Polish community organisations. Thus, over 50 participants were involved in the study (for more details see Ryan et al, 2008; Ryan et al, 2009; Ryan and Sales, 2013).

Muslims in the London Borough of Barnet

The next data set I draw upon in this book is from a study commissioned by Barnet Muslim Engagement Partnership. As explained in the Introduction, this local initiative brought together diverse Muslim groups across the borough with a view to understanding the varied needs of the communities and their experiences of living in Barnet, especially in the wake of the 2005 London bombings. Between September 2009 and May 2010, three focus groups were conducted with the support of Muslim community organisations. 23 women took part in the focus groups. In addition, ten in-depth interviews were undertaken with individual women. Two of the women from the focus groups also took part in individual interviews. Hence, a total of 31 women took part in this project. Most participants were aged in their 30s and 40s and varied enormously in terms of their educational background and employment status. Unlike many other studies that focus on one ethnic group, these participants were drawn from a range of ethnic backgrounds. As well as those of South Asian origin, there were also newer waves of migrants from Somalia, Afghanistan and Iran. The participants were not only ethnically diverse but also varied in their levels of religiosity (see Ryan, 2011b).

French highly skilled migrants in the financial sector (2010–2013)

Between 2010 and 2013, Jon Mulholland and I undertook a study of French highly skilled migrants in London's financial sector (French Capital), funded by the Economic and Social Research Council (grant number RES-000-22-4240). The first wave of interviews (2010–11) focused on migration trajectories and motivations, accessing the labour market, negotiating identity and belonging, as well as processes of networking both in terms of making business connections (Mulholland and Ryan, 2014a) and through social activities, especially around family life (Ryan and Mulholland, 2014b). In an attempt to collect richer data on particular themes, in 2013 we reinterviewed a sample of our original participants (resulting in 14 second-round interviews). A total of 40 participants took part in the study, 19 men and 21 women, the bulk aged between 35 and 44. Most had arrived in the

UK in the early 2000s. 26 were married, five were cohabiting and nine were single, with 28 parents. A snowballing technique was used to recruit participants, with purposive sampling, to ensure a sufficient range of key demographic categories: gender, age (capturing a life course spectrum), family status and length of residence in London. In 2018, two years after the Brexit referendum, Jon and I re-contacted those initial 40 participants using asynchronous methods and succeeded in carrying out email interviews with 18 of them (Mulholland and Ryan, 2022).

Irish highly qualified migrants in Britain post-economic recession (2013–2014)

Continuing with the theme of highly qualified and highly skilled migrants, recognising that those are not necessarily the same, my next data set concerned recent Irish migrants. Commissioned by an Irish migrant organisation – The Irish in Britain – this was a study of teaching graduates who had left Ireland following the collapse of the Celtic Tiger economy in 2008–9. Mixed methods were used with an online questionnaire, in-depth interviews plus one focus group. A total of 114 participants took part in the study which aimed to explore the expectations and experiences of Irish migrants, working in the teaching profession, who had arrived in Britain since the economic recession in 2008–9 (Ryan and Kurdi, 2015). Qualitative interviews were undertaken to obtain deeper insights into issues such as migration trajectories, career progression and social networks. 24 participants (19 women and five men) took part in the qualitative part of the study. Their average age was 28 years and most were single and childless. Most participants had arrived in Britain between 2008 and 2010 (Ryan, 2015b). This book draws upon the in-depth interviews.

Polish migrants in London: ten years since accession (2014)

In 2014, on the tenth anniversary of Polish accession to the EU, I undertook a small study with 20 Polish migrants in London, several of whom had been interviewed as part of previous studies (Ryan, 2016; 2019). The majority of the participants (17 out of 20) were women. The average age was 36 years. The mean year of arrival was 2005, with the majority of participants moving to the UK between 2004 and 2007. 13 were married, five divorced and two were currently single. There was an even split between those with and without children (10/20). The main aim of that study was to understand changing migration strategies, experiences and plans over time as migrants who had initially arrived with rather short-term plans had gradually extended their stay over ten years. Social networks, employment, family life and issues of identity and belonging were key themes in the interviews. In 2016, in the period immediately following the Brexit referendum, I re-contacted those 20 people using asynchronous methods and succeeded in obtaining email interviews with 14 of them.

Older migrants in London (2017–2019)

The final data set I draw upon in this book brings me back to my interest in ageing and the memories of earlier waves of migrants. This formed part of a large research programme funded by the Economic and Social Research Council for Sustainable Care: connecting people and systems programme, Grant reference: ES/P009255/1, 2017–21, Principal Investigator Sue Yeandle, University of Sheffield. As part of our work package on ageing and migration, my colleagues Majella Kilkey, Magdolna Lőrinc, Obert Tawodzera and I interviewed 45 older people, with an average age of 81 years, though some were over 90, who came from Ireland, Poland and various parts of the Caribbean in the post-war period. The interviews involved two rounds: an initial semi-structured interview in 2018 and a follow-up, walking interview, with a sub-sample of participants, in the summer of 2019 (Lőrinc et al, 2021). Field work was conducted in Yorkshire and London (Ryan et al, 2021). I am grateful to my colleagues for their agreement to include some of those interviews in this book. To maintain the overall coherence of this book, I will only draw upon London data that I collected (often with Magdolna Lőrinc).

Notes

Introduction

1. https://bigbangtrans.wordpress.com/series-2-episode-13-the-friendship-algorithm/.
2. Charlton, B. G. (2008). Crick's gossip test and Watson's boredom principle: a pseudo-mathematical analysis of effort in scientific research, *Medical Hypotheses*, 70(1), 1–3, ISSN 0306-9877.
3. The precise data sets used in this book are summarised in the Appendix.
4. I am grateful to my colleagues for their agreement to include some of those interviews in this book.
5. Ó Direáin, M., *Selected Poems/Rogha Dánta*, edited and translated by Frank Sewell (Cló Iar-Chonnacht). I am grateful to Cló Iar-Chonnacht for permission and to Dr. Isobel Ni Riain, University College Cork, for sourcing the translation.
6. All names have been changed with culturally appropriate pseudonyms. The information in brackets is country of origin and decade of migration to Britain.

Chapter 3

1. In the Appendix, I summarise the various studies from which my data are drawn.
2. One participant, Damien, was interviewed by Jon Mulholland, though followed up asynchronously by me. The research assistant, Agnes Agoston, was present during the follow-up interview with Irène. Agnieszka was initially interviewed in Polish by the research fellow Bernadetta Siara but twice followed up and interviewed by me. My colleague Magdolna Lőrinc was present during several interviews with the older Caribbean participants. Edina Kurdi was the research assistant on the Irish Migrant Teachers project and was present during some interviews. The teams involved in all the projects are summarised in the Appendix.
3. When I use the term 'Irish migrants', I am referring to people who migrated from the island of Ireland and who identify as 'Irish'. In a few cases, this included people from Northern Ireland. Although technically people from Northern Ireland are not migrants in Britain, I am aware that this is a complex and highly politicised issue (see Trew, 2016). I respected my participants' self-identification as 'Irish' regardless of where on the island of Ireland they originated. I am grateful to my former PhD student Maev MacDaid for our interesting discussions about the self-identifications of people from the north of Ireland.
4. The interviews discussed in this book were conducted in English, apart from three translated from Polish by Bernadetta Siara. I have worked with interpreters on several projects so I am keenly aware of how the research process is mediated by language. While conscious that only interviewing in English could shape the diversity of participants,

NOTES

nonetheless, many participants had lived in London for many years and hence had developed good English language skills and consented to be interviewed by me in English.
5   I am grateful to my former PhD student Xia Lin for her insights into the dance of positionality in interviewing.
6   Anne Golden was the researcher on the Depression in Irish Migrants survey; together, we came across the Measure of Support (MoS) scale, which posed very specific questions about who provides particular forms of care. Such precise questions can help to overcome some vague, metaphorical use of network.
7   My former PhD student, Elisavet Tapini, shared her experience of also using paper-based sociograms.
8   'Closeness' is defined by Wellman as 'the single most important defining characteristic of helpful intimate relationship' (Wellman, 1979: 1223).

Chapter 4
1   See the Appendix for details on all the projects drawn upon in this book.
2   I appreciated conversations with my former PhD student Elena Samarsky about migrant couples and reunion strategies.
3   For a wider discussion of agency recruitment into the care sector, see Elrick and Lewandowska (2008).
4   Within the world of highly skilled migration, the term 'ex-patriot' (or expat) has a very specific technical meaning with implications for particular contractual arrangements and often includes relocation packages. These types of expat contracts tend to be used within large international corporations, including banks.

Chapter 5
1   Postgraduate Certificate in Education.
2   Freedom of movement between Ireland and Britain derives from the former colonial relationship and, following the independence of the Irish Republic, the Common Travel Area agreement was put in place. However, the ease of movement between the two states can cause some migrants to underestimate the different rules and systems that operate in each country. Such differences, of course, have been exacerbated following Brexit, as the Irish Republic remains a member of the EU.
3   Equivalent to English 'A levels' and thus a more advanced qualification than the required 'O levels'.
4   This is an extract from a song Cricklewood, based on a poem by the Irish writer John B Keane, used here with permission of the Keane family. The poem appeared in the collection The Street by John B. Keane, (2003) Mercier Press: Cork.
5   County in the west of Ireland.
6   Suburb in South London.

Chapter 6
1   Lycee Francais Charles de Gaulle in Kensington, West London.
2   I interviewed Rory in 2013. In 2015 Ireland became the first country in the world to introduce full marriage equality and in 2017 Leo Varadkar became Ireland's first openly gay 'Taoiseach' (prime minister).
3   The notion of who is 'British' is of course open to interpretation. Some participants referred to English people specifically, by which they meant people who were born in England. For example, some participants said they had a Welsh or a Scottish friend

but no English friends. However, several participants used the terms English and British interchangeably.
4. Lord Mountbatten, a senior member of the British royal family, was killed by the Irish Republican Army in 1979.
5. 'Sister' or 'ward sister' is a British nursing grade.
6. Bombing of the World Trade Center in New York in 2001.
7. In combining my data sets from various projects, I realised that I had given some participants the same pseudonyms; for example, traditional Gaelic names Deirdre and Cliona were used for both Irish nurses from the 1940s to the 1960s and Irish teachers from the 2000s. As I had published about both in different articles, I decided to retain these names but use decade of arrival to clearly differentiate.
8. All these are located close together in south-west London.
9. These are very affluent areas in North London.
10. I interviewed Lilian and Barry at the same day centre. My colleague Magdolna Lőrinc was also present during both interviews.

Chapter 7
1. Darek was interviewed in Polish by Bernadetta Siara (see Ryan et al, 2009).
2. Divorce was legalised in Ireland in 1996.
3. I am grateful to my former PhD student, Obert Tawodzera, for our conversations about the enduring relevance of the telephone, including landlines, for older migrants.
4. 'Sister tutor' was a higher grade within British nursing.

Chapter 8
1. https://commonslibrary.parliament.uk/research-briefings/cbp-7960/.
2. For overseas hgv drivers www.gov.uk/guidance/concession-for-temporary-leave-to-allow-employment-as-hgv-fuel-drivers and also for overseas care workers https://www.bbc.co.uk/news/uk-politics-59785227.
3. The so-called Windrush scandal emerged in 2018 as long-term British residents, mainly Caribbean-born, were targeted by immigration officials as 'over-stayers' because they did not have British citizenship. Having arrived in the 1950s and 1960s, as British subjects, their status changed as origin countries gained independence.
4. My latest research project involves working with recently arrived Afghan refugees in London and this is likely to be the subject of future publications – www.londonmet.ac.uk/afghan-migrants-in-london.
5. I reconnected with participants from my ongoing work with Polish migrants in 2016, while participants from the project with French migrants were re-contacted in 2018 with my colleague Jon Mulholland.
6. For a fuller discussion of how the French participants reacted to Brexit, see Mulholland and Ryan (2022).

References

Ackers, L. (2004). Managing relationships in peripatetic careers: scientific mobility in the European Union. *Women's Studies International Forum*, 27(3), 189–201.

Adam, B. (2000). The temporal gaze: the challenge for social theory in the context of GM food. *The British Journal of Sociology*, 51(1), 125–42.

Altissimo, A. (2016). Combining egocentric network maps and narratives: an applied analysis of qualitative network map interviews. *Sociological Research Online*, 21(2), 152–64.

Amelina, A. and Faist, T. (2012). De-naturalizing the national in research methodologies: key concepts of transnational studies in migration. *Ethnic and Racial Studies*, 35(10), 1707–24.

Anthias, F. (2007). Ethnic ties: social capital and the question of mobilisability. *The Sociological Review*, 55(4), 788–805.

Anthias, F. and Cederberg, M. (2009). Using ethnic bonds in self-employment and the issue of social capital. *Journal of Ethnic and Migration Studies*, 35(6), 901–17.

Azarian, R. (2010). Social ties: elements of a substantive conceptualization. *Acta Sociologica*, 53(4), 323–38.

Azarian, R. (2017). Joint actions, stories and symbolic structures: a contribution to Herbert Blumer's conceptual framework. *Sociology*, 51(3), 685–700.

Back, L. (2015). Why everyday life matters: class, community and making life livable. *Sociology*, 49(5), 820–36.

Back, L. and Sinha, S. (2018). *Migrant City*. Abingdon: Routledge.

Badwi, R., Ablo, A. D. and Overå, R. (2018). The importance and limitations of social networks and social identities for labour market integration: the case of Ghanaian immigrants in Bergen, Norway. *Norsk Geografisk Tidsskrift-Norwegian Journal of Geography*, 72(1), 27–36.

Bagchi, A. D. (2001). Migrant networks and the immigrant professional: an analysis of the role of weak ties. *Population Research and Policy Review*, 20(1), 9–31.

Barnes, J. A. (1969). Network and political process. In J. C. Mitchell (ed.), *Social Networks in Urban Situations: Analysis of Personal Relationships in Central African Towns* (pp 51–76). Manchester: Manchester University Press.

Bauer, E. (2018). Racialized citizenship, respectability and mothering among Caribbean mothers in Britain. *Ethnic and Racial Studies*, 41(1), 151–69.

Beaverstock, J. V. (2005). Transnational elites in the city: British highly-skilled inter-company transferees in New York City's financial district. *Journal of Ethnic and Migration Studies*, 31(2), 245–68.

Beaverstock, J. V. and Smith, J. (1996). Lending jobs to global cities: skilled international labour migration, investment banking and the City of London. *Urban Studies*, 33(8), 1377–94.

Behtoui, A. (2022). Social capital, immigrants and their descendants – the case of Sweden. In E. Keskiner, M. Eve and L. Ryan (eds.), *Revisiting Migrant Networks* (pp 121–38). Amsterdam: Springer.

Bell, J. and Bivand Erdal, M. (2015). Limited but enduring transnational ties? Transnational family life among Polish migrants in Norway. *Studia Migracyjne-Przegląd Polonijny*, 41(3), 77–98.

Bellotti, E. (2015). *Qualitative Networks: Mixed Methods in Sociological Research*. Abingdon: Routledge.

Berg, M. L. and Sigona, N. (2013). Ethnography, diversity and urban space. *Identities*, 20(4), 347–60.

Bernhard, S. (2021). Reaching in: meaning-making, receiving context and inequalities in refugees' support networks. *The Sociological Review*, 69(1), 72–89.

Bhopal, K. and Preston, J. (2012). Introduction: intersectionality and 'race' in education: theorising difference: Kalwant Bhopal and John Preston. In *Intersectionality and Race in Education* (pp 9–18). Abingdon: Routledge.

Bidart, C. and Lavenu, D. (2005). Evolutions of personal networks and life events. *Social Networks*, 27(4), 359–76.

Bilecen, B. (2014). *International Student Mobility and Transnational Friendships*. London: Palgrave Macmillan.

Bilecen, B. (2020). Asymmetries in transnational social protection: perspectives of migrants and nonmigrants. *The Annals of the American Academy of Political and Social Science*, 689(1), 168–91.

Bilecen, B. (2021). Personal network analysis from an intersectional perspective: how to overcome ethnicity bias in migration research. *Global Networks*, 21(3), 470–86.

Bilecen, B. and Sienkiewicz, J. J. (2015). Informal social protection networks of migrants: typical patterns in different transnational social spaces. *Population, Space and Place*, 21(3), 227–43.

Bilecen, B., Çatır, G. and Orhon, A. (2015). Turkish–German transnational social space: stitching across borders. *Population, Space and Place*, 21(3), 244–56.

Bilecen, B., Gamper, M. and Lubbers, M. J. (2018). The missing link: social network analysis in migration and transnationalism. *Social Networks*, 53, 1–3.

Block, P. and Grund, T. (2014). Multidimensional homophily in friendship networks. *Network Science*, 2(2), 189–212.

Boccagni, P. (2015). Burden, blessing or both? On the mixed role of transnational ties in migrant informal social support. *International Sociology*, 30(3), 250–68.

Bojarczuk, S. and Mühlau, P. (2018). Mobilising social network support for childcare: the case of Polish migrant mothers in Dublin. *Social Networks*, 53, 101–10.

Borgatti, S. P. and Ofem, B. (2010). Overview: social network theory and analysis. In A.J. Daly (ed.), *Social Network Theory and Educational Change* (pp 17–30). Cambridge, MA: Harvard Education Press.

Borgatti, S. P., Mehra, A., Brass, D. J. and Labianca, G. (2009). Network analysis in the social sciences. *Science*, 323(5916), 892–5.

Bott, E. (1957). *Family and Social Network*. London: Tavistock Publications.

Botterill, K. (2014). Family and mobility in second modernity: Polish migrant narratives of individualization and family life. *Sociology*, 48(2), 233–50.

Botterill, K. (2015). 'We don't see things as they are, we see things as we are': questioning the 'outsider' in Polish migration research. *Forum: Qualitative Social Research*, 16(2). https://doi.org/10.17169/fqs-16.2.2331.

Bourdieu, P. (1986). The forms of capital. In J. Richardson (ed.), *Handbook of Theory and Research for the Sociology of Education* (pp 241–58). New York: Greenwood Press.

Boyd, D. (2012). Participating in the always-on lifestyle. In M. Mandiberg (ed.), *The Social Media Reader* (pp 71–6). New York: New York University Press.

Boyd, M. (1989). Family and personal networks in international migration: recent developments and new agendas. *International Migration Review*, 23(3), 638–70.

Brannen, J. (2013). Life story talk: Some reflections on narrative in qualitative interviews. *Sociological Research Online*, 18(2), 48–58.

Brannen, J., Elliott, H. and Phoenix, A. (2016). Narratives of success among Irish and African Caribbean migrants. *Ethnic and Racial Studies*, 39(10), 1755–72.

Bronfenbrenner, U. (1992). *Ecological Systems Theory*. Philadelphia: Jessica Kingsley Publishers.

Bryceson, D. and Vuorela, U. (eds.) (2020). *The Transnational Family: New European Frontiers and Global Networks*. Abingdon: Routledge.

Buffel, T. (2017). Ageing migrants and the creation of home: mobility and the maintenance of transnational ties. *Population, Space and Place*, 23(5), e1994.

Bunnell, T., Yea, S., Peake, L., Skelton, T. and Smith, M. (2012). Geographies of friendships. *Progress in Human Geography*, 36(4), 490–507.

Burns, E. (2010). Developing email interview practices in qualitative research. *Sociological Research Online*, 15(4), 24–35.

Burrell, K. (2006). *Moving Lives: Narratives of Nation and Migration among Europeans in Post-War Britain*. Abingdon: Ashgate Publishing.

Burt, R. S. (1992). *Structural Holes*. Cambridge, MA: Harvard University Press.

Burt, R. S. (2009). *Structural Holes: The Social Structure of Competition*. Cambridge, MA: Harvard University Press.

Butcher, M. (2010). From 'fish out of water' to 'fitting in': the challenge of re-placing home in a mobile world. *Population, Space and Place*, 16(1), 23–36.

Byron, M. (1994). *Post-War Caribbean Migration to Britain: The Unfinished Cycle*. Aldershot: Avebury.

Carrasco, J. A., Hogan, B., Wellman, B. and Miller, E. J. (2008). Collecting social network data to study social activity-travel behavior: an egocentric approach. *Environment and Planning B: Planning and Design*, 35(6), 961–80.

Castles, S. and Miller, M. J. (2003). *The Age of Migration: International Population Movements in the Modern World*. New York: The Guilford Press.

Cattell, V. (2001). Poor people, poor places, and poor health: the mediating role of social networks and social capital. *Social Science & Medicine*, 52(10), 1501–16.

Cederberg, M. (2015). Embodied cultural capital and the study of ethnic inequalities. In L. Ryan, U. Erel and A. D'Angelo (eds.), *Migrant Capital* (pp 33–47). London: Palgrave Macmillan.

Chamberlain, M. (1997). Gender and the narratives of migration. *History Workshop Journal*, 43, 87–108.

Chamberlain, M. (ed.) (2002). *Caribbean Migration: Globalized Identities*. Abingdon: Routledge.

Chamberlain, M. (2017). *Family Love in the Diaspora: Migration and the Anglo-Caribbean Experience*. Abingdon: Routledge.

Christou, A. (2006). Crossing boundaries – ethnicizing employment – gendering labor: gender, ethnicity and social networks in return migration. *Social & Cultural Geography*, 7(1), 87–102.

Chua, V., Madej, J. and Wellman, B. (2011). Personal communities: the world according to me. In J. Scott and P. J. Carrington (eds.) *The SAGE Handbook of Social Network Analysis* (pp 101–15). London: SAGE.

Ciobanu, R. O. and Fokkema, T. (2017). The role of religion in protecting older Romanian migrants from loneliness. *Journal of Ethnic and Migration Studies*, 43(2), 199–217.

Coleman, J. S. (1988). Social capital in the creation of human capital. *American Journal of Sociology*, 94, S95–S120.

Coleman, J. S. (1990). *Foundations of Social Theory*. Cambridge: Harvard University Press.

Collier, M. J. and Muneri, C. (2016). A call for critical reflexivity: reflections on research with nongovernmental and nonprofit organizations in Zimbabwe and Kenya. *Western Journal of Communication*, 80(5), 638–58.

Collins, F. L. and Shubin, S. (2015). Migrant times beyond the life course: the temporalities of foreign English teachers in South Korea. *Geoforum*, 62, 96–104.

Collins, P. H. and Bilge, S. (2020). *Intersectionality*. Cambridge: Polity Press.

Conradson, D. and Latham, A. (2005). Friendship, networks and transnationality in a world city: Antipodean transmigrants in London. *Journal of Ethnic and Migration Studies*, 31(2), 287–305.

Conway, S. (2014). A cautionary note on data inputs and visual outputs in social network analysis. *British Journal of Management*, 25(1), 102–17.

Cowley, U. (2011). *The Men Who Built Britain: A History of Irish Labour in British Construction*. Mayo: Potter's Yard Press.

Crawford, E. M. (1997). Migrant maladies: unseen lethal baggage. In *The Hungry Stream: Essays on Emigration and Famine* (pp 137–50). Ulster: Institute of Irish Studies.

Crossley, N. (2015). Relational sociology and culture: a preliminary framework. *International Review of Sociology*, 25(1), 65–85.

Crossley, N. and Edwards, G. (2016). Cases, mechanisms and the real: the theory and methodology of mixed-method social network analysis. *Sociological Research Online*, 21(2), 217–85.

Crul, M. and Schneider, J. (2010). Comparative integration context theory: participation and belonging in new diverse European cities. *Ethnic and Racial Studies*, 33(7), 1249–68.

Curran, S., Garip, F. and Chung, C. (2005). Advancing theory and evidence about migration and cumulative causation: destination and gender in Thailand. Center for Migration and Development Working Paper.

Dahinden, J. (2005). Contesting transnationalism? Lessons from the study of Albanian migration networks from former Yugoslavia. *Global Networks*, 5(2), 191–208.

Dahinden, J. (2016). A plea for the 'de-migranticization' of research on migration and integration. *Ethnic and Racial Studies*, 39(13), 2207–25.

Damstra, A. and Tillie, J. (2016). How crosscutting weak ties are established – the case of Muslims in Europe. *Journal of Ethnic and Migration Studies*, 42(2), 237–60.

D'Angelo, A. and Ryan, L. (2021). The presentation of the networked self: ethics and epistemology in social network analysis. *Social Networks*, 67, 20–8.

Darwen, L., MacRaild, D. M., Gurrin, B. and Kennedy, L. (2020). 'Irish fever' in Britain during the Great Famine: immigration, disease and the legacy of 'Black' 47. *Irish Historical Studies*, 44(166), 270–94.

De Fina, A. (2011). Researcher and informant roles in narrative interactions: constructions of belonging and foreign-ness. *Language in Society*, 40(1), 27–38.

De Haas, H. and Fokkema, T. (2011). The effects of integration and transnational ties on international return migration intentions. *Demographic Research*, 25, 755–82.

De Klepper, M., Sleebos, E., Van de Bunt, G. and Agneessens, F. (2010). Similarity in friendship networks: selection or influence? The effect of constraining contexts and non-visible individual attributes. *Social Networks*, 32(1), 82–90.

Dekker, R. and Engbersen, G. (2014). How social media transform migrant networks and facilitate migration. *Global Networks*, 14(4), 401–18.

Delaney, E. (2000). *Demography, State and Society: Irish Migration to Britain, 1921–1971* (Vol. 34). Belfast: McGill-Queen's Press-MQUP.

Del Real, D. (2019). Toxic ties: the reproduction of legal violence within mixed-status intimate partners, relatives, and friends. *International Migration Review*, 53(2), 548–70.

Denzin, N. K. (2001). *Interpretive Interactionism* (Vol. 16). London: SAGE.

Duval, D. T. (2004). Linking return visits and return migration among Commonwealth Eastern Caribbean migrants in Toronto. *Global Networks*, 4(1), 51–67.

Duvell, F. and Jordan, B. (2003). *Migration: The Boundaries of Equality and Justice*. Cambridge: Polity.

Easthope, H. (2009). Fixed identities in a mobile world? The relationship between mobility, place, and identity. *Identities: Global Studies in Culture and Power*, 16(1), 61–82.

Elder, G. H. (1994). Time, human agency, and social change: perspectives on the life course. *Social Psychology Quarterly*, 57(1), 4–15.

Elder, G. H., Johnson, M. K. and Crosnoe, R. (2003). The emergence and development of life course theory. In J.T. Mortimer and M.J. Shanahan (eds.), *Handbook of the Life Course* (pp 3–19). New York: Kluwer Academic/Plenum Publishers.

Elrick, T. and Lewandowska, E. (2008). Matching and making labour demand and supply: agents in Polish migrant networks of domestic elderly care in Germany and Italy. *Journal of Ethnic and Migration Studies*, 34(5), 717–34.

Endelstein, L. and Ryan, L. (2013). Dressing religious bodies in public spaces: gender, clothing and negotiations of stigma among Jews in Paris and Muslims in London. *Integrative Psychological and Behavioral Science*, 47(2), 249–64.

Erel, U. (2010). Migrating cultural capital: Bourdieu in migration studies. *Sociology*, 44(4), 642–60.

Erel, U. and Ryan, L. (2019). Migrant capitals: proposing a multi-level spatio-temporal analytical framework. *Sociology*, 53(2), 246–63.

Erel, U., Reynolds, T. and Kaptani, E. (2018). Migrant mothers' creative interventions into racialized citizenship. *Ethnic and Racial Studies*, 41(1), 55–72.

Eve, M. (2002). Is friendship a sociological topic? *European Journal of Sociology*, 43(3), 386–409.

Eve, M. (2010). Integrating via networks: foreigners and others. *Ethnic and Racial Studies*, 33(7), 1231–48.

Eve, M. (2022). Networks in migration processes. In E. Keskiner, M. Eve and L. Ryan (eds.), *Revisiting Migrant Networks* (pp 179–204). Amsterdam: Springer.

Everett, M. G. and Borgatti, S. P. (2014). Networks containing negative ties. *Social Networks*, 38, 111–20.

Faist, T. and Ozveren, E. (2004). *Transnational Social Spaces: Agents, Networks and Institutions*. Aldershot: Ashgate.

Farrall, S., Hunter, B., Sharpe, G. and Calverley, A. (2016). What 'works' when retracing sample members in a qualitative longitudinal study? *International Journal of Social Research Methodology*, 19(3), 287–300.

Felder, M. (2020). Strong, weak and invisible ties: a relational perspective on urban coexistence. *Sociology*, 54(4), 675–92.

Foner, N. (1997). What's new about transnationalism? New York immigrants today and at the turn of the century. *Diaspora: A Journal of Transnational Studies*, 6(3), 355–75.

Fortier, A. M. (2000). *Migrant Belongings: Memory, Space, Identity*. London: Berg.

Freeman, L. C. (2000). Visualizing social networks. *Journal of Social Structure*, 1(1), www.cmu.edu/joss/content/articles/volume1/Freeman.html.

Fritz, R. L. and Vandermause, R. (2018). Data collection via in-depth email interviewing: lessons from the field. *Qualitative Health Research*, 28(10), 1640–9.

Gardner, K. (1999). Narrating location: space, age and gender among Bengali elders in East London. *Oral History*, 27(1), 65–74.

Garg, R. and Telang, R. (2018). To be or not to be linked: online social networks and job search by unemployed workforce. *Management Science*, 64(8), 3926–41.

Gericke, D., Burmeister, A., Löwe, J., Deller, J. and Pundt, L. (2018). How do refugees use their social capital for successful labor market integration? An exploratory analysis in Germany. *Journal of Vocational Behavior*, 105, 46–61.

Geys, B. and Murdoch, Z. (2010). Measuring the 'bridging' versus 'bonding' nature of social networks: a proposal for integrating existing measures. *Sociology*, 44(3), 523–40.

Gibson, L. (2010). Using email interviews to research popular music and the life course. https://research.edgehill.ac.uk/en/publications/using-email-interviews-to-research-popular-music-and-the-life-cou-2.

Gill, N. and Bialski, P. (2011). New friends in new places: network formation during the migration process among Poles in the UK. *Geoforum*, 42(2), 241–9.

Gilmartin, M. and Migge, B. (2015). European migrants in Ireland: pathways to integration. *European Urban and Regional Studies*, 22(3), 285–99.

Gilmartin, M. and Migge, B. (2016). Migrant mothers and the geographies of belonging. *Gender, Place & Culture*, 23(2), 147–61.

Glynn, I., Kelly, T. and MacÉinrí, P. (2013). *Irish Emigration in an Age of Austerity*. Cork: Department of Geography & Institute for the Social Sciences in the 21st Century, University College Cork.

Goffman, E. (1978). *The Presentation of Self in Everyday Life* (Vol. 21). London: Harmondsworth.

Goulbourne, H., Reynolds, T., Solomos, J. and Zontini, E. (2010). *Transnational Families: Ethnicities, Identities and Social Capital*. Abingdon: Routledge.

Grabowska, I. and Garapich, M. P. (2016). Social remittances and intra-EU mobility: non-financial transfers between UK and Poland. *Journal of Ethnic and Migration Studies*, 42(13), 2146–62.

Granovetter, M. S. (1973). The strength of weak ties. *American Journal of Sociology*, 78(6), 1360–80.

Granovetter, M. (1983). The strength of weak ties: a network theory revisited, *Sociological Theory*, 1, 201–33.

Gray, B. (2004). *Women and the Irish Diaspora*. Abingdon: Routledge.

Grzymala-Kazlowska, A. (2018). From connecting to social anchoring: Adaptation and 'settlement' of Polish migrants in the UK. *Journal of Ethnic and Migration Studies*, 44(2), 252–69.

Greif, G. L. and Deal, K. H. (2012). The impact of divorce on friendships with couples and individuals. *Journal of Divorce & Remarriage*, 53(6), 421–35.

Gurak, D. T. and Caces, F. (1992). Migration networks and the shaping of migration systems. In M. Kritz, L. Lim, and H. Zlotnik (eds.), *International Migration Systems: A Global Approach* (pp 150–76). Oxford: Clarendon Press.

Harris, A., Baldassar, L. and Robertson, S. (2020). Settling down in time and place? Changing intimacies in mobile young people's migration and life courses. *Population, Space and Place*, 26(8), e2357.

Harvey, W. S. (2008). The social networks of British and Indian expatriate scientists in Boston. *Geoforum*, 39(5), 1756–65.

Hari, A., Nardon, L. and Zhang, H. (2021). A transnational lens into international student experiences of the COVID-19 pandemic. *Global Networks*. https://doi.org/10.1111/glob.12332.

Haug, S. (2008). Migration networks and migration decision-making. *Journal of Ethnic and Migration Studies*, 34(4), 585–605.

Healy, K. (2015). The performativity of networks. *European Journal of Sociology/Archives Européennes de Sociologie*, 56(2), 175–205.

Heath, S., Fuller, A. and Johnston, B. (2009). Chasing shadows: defining network boundaries in qualitative social network analysis. *Qualitative Research*, 9(5), 645–61.

Heering, L., Van Der Erf, R. and Van Wissen, L. (2004). The role of family networks and migration culture in the continuation of Moroccan emigration: a gender perspective. *Journal of Ethnic and Migration Studies*, 30(2), 323–37.

Henderson, S., Holland, J., McGrellis, S., Sharpe, S. and Thomson, R. (2012). Storying qualitative longitudinal research: sequence, voice and motif. *Qualitative Research*, 12(1), 16–34.

Hersberger, J. (2003). A qualitative approach to examining information transfer via social networks among homeless populations. *The New Review of Information Behaviour Research*, 4(1), 95–108.

Herz, A. and Altissimo, A. (2021). Understanding the structures of transnational youth im/mobility: a qualitative network analysis. *Global Networks*. https://onlinelibrary.wiley.com/doi/full/10.1111/glob.12315.

Hickman, M. J. (1995). *Religion, Class, and Identity: The State, the Catholic Church, and the Education of the Irish in Britain*. Aldershot: Ashgate.

Hickman, M. J. and Mai, N. (2015). Migration and social cohesion: appraising the resilience of place in London. *Population, Space and Place*, 21(5), 421–32.

Hickman, M. J. and Ryan, L. (2020). The 'Irish question': marginalizations at the nexus of sociology of migration and ethnic and racial studies in Britain. *Ethnic and Racial Studies*, 43(16), 96–114.

Ho, E. L. E. (2011). Migration trajectories of 'highly skilled' middling transnationals: Singaporean transmigrants in London. *Population, Space and Place*, 17(1), 116–29.

Hogan, B. (2010). The presentation of self in the age of social media: distinguishing performances and exhibitions online. *Bulletin of Science, Technology & Society*, 30(6), 377–86.

Hogan, B., Carrasco, J. A. and Wellman, B. (2007). Visualizing personal networks: working with participant-aided sociograms. *Field Methods*, 19(2), 116–44.

Hollstein, B. (2011). Qualitative approaches. In J. Scott and P.J. Carrington (eds.), *The SAGE Handbook of Social Network Analysis* (pp 404–16). London; New Delhi: SAGE.

Hosnedlová, R. (2017). Ties that bother – ties that matter. *Bulletin of Sociological Methodology/Bulletin de Méthodologie Sociologique*, 133(1), 29–45.

Huang, W., Hong, S. H. and Eades, P. (2007). Effects of sociogram drawing conventions and edge crossings in social network visualization. *J. Graph Algorithms Appl.*, 11(2), 397–429.

Hugo, G. J. (1982). Circular migration in Indonesia. *Population and Development Review*, 8(1), 59–83.

Ibarra, H. and Deshpande, P. H. (2007). Networks and identities: reciprocal influences on career processes and outcomes. In H. Gunz and M. Peiperl (eds.), *Handbook of Career Studies* (pp 268–82). Los Angeles, CA: SAGE.

James, W. (1992). Migration, racism and identity: the Caribbean experience in Britain. *New Left Review*, 1(193), 15.

James, W. and Harris, C. (eds.) (1993). *Inside Babylon: The Caribbean Diaspora in Britain*. London: Verso.

Janta, H. and Ladkin, A. (2013). In search of employment: online technologies and Polish migrants. *New Technology, Work and Employment*, 28(3), 241–53.

Kaczan, D. J. and Orgill-Meyer, J. (2020). The impact of climate change on migration: a synthesis of recent empirical insights. *Climatic Change*, 158(3), 281–300.

Kalter, F. and Kogan, I. (2014). Migrant networks and labor market integration of immigrants from the former Soviet Union in Germany. *Social Forces*, 92(4), 1435–56.

Kawai, N. (2012). The influence of external network ties on organisational performance: evidence from Japanese manufacturing subsidiaries in Europe. *European Journal of International Management*, 6(2), 221–42.

Kay, R. and Trevena, P. (2021). (Not) a good place to stay! – East European migrants' experiences of settlement in disadvantaged neighbourhoods in Scotland. *Journal of Ethnic and Migration Studies*, 1–19. https://doi.org/10.1080/1369183X.2021.1886061.

Kelly, P. and Lusis, T. (2006). Migration and the transnational habitus: evidence from Canada and the Philippines. *Environment and Planning A*, 38(5), 831–47.

Kennedy, P. (2004). Making global society: friendship networks among transnational professionals in the building design industry. *Global Networks*, 4(2), 157–79.

Keskiner, E., Eve, M. and Ryan, L. (eds.) (2022). *Revisiting Migrant Networks*. Amsterdam: Springer.

Kilkey, M. and Ryan, L. (2021). Unsettling events: understanding migrants' responses to geopolitical transformative episodes through a life-course lens. *International Migration Review*, 55(1), 227–53.

Kindler, M. (2021). Networking in contexts: qualitative social network analysis insights into migration processes. *Global Networks*, 21(3), 513–28.

King, R. (2002). Towards a new map of European migration. *International Journal of Population Geography*, 8(2), 89–106.

King, R. (2021). On Europe, immigration and inequality: Brexit as a 'wicked problem'. *Journal of Immigrant & Refugee Studies*, 19(1), 25–38.

King, R. and Christou, A. (2011). Of counter-diaspora and reverse transnationalism: return mobilities to and from the ancestral homeland. *Mobilities*, 6(4), 451–66.

King, R. and Della Puppa, F. (2021). Times of work and social life: Bangladeshi migrants in Northeast Italy and London. *International Migration Review*, 55(2), 402–30.

King-O'Riain, R. C. (2015). Emotional streaming and transconnectivity: Skype and emotion practices in transnational families in Ireland. *Global Networks*, 15(2), 256–73.

Kim, J. (2019). 'Ethnic capital' and 'flexible citizenship' in unfavourable legal contexts: stepwise migration of the Korean Chinese within and beyond northeast Asia. *Journal of Ethnic and Migration Studies*, 45(6), 939–57.

Kloc-Nowak, W. and Ryan, L. (2022). Negotiating long distance caring relations: migrants in the UK and their families in Poland. In J. Waters and B. Yeoh (eds.), *Handbook of Migration and Family*. Cheltenham: Edward Elgar Publishing.

Knox, H., Savage, M. and Harvey, P. (2006). Social networks and the study of relations: networks as method, metaphor and form. *Economy and Society*, 35(1), 113–40.

Koelet, S., Van Mol, C. and De Valk, H. A. (2017). Social embeddedness in a harmonized Europe: the social networks of European migrants with a native partner in Belgium and the Netherlands. *Global Networks*, 17(3), 441–59.

Kofman, E., Phizacklea, A., Raghuram, P. and Sales, R. (2005). *Gender and International Migration in Europe: Employment, Welfare and Politics*. Abingdon: Routledge.

Kordasiewicz, A., Radziwinowiczówna, A. and Kloc-Nowak, W. (2018). Ethnomoralities of care in transnational families: care intentions as a missing link between norms and arrangements. *Journal of Family Studies*, 24(1), 76–93.

Krackhardt, D. (1987). Cognitive social structures. *Social Networks*, 9(2), 109–34.

Kraler, A., Kofman, E., Kohli, M. and Schmoll, C. (2011). *Gender, Generations and the Family in International Migration*. Amsterdam: Amsterdam University Press.

Kraut, A. M. (1995). *Silent Travelers: Germs, Genes, and the Immigrant Menace*. Baltimore: JHU Press.

Kuhn, P. and Mansour, H. (2014). Is internet job search still ineffective? *The Economic Journal*, 124(581), 1213–33.

Labianca, G., Brass, D. J. and Gray, B. (1998). Social networks and perceptions of intergroup conflict: the role of negative relationships and third parties. *Academy of Management Journal*, 41(1), 55–67.

Lancee, B. (2010). The economic returns of immigrants' bonding and bridging social capital: the case of the Netherlands. *International Migration Review*, 44(1), 202–26.

Lancee, B. and Hartung, A. (2012). Turkish migrants and native Germans compared: the effects of inter-ethnic and intra-ethnic friendships on the transition from unemployment to work. *International Migration*, 50(1), 39–54.

Lang, C., Pott, A. and Schneider, J. (2022). Context matters: the varying roles of social ties for professional careers of immigrants' descendants. In E. Keskiner, M. Eve and L. Ryan (eds.), *Revisiting Migrant Networks* (pp 61–81). Amsterdam: Springer.

Lazarsfeld, P. F. and Merton, R. K. (1954). Friendship as a social process: a substantive and methodological analysis. *Freedom and Control in Modern Society*, 18(1), 18–66.

Lazer, D. (2001). The co-evolution of individual and network. *Journal of Mathematical Sociology*, 25, 69–108.

Leszczensky, L. (2013). Do national identification and interethnic friendships affect one another? A longitudinal test with adolescents of Turkish origin in Germany. *Social Science Research*, 42(3), 775–88.

Leung, M. (2015). 'Talk to her, she is also Chinese': a reflection on the spatial-temporal reach of co-ethnicity in migration research. *Forum Qualitative Sozialforschung/Forum: Qualitative Social Research*, 16(2), https://doi.org/10.17169/fqs-16.2.2332.

Lin, N. (2000). Inequality in social capital. *Contemporary Sociology*, 29(6), 785–95.

Lopez Rodriguez, M. (2010). Migration and a quest for 'normalcy': Polish migrant mothers and the capitalization of meritocratic opportunities in the UK. *Social Identities*, 16(3), 339–58.

Lőrinc, M., Kilkey, M., Ryan, L. and Tawodzera, O. (2021). 'You still want to go lots of places': exploring walking interviews in research with older migrants. *The Gerontologist*, https://doi.org/10.1093/geront/gnab152.

Lubbers, M. J., Molina, J. L. and McCarty, C. (2021). How do migrants' processes of social embedding unfold over time? *Global Networks*, 21(3), 529–50.

Lubbers, M. J., Molina, J. L., Lerner, J., Brandes, U., Ávila, J. and McCarty, C. (2010). Longitudinal analysis of personal networks: the case of Argentinean migrants in Spain. *Social Networks*, 32(1), 91–104.

MacRaild, D. M. (1999). *Irish Migrants in Modern Britain, 1750–1922*. Basingstoke: Macmillan International Higher Education.

Madianou, M. (2016). Ambient co-presence: transnational family practices in polymedia environments. *Global Networks*, 16(2), 183–201.

Madianou, M. and Miller, D. (2013). *Migration and New Media: Transnational Families and Polymedia*. London: Routledge.

Madziva, R. and Zontini, E. (2012). Transnational mothering and forced migration: understanding the experiences of Zimbabwean mothers in the UK. *European Journal of Women's Studies*, 19(4), 428–43.

Madziva, R., McGrath, S. and Thondhlana, J. (2016). Communicating employability: the role of communicative competence for Zimbabwean highly skilled migrants in the UK. *Journal of International Migration and Integration*, 17(1), 235–52.

Maltseva, D. and Batagelj, V. (2019). Social network analysis as a field of invasions: bibliographic approach to study SNA development. *Scientometrics*, 121, 1085–128.

Mason, J. (2004). Personal narratives, relational selves: residential histories in the living and telling. *The Sociological Review*, 52(2), 162–79.

Massey, D. (2007). *World City*. Cambridge: Polity.

Massey, D. S. (1986). The settlement process among Mexican migrants to the United States. *American Sociological Review*, 51(5), 670–84.

Massey, D. S. and España, F. G. (1987). The social process of international migration. *Science*, 237(4816), 733–8.

Mauthner, N. and Doucet, A. (2003). Reflexive accounts and accounts of reflexivity in qualitative data analysis. *Sociology*, 37(3), 413–31.

May, V. (2019). *Sociology of Personal Life*. Basingstoke: Macmillan International Higher Education.

Mayblin, L. (2019). *Impoverishment and Asylum: Social Policy as Slow Violence*. Abingdon: Routledge.

Mazzucato, V. (2021). Mixed-method social network analysis for multi-sited transnational migration research. *Global Networks*, 21(3), 551–66.

McKie, L., Gregory, S. and Bowlby, S. (2002). Shadow times: the temporal and spatial frameworks and experiences of caring and working. *Sociology*, 36(4), 897–924.

McLeod, J. (2003). Why we interview now – reflexivity and perspective in a longitudinal study. *International Journal of Social Research Methodology*, 6(3), 201–11.

McPherson, M., Smith-Lovin, L. and Cook, J. M. (2001). Birds of a feather: homophily in social networks. *Annual Review of Sociology*, 27(1), 415–44.

Meer, N. and Modood, T. (2012). For 'Jewish' read 'Muslim'? Islamophobia as a form of racialisation of ethno-religious groups in Britain today. *Islamophobia Studies Journal*, 1(1), 34–53.

Meho, L. I. (2006). E-mail interviewing in qualitative research: a methodological discussion. *Journal of the American Society for Information Science and Technology*, 57(10), 1284–95.

Mehra, A., Borgatti, S. P., Soltis, S., Floyd, T., Halgin, D. S., Ofem, B. and Lopez-Kidwell, V. (2014). Imaginary worlds: using visual network scales to capture perceptions of social networks. In D. J. Brass, G. Labianca, A. Mehra, D. S. Halgin and S. P. Borgatti (eds.), *Contemporary Perspectives on Organizational Social Networks* (pp 315–36). Bingley: Emerald Group Publishing Limited.

Meier, L. (2014). Introduction: local lives, work and social identities of migrant professionals in the city. In L. Meier (ed.), *Migrant Professionals in the City* (pp 13–30). Abingdon: Routledge.

Merluzzi, J. and Burt, R. S. (2013). How many names are enough? Identifying network effects with the least set of listed contacts. *Social Networks*, 35(3), 331–7.

Merton, R. K. (1957). *Social Theory and Social Structure*. New York: Free Press.

Miller, T. (2015). Going back: 'stalking', talking and researcher responsibilities in qualitative longitudinal research. *International Journal of Social Research Methodology*, 18(3), 293–305.

Mirza, H. S. (2013). 'A second skin': embodied intersectionality, transnationalism and narratives of identity and belonging among Muslim women in Britain. *Women's Studies International Forum*, 36, 5–15.

Mische, A. and White, H. (1998). Between conversation and situation: public switching dynamics across network domains. *Social Research*, 65(3), 695–724.

Mitchell, J. C. (1969). The concept and use of social networks. In J. C. Mitchell (ed.), *Social Networks in Urban Situations. Analysis of Personal Relationships in Central African Towns* (pp 1–50). Manchester: Manchester University Press.

Mok, A., Morris, M. W., Benet-Martinez, V. and Karakitapoğlu-Aygün, Z. (2007). Embracing American culture: structures of social identity and social networks among first-generation biculturals. *Journal of Cross-Cultural Psychology*, 38(5), 629–35.

Molina, J. L., Valenzuela-Garía, H., Lubbers, M. J., García-Macías, A. and Pampalona, J. (2015). Looking inside the ethnic enclave: Inequality, social capital and transnationalism. In L. Ryan, U. Erel and A. D'Angelo (eds.), *Migrant Capital* (pp 154–71). London: Palgrave Macmillan.

Morosanu, L. (2013). Between fragmented ties and 'soul friendships': the cross-border social connections of young Romanians in London. *Journal of Ethnic and Migration Studies*, 39(3), 353–72.

Moskal, M. and Tyrrell, N. (2016). Family migration decision-making, step-migration and separation: children's experiences in European migrant worker families. *Children's Geographies*, 14(4), 453–67.

Mulholland, J. and Ryan, L. (2014). Doing the business: variegation, opportunity and intercultural experience among intra-EU highly-skilled migrants. *International Migration*, 52(3), 55–68.

Mulholland, J. and Ryan, L. (2022). Advancing the embedding framework: using longitudinal methods to revisit French highly skilled migrants in the context of Brexit. *Journal of Ethnic and Migration Studies*, www.tandfonline.com/doi/full/10.1080/1369183X.2022.2057282.

Muttarak, R. (2014). Generation, ethnic and religious diversity in friendship choice: exploring interethnic close ties in Britain. *Ethnic and Racial Studies*, 37(1), 71–98.

Nannestad, P., Lind Haase Svendsen, G. and Tinggaard Svendsen, G. (2008). Bridge over troubled water? Migration and social capital. *Journal of Ethnic and Migration Studies*, 34(4), 607–31.

Ni Laoire, C. (2014). 'Settling back'? A biographical and life-course perspective on Ireland's recent return migration. *Irish Geography*, 41(2), 195–210.

Nowicka, M. (2013). Positioning strategies of Polish entrepreneurs in Germany: transnationalizing Bourdieu's notion of capital. *International Sociology*, 28(1), 29–47.

Nowicka, M. (2020). (Dis)connecting migration: transnationalism and nationalism beyond connectivity. *Comparative Migration Studies*, 8(1), 1–13.

Nowicka, M. and Ryan, L. (2015). Beyond insiders and outsiders in migration research: rejecting a priori commonalities. Introduction to thematic section on 'researcher, migrant, woman: methodological implications of multiple positionalities in migration studies'. *Forum Qualitative Sozialforschung/Forum: Qualitative Social Research*, 16(2), https://doi.org/10.17169/fqs-16.2.2342.

Nunes, R. (2014). Organisation of the organisationless: collective action after networks. spheres. *Journal for Digital Cultures*, 1, 1–15.

Oberst, U., Wegmann, E., Stodt, B., Brand, M. and Chamarro, A. (2017). Negative consequences from heavy social networking in adolescents: the mediating role of fear of missing out. *Journal of Adolescence*, 55, 51–60.

Oliver, C. (2012). *Retirement Migration: Paradoxes of Ageing*. Abingdon: Routledge.

Olwig, K. F. (2007). *Caribbean Journeys: An Ethnography of Migration and Home in Three Family Networks*. Durham, NC: Duke University Press.

Pahl, R. and Spencer, L. (2004). Personal communities: not simply families of fate or choice. *Current Sociology*, 52, 199–221.

Pahl, R. and Pevalin, D. (2005). Between family and friends: a longitudinal study of friendship choice. *British Journal of Sociology*, 56(3): 433–50.

Palmberger, M. (2017). Social ties and embeddedness in old age: older Turkish labour migrants in Vienna. *Journal of Ethnic and Migration Studies*, 43(2), 235–49.

Panayi, P. (2020). *Migrant City*. New Haven, CT: Yale University Press.

Parreñas, R. (2005). Long distance intimacy: class, gender and intergenerational relations between mothers and children in Filipino transnational families. *Global Networks*, 5(4), 317–36.

Parutis, V. (2014). 'Economic migrants' or 'middling transnationals'? East European migrants' experiences of work in the UK. *International Migration*, 52(1), 36–55.

Patulny, R. (2015). A spectrum of integration: examining combinations of bonding and bridging social capital and network heterogeneity among Australian refugee and skilled migrants. In L. Ryan, U. Erel and A. D'Angelo (eds.), *Migrant Capital* (pp 207–29). London: Palgrave Macmillan.

Patulny, R. V. and Svendsen, G. L. H. (2007). Exploring the social capital grid: bonding, bridging, qualitative, quantitative. *International Journal of Sociology and Social Policy*, 27(1/2), 32–51.

Phillips, D. and Robinson, D. (2015). Reflections on migration, community, and place. *Population, Space and Place*, 21(5), 409–20.

Phoenix, A. and Bauer, E. (2012). Challenging gender practices: intersectional narratives of sibling relations and parent–child engagements in transnational serial migration. *European Journal of Women's Studies*, 19(4), 490–504.

Phoenix, A. and Brannen, J. (2014). Researching family practices in everyday life: methodological reflections from two studies. *International Journal of Social Research Methodology*, 17(1), 11–26.

Phoenix, A. and Pattynama, P. (2006). Intersectionality. *European Journal of Women's Studies*, 13(3), 187–92.

Pillow, W. (2003). Confession, catharsis or cure? Rethinking the uses of reflexivity as methodological power in qualitative research. *Qualitative Studies in Education*, 16(2), 175–96.

Plummer, K. (2002). *Telling Sexual Stories: Power, Change and Social Worlds*. Abingdon: Routledge.

Ponterotto, J. G. (2006). Brief note on the origins, evolution, and meaning of the qualitative research concept thick description. *The Qualitative Report*, 11(3), 538–49.

Portes, A. (1998). Social capital: its origins and applications in modern sociology. *Annual Review of Sociology*, 24(1), 1–24.

Portes, A. (2000). The two meanings of social capital. *Sociological Forum*, 15(1), 1–12.

Portes, A. and Landolt, P. (2000). Social capital: promise and pitfalls of its role in development. *Journal of Latin American Studies*, 32(2), 529–47.

Portes, A. and Sensenbrenner, J. (1993). Embeddedness and immigration: notes on the social determinants of economic action. *American Journal of Sociology*, 98(6), 1320–50.

Pustułka, P. and Ślusarczyk, M. (2016). Cultivation, compensation and indulgence: transnational short-term returns to Poland across three family generations. *Transnational Social Review*, 6(1–2), 78–92.

Putnam, R. D. (2000). *Bowling Alone: The Collapse and Revival of American Community*. New York: Simon and Schuster.

Rainbird, S. (2012). Distrust and collaboration: exploring identity negotiation among asylum seekers in East Anglia, Britain. *Journal of Intercultural Studies*, 33(2), 139–56.

Razon, N. A. and Ross, K. (2012). Negotiating fluid identities: alliance-building in qualitative interviews. *Qualitative Inquiry*, 18(6), 494–503.

Reimer, B., Lyons, T., Ferguson, N. and Polanco, G. (2008). Social capital as social relations: the contribution of normative structures. *The Sociological Review*, 56(2), 256–74.

Retzer, S., Yoong, P. and Hooper, V. (2012). Inter-organisational knowledge transfer in social networks: a definition of intermediate ties. *Information Systems Frontiers*, 14(2), 343–61.

Reynolds, T. A. (2013). 'Them and us': 'Black neighbourhoods' as a social capital resource among black youths living in inner-city London. *Urban Studies*, 50(3), 484–98.

Reynolds, T. A. (2010). Transnational family relationships, social networks and return migration among British-Caribbean young people. *Ethnic and Racial Studies*, 33(5), 797–815.

Reynolds, T. A. (2012). 'Birds of a feather stick together'? Negotiating community, family and intimate relationships between 'established' and 'newcomer' Caribbean migrants in Britain. *Community, Work & Family*, 15(1), 69–84.

Rezai, S. and Keskiner, E. (2022). Activating social capital: steep mobility of descendants of Turkish immigrants at the top of the corporate business sector. In E. Keskiner, M. Eve and L. Ryan (eds.), *Revisiting Migrant Networks* (pp 139–57). Amsterdam: Springer.

Richter, M. and Nollert, M. (2014). Transnational networks and transcultural belonging: a study of the Spanish second generation in Switzerland. *Global Networks*, 14(4), 458–76.

Ripley Smith, L. (2013). Female refugee networks: rebuilding post-conflict identity. *International Journal of Intercultural Relations*, 37(1), 11–27.

Ritivoi, A. (2002) *Yesterday's Self: Nostalgia and the Immigrant Identity*. Lanham, MD: Rowman and Littlefield.

Robertson, S. (2018). Friendship networks and encounters in student-migrants' negotiations of translocal subjectivity. *Urban Studies*, 55(3), 538–53.

Ryan, L. (2003). Moving spaces and changing places: Irish women's memories of emigration to Britain in the 1930s. *Journal of Ethnic and Migration Studies*, 29(1), 67–82.

Ryan, L. (2004). Family matters:(e) migration, familial networks and Irish women in Britain. *The Sociological Review*, 52(3), 351–70.

Ryan, L. (2007a). Migrant women, social networks and motherhood: the experiences of Irish nurses in Britain. *Sociology*, 41(2), 295–312.

Ryan, L. (2007b). Who do you think you are? Irish nurses encountering ethnicity and constructing identity in Britain. *Ethnic and Racial Studies*, 30(3), 416–38.

Ryan, L. (2008a). Navigating the emotional terrain of families "here" and "there": Women, migration and the management of emotions. *Journal of Intercultural Studies*, 29(3), 299–313.

Ryan, L. (2008b). 'I had a sister in England': family-led migration, social networks and Irish nurses. *Journal of Ethnic and Migration Studies*, 34(3), 453–70.

Ryan, L. (2010). Becoming Polish in London: Negotiating ethnicity through migration. *Social Identities*, 16(3), 359–76.

Ryan, L. (2011a). Migrants' social networks and weak ties: accessing resources and constructing relationships post-migration. *The Sociological Review*, 59(4), 707–24.

Ryan, L. (2011b). Muslim women negotiating collective stigmatization: 'we're just normal people'. *Sociology*, 45(6), 1045–60.

Ryan, L. (2015a). Friendship-making: exploring network formations through the narratives of Irish highly qualified migrants in Britain. *Journal of Ethnic and Migration Studies*, 41(10), 1664–83.

Ryan, L. (2015b). 'It's different now': a narrative analysis of recent Irish migrants making sense of migration and comparing themselves with previous waves of migrants. *Irish Journal of Sociology*, 23(2), 114–32.

Ryan, L. (2015c). 'Inside' and 'outside' of what or where? Researching migration through multi-positionalities. *Forum: Qualitative Social Research*, 16(2), https://doi.org/10.17169/fqs-16.2.2333.

Ryan, L. (2016). Looking for weak ties: using a mixed methods approach to capture elusive connections. *The Sociological Review*, 64(4), 951–69.

Ryan, L. (2018). Differentiated embedding: Polish migrants in London negotiating belonging over time. *Journal of Ethnic and Migration Studies*, 44(2), 233–51.

Ryan, L. (2019). Narratives of settling in contexts of mobility: A comparative analysis of Irish and Polish highly qualified women migrants in London. *International Migration*, 57(3), 177–91.

Ryan, L. (2021). Telling network stories: researching migrants' changing social relations in places over time. *Global Networks*, 21(3), 567–84.

Ryan, L. (2022). The direct and indirect role of migrants' networks in accessing diverse labour market sectors: an analysis of the weak/strong ties continuum. In E. Keskiner, M. Eve and L. Ryan (eds.), *Revisiting Migrant Networks* (pp 23–40). Amsterdam: Springer.

Ryan, L. and Golden, A. (2006). 'Tick the box please': a reflexive approach to doing quantitative social research. *Sociology*, 40(6), 1191–200.

Ryan, L. and Sales, R. (2013). Family migration: the role of children and education in family decision-making strategies of Polish migrants in London. *International Migration*, 51(2), 90–103.

Ryan, L. and Mulholland, J. (2014a). Trading places: French highly skilled migrants negotiating mobility and emplacement in London. *Journal of Ethnic and Migration Studies*, 40(4), 584–600.

Ryan, L. and Mulholland, J. (2014b). French connections: the networking strategies of French highly skilled migrants in London. *Global Networks*, 14(2), 148–66.

Ryan, L. and Mulholland, J. (2014c). 'Wives are the route to social life': an analysis of family life and networking amongst highly skilled migrants in London. *Sociology*, 48(2), 251–67.

Ryan, L. and Kurdi, E. (2015). 'Always up for the craic': young Irish professional migrants narrating ambiguous positioning in contemporary Britain. *Social Identities*, 21(3), 257–72.

Ryan, L. and Mulholland, J. (2015). Embedding in motion: analysing relational, spatial and temporal dynamics among highly skilled migrants. In L. Ryan, U. Erel and A. D'Angelo (eds.), *Migrant Capital* (pp 135–53). London: Palgrave Macmillan.

Ryan, L. and D'Angelo, A. (2018). Changing times: migrants' social network analysis and the challenges of longitudinal research. *Social Networks*, 53, 148–58.

Ryan, L. and Dahinden, J. (2021). Qualitative network analysis for migration studies: beyond metaphors and epistemological pitfalls. *Global Networks*, 21(3), 459–69.

Ryan, L. and Webster, W. (eds.) (2008). *Gendering Migration: Masculinity, Femininity and Ethnicity in Post-War Britain*. Aldershot: Ashgate.

Ryan, L., Mulholland, J. and Agoston, A. (2014). Talking ties: reflecting on network visualisation and qualitative interviewing. *Sociological Research Online*, 19(2), 1–12.

Ryan, L., Eve, M. and Keskiner, E. (2022). Introduction: Revisiting Networks: Setting the Conceptual and Methodological Scene. In E. Keskiner, M. Eve and L. Ryan (eds.), *Revisiting Migrant Networks* (pp 1–22). Amsterdam: Springer.

Ryan, L., Erel, U. and D'Angelo, A. (2015). *Migrant Capital*. London: Palgrave Macmillan.

Ryan, L., Rodriguez, M. L. and Trevena, P. (2016). Opportunities and challenges of unplanned follow-up interviews: experiences with Polish migrants in London. *Forum Qualitative Sozialforschung/Forum: Qualitative Social Research*, 17(2), 1–20.

Ryan, L., Sales, R., Tilki, M. and Siara, B. (2008). Social networks, social support and social capital: the experiences of recent Polish migrants in London. *Sociology*, 42(4), 672–90.

Ryan, L., Sales, R., Tilki, M. and Siara, B. (2009). Family strategies and transnational migration: recent Polish migrants in London. *Journal of Ethnic and Migration Studies*, 35(1), 61–77.

Ryan, L., D'Angelo, A., Kaye, N. and Lőrinc, M. (2019). Young people, school engagement and perceptions of support: a mixed methods analysis. *Journal of Youth Studies*, 22(9), 1272–88.

Ryan, L., Kilkey, M., Lőrinc, M. and Tawodzera, O. (2021). Analysing migrants' ageing in place as embodied practices of embedding through time: 'Kilburn is not Kilburn any more'. *Population, Space and Place*, 27(3), e2420.

Ryan, L., Leavey, G., Golden, A., Blizard, R. and King, M. (2006). Depression in Irish migrants living in London: case-control study. *The British Journal of Psychiatry*, 188(6), 560–6.

Rzepnikowska, A. (2019). Racism and xenophobia experienced by Polish migrants in the UK before and after Brexit vote. *Journal of Ethnic and Migration Studies*, 45(1), 61–77.

Salaff, J. W. and Greve, A. (2013). Social networks and family relations in return migration. In *International Handbook of Chinese Families* (pp 77–90). New York, NY: Springer.

Samuelsson, M., Thernlund, G. and Ringström, J. (1996). Using the five field map to describe the social network of children: a methodological study. *International Journal of Behavioral Development*, 19(2), 327–45.

Sanders, J., Nee, V. and Sernau, S. (2002). Asian immigrants' reliance on social ties in a multiethnic labor market. *Social Forces*, 81(1), 281–314.

Schapendonk, J. (2015). What if networks move? Dynamic social networking in the context of African migration to Europe. *Population, Space and Place*, 21(8), 809–19.

Schiller, N.G., Basch, L. and Blanc-Szanton, C. (1992). Towards a transnationalization of migration. *The Annals of the New York Academy of Science*, 645, 1–24.

Schiller, N. G., Çağlar, A. and Guldbrandsen, T. C. (2006). Beyond the ethnic lens: locality, globality, and born-again incorporation. *American Ethnologist*, 33(4), 612–33.

Schiller, N. G. and Çağlar, A. (2009). Towards a comparative theory of locality in migration studies: migrant incorporation and city scale. *Journal of Ethnic and Migration Studies*, 35(2), 177–202.

Schnell, P., Kohlbacher, J. and Reeger, U. (2015). Network embeddedness of migrants: exploring variations across three neighbourhoods in Vienna. In L. Ryan, U. Erel and A. D'Angelo (eds.), *Migrant Capital* (pp 188–206). London: Palgrave Macmillan.

Scott, J. (1988). Social network analysis. *Sociology*, 22(1), 109–27.
Scott, J. (2011). Social network analysis: developments, advances, and prospects. *Social Network Analysis and Mining*, 1(1), 21–6.
Scott, S. (2006). The social morphology of skilled migration: the case of the British middle class in Paris. *Journal of Ethnic and Migration Studies*, 32(7), 1105–29.
Sime, D. (2018). Belonging and ontological security among Eastern European migrant parents and their children. *Central and Eastern European Migration Review*, 7(1), 35–53.
Skrbiš, Z. (2008). Transnational families: theorising migration, emotions and belonging. *Journal of Intercultural Studies*, 29(3), 231–46.
Smith, S. S. (2005). 'Don't put my name on it': social capital activation and job-finding assistance among the black urban poor. *American Journal of Sociology*, 111(1), 1–57.
Snijders, T. A. (2005). Models for longitudinal network data. *Models and Methods in Social Network Analysis*, 1, 215–47.
Somers, M. R. (1994). The narrative constitution of identity: a relational and network approach. *Theory and Society*, 23(5), 605–49.
Sommer, E. and Gamper, M. (2021). Beyond structural determinism: advantages and challenges of qualitative social network analysis for studying social capital of migrants. *Global Networks*, 21(3), 608–25.
Souto-Manning, M. (2014). Critical narrative analysis: the interplay of critical discourse and narrative analyses. *International Journal of Qualitative Studies in Education*, 27(2), 159–80.
Spalter, T. (2010). Social capital and intimate partnership in later life: a gendered perspective on 60+ year-old Israelis. *Social Networks*, 32(4), 330–8.
Speed, F., Scurry, T., Edward, P. and Moufahim, M. (2021). Networks amongst Syrians: situated migrant positionalities and the impact on relational embedding. *Social Inclusion*, 9(4), 243–53.
Stanley, L. (2015). The scriptural economy, the Forbes figuration and the racial order: everyday life in South Africa 1850–1930. *Sociology*, 49(5), 837–52.
Sutton, C. R. (2004). Celebrating ourselves: the family reunion rituals of African-Caribbean transnational families. *Global Networks*, 4(3), 243–57.
Sword, K. (1996). *Identity in Flux. The Polish Community in Britain* (Vol. 36). London: UCL School of Slavonic and East European Studies (SSEES).
Thomas, W. I. and Znaniecki, F. (1919). *The Polish Peasant in Europe and America: Monograph of an Immigrant Group* (Vol. 3). Chicago, IL: University of Chicago Press.
Thomson, A. (2019). Anzac memories revisited: trauma, memory and oral history. *The Oral History Review*, 42(1), 1–29.

Thomson, R. (2007). The qualitative longitudinal case history: practical, methodological and ethical reflections. *Social Policy and Society*, 6(4), 571–82.

Thomson, R. and McLeod, J. (2015). New frontiers in qualitative longitudinal research: an agenda for research. *International Journal of Social Research Methodology*, 18(3), 243–50.

Thondhlana, J., Madziva, R. and McGrath, S. (2016). Negotiating employability: migrant capitals and networking strategies for Zimbabwean highly skilled migrants in the UK. *The Sociological Review*, 64(3), 575–92.

Tilly, C. and Brown, C. H. (1967). On uprooting, kinship, and the auspices of migration. *International Journal of Comparative Sociology*, 8, 139–64.

Toma, S. (2016). The role of migrant networks in the labour market outcomes of Senegalese men: how destination contexts matter. *Ethnic and Racial Studies*, 39(4), 593–613.

Trevena, P. (2013). Why do highly educated migrants go for low-skilled jobs? A case study of Polish graduates working in London. In B. Glorius, I. Grabowska-Lusinska and A. Kuvik (eds.), *Mobility in Transition: Migration Patterns After EU Enlargement* (pp 169–90). Amsterdam: Amsterdam University Press.

Trew, J. D. (2016). *Leaving the North: Migration and Memory, Northern Ireland 1921–2011*. Oxford: Oxford University Press.

Tubaro, P., Ryan, L. and D'Angelo, A. (2016). The visual sociogram in qualitative and mixed-methods research. *Sociological Research Online*, 21(2), 180–97.

Tubaro, P., Ryan, L., Casilli, A. A. and D'Angelo, A. (2021). Social network analysis: new ethical approaches through collective reflexivity. *Social Networks*, 67, 1–8.

Twine, F. W. (2010). *A White Side of Black Britain: Interracial Intimacy and Racial Literacy*. Durham, NC: Duke University Press.

Van Kessel, F. G., Oerlemans, L. A. and Van Stroe-Biezen, S. A. (2014). No creative person is an island: organisational culture, academic project-based creativity, and the mediating role of intra-organisational social ties. *South African Journal of Economic and Management Sciences*, 17(1), 46–69.

Van Riemsdijk, M. (2014). International migration and local emplacement: everyday place-making practices of skilled migrants in Oslo, Norway. *Environment and Planning A*, 46(4), 963–79.

Vincent, C., Neal, S. and Iqbal, H. (2018). *Friendship and Diversity: Class, Ethnicity and Social Relationships in the City*. Amsterdam: Springer.

Von Koppenfels, A. K., Mulholland, J. and Ryan, L. (2015). 'Gotta go visit family': reconsidering the relationship between tourism and transnationalism. *Population, Space and Place*, 21(7), 612–24.

Walter, B. (1989). *Irish Women in London: The Ealing Dimension*. London: Ealing Women's Unit.

Walter, B. (2001). *Outsiders Inside: Whiteness, Place, and Irish Women*. Abingdon: Routledge.

Walter, B. and Hickman, M. J. (1997). *Discrimination and the Irish community in Britain*. London: Commission for Racial Equality Report.

Wang, H. and Wellman, B. (2010). Social connectivity in America: changes in adult friendship network size from 2002 to 2007. *American Behavioral Scientist*, 53(8), 1148–69.

Webster, W. (2005). *Imagining Home: Gender, Race and National Identity, 1945–1964*. Abingdon: Routledge.

Webster, W. (2018). *Mixing It: Diversity in World War Two Britain*. Oxford: Oxford University Press.

Wellman, B. (1979). The community question: the intimate networks of East Yorkers. *American Journal of Sociology*, 84(5), 1201–31.

Wellman, B. (1984). *Domestic Work, Paid Work and Network*. Toronto: Centre for Urban and Community Studies, University of Toronto. https://tspace.library.utoronto.ca/handle/1807/94573.

Wellman, B. and Wortley, S. (1990). Different strokes from different folks: community ties and social support. *American Journal of Sociology*, 96(3), 558–88.

Wellman, B. (1997). Structural analysis: from method and metaphor to theory and substance. *Contemporary Studies in Sociology*, 15, 19–61.

Wessendorf, S. and Phillimore, J. (2019). New migrants' social integration, embedding and emplacement in superdiverse contexts. *Sociology*, 53(1), 123–38.

White, A. (2014). Polish return and double return migration. *Europe-Asia Studies*, 66(1), 25–49.

White, A. (2017). *Polish Families and Migration since EU Accession*. Bristol: Policy Press.

White, A., Grabowska, I., Kaczmarczyk, P. and Slany, K. (2018). *The Impact of Migration on Poland: EU Mobility and Social Change*. London: UCL Press.

White, J. and Drew, S. (2011). Collecting data or creating meaning. *Qualitative Research Journal*, 11(1), 3–12.

Widmer, E. D. (2006). Who are my family members? Bridging and binding social capital in family configurations. *Journal of Social and Personal Relationships*, 23(6), 979–98.

Wierzbicki, S. (2004). *Beyond the Immigrant Enclave: Network Change and Assimilation*. New York: LFB Scholarly Publishing.

Wilding, R. and Baldassar, L. (2009). Transnational family–work balance: experiences of Australian migrants caring for ageing parents and young children across distance and borders. *Journal of Family Studies*, 15(2), 177–87.

Wimmer, A. (2004). Does ethnicity matter? Everyday group formation in three Swiss immigrant neighbourhoods. *Ethnic and Racial Studies*, 27(1), 1–36.

Wimmer, A. (2009). Herder's heritage and the boundary-making approach: studying ethnicity in immigrant societies. *Sociological Theory*, 27(3), 244–70.

Wissink, M. and Mazzucato, V. (2018). In transit: changing social networks of sub-Saharan African migrants in Turkey and Greece. *Social Networks*, 53, 30–41.

Wojtyńska, A. and Skaptadóttir, U. D. (2020). Re-creational travelling: Polish migrants visiting their families in Poland. *Emotion, Space and Society*, 34, 100634.

Yuval-Davis, N., Wemyss, G. and Cassidy, K. (2019). *Bordering*. London: John Wiley & Sons.

Zubrzycki, J. (2013). *Polish Immigrants in Britain: A Study of Adjustment* (Vol. 3). Berlin: Springer Science & Business Media.

Index

References to figures appear in *italic* type.

9/11 116

A

Actor Network Theory (ANT) 21, 78
Adam, Barbara 27
Adele (research participant) 54
Adrianna (research participant) 53–4, 86, 108, 138
Afghanistan, refugees and migrants from 162, 164, 167
   Rukhsana (research participant) 71, 111, 141, 149
ageing *see* older migrants
Agnieszka (research participant) 73, 129–31, *130*, 135, 136, 160
Agoston, Agnes 51–2
Aisling (research participant) 123, 124, 134
Angelika (research participant) 115, 139
anonymisation 43, 49
ANT (Actor Network Theory) 21, 78
antecedents of social ties 15, 21–2, 26, 88–9, 159
Aoife (research participant) 110, 112, 133
arrival stories 59–60, 79–80, 156–7
   fragile, fleeting and loose connections 75–8
   Howard's story 60–1, 116–17, 141, 157
   and the internet 60, 72–5
   negative ties 70–2
   organisational ties 78–9
   romance and marriage migration 67–70
   strong ties 60, 61–5
   weak ties 60, 65–7
Azarian, R. 32

B

Barnet Muslim Engagement Partnership 6
Barry (research participant) 96–7, 124–5, 140–1
Bauer, Elaine 45
Behtoui, Alireza 28
'benefit trap' 17, 34

Bernadette (research participant) 61–2, 99–100, 110
Bidart, C. 27–8, 121
Bilecen, B. 14, 19
biographical time 27, 29
   see also life course perspective
Blaithin (research participant) 77, 112, 132, 145
Block, P. 105
bonding social capital 16, 22, 35, 154
Borgatti, S. P. 21, 59
Bott, Elisabeth 19–20, 28, 33, 38, 99, 164
Bourdieu, Pierre 3, 22, 24, 85
'bowling alone' thesis (Putnam) 20
Boyd, Danah 138
Boyd, Monica 14, 20, 38
Brannen, Julia 48
Brexit 49, 106, 123, 145
   migrants' responses to 162–4
bridging social capital 16, 22, 35, 56, 154
British people, friendships with 107, 113–17, 160
Bronfenbrenner, U. 29
Burt, R. S. 51, 82

C

Canada, migrants' relatives in 133
care relationships
   physical co-presence in 10
   transnational, and propinquity 142–5
   see also childcare; older migrants
care work 73
Caribbean, migrants from
   racism towards 91–2, 119
   research participants
      Hannah 92, 119, 144–5, 148, 158
      Lilian 125–6, 142, 147
      Phyllis 65–6, 67, 73, 77, 91–2, 97, 115, 126, 145, 146–7, 157, 161
   return migration 146–7
   scholarship on 8
   Windrush scandal 162

case studies *see* thick descriptions
Catriona (research participant) 9, 88, 110
Celine (research participant) 86
Chamberlain, Mary 48
Chantal (research participant) 2, 10, 68, 115, 118, 132, 142–3, 163
Charles (research participant) 114
child-based sociality 107–8
childcare 82, 98, 99–101, 158
  and neighbour relationships 118
  transnational care networks 142–4
Ciara (research participant) 131
Ciobanu, R. O. 125
class privilege, networks as protection of 85
climate emergency 162
Cliona (research participant) 116, 133, 143
Clodagh (research participant) 135, 137
co-construction of networks 31, 53
Coleman, J. S. 114
Colette (research participant) 76–7, 86–7, 90, 108, 114, 132, 136, 145, 147, 157
Collier, M. J. 43, 44
computer software, for network visualisation 50, 52
consequences of social ties 15, 21–2, 26, 88, 159
construction industry 83, 96–7
COVID-19 pandemic 10, 39, 161, 162
  lockdowns 8
Crick's gossip test 2
Crossley, Nick 21
cultural capital, and employment 17, 24, 82, 88–91, 95–6, 98, 158, 160
culture, and friendship formation 115

D

Dahinden, Janine 23, 128
Dalceggio, Alessia 164
Damien (research participant) 73–4, 108, 114, 132, 162
D'Angelo, Alessio 5, 8, 31, 53
Daragh (research participant) 67, 83–4, 96, 158
Darek (research participant) 131–2
De Fina, A. 45
Deirdre (research participant) 64, 116, 118, 138, 139, 145
Denzin, N. K. 40, 43
deprived neighbourhoods, stigmatisation of 123–4
deskilling 24, 55, 82, 90, 91, 99, 156, 158
Desmond (research participant) 72, 131
'differentiated embedding' 6
discrimination 42, 115
  hostile working environments 91–6, 102, 158
  see also racism
disease
  and migration 11

Dominik (research participant) 115, 137, 147, 161
downward social mobility 24, 55, 81, 91, 123–4, 160
Dymphna (research participant) 66–7, 77

E

ecosystems 29
ego networks 50, 51
Eileen (research participant) 140, 146, 147–8
Eithne (research participant) 101, 109–10
Elder, Glen H. 27, 29, 37, 38, 48, 57, 82, 115, 156
email, interviewing via 49–50
embedding 6, 105
  see also friendship
Emer (research participant) 65, 148–9, 153, 161
employment 81–3, 101–3, 158
  co-ethnic negative social ties 81, 83, 96–7
  and cultural capital 17, 24, 82, 88–91, 95–6, 98, 158, 160
  Daragh's story 67, 83–4, 96, 158
  deskilling 24, 55, 82, 90, 91, 99, 156, 158
  exploitation 96–7
  family life stages 82, 98–101
  hostile working environments 91–6, 102, 158
  networking, in London's financial district 82, 84–7
  reluctance to share information about job opportunities 24–5
  role of the internet in 73–4, 85
Erel, Umut 8
España, F. G. 14
ethical issues 156
  interviewing 49
  sociograms 53–4
  thick descriptions 43
ethnic ties
  negative aspects of 96–7
  non-assumption of benefits of 15, 44, 81
  social capital 23–4, 35
  strong and weak 25–6
Eve, Michael 8, 15, 28, 159
Everett, M. G. 21
Ewa (research participant) 53, 75, 89–90, 108, 113, 114, 122, 123, 143, 162–3, 163–4
Ewelina (research participant) 108, 118, 139, 143–4
ex-patriot contracts, ICT (information and communication technology) organisations 78–9

F

Facebook 86, 138, 139
faith groups, as source of friendship and social support 116, 125

INDEX

family life stages, and employment 82, 98–101
family reunion migration 67–8
Farrall, S. 49
fear of missing out 138
Fidelma (research participant) 134
financial sector
  highly skilled migrants from France research project 167–8
  networking in 82, 84–7
  see also France, highly skilled migrants in the financial sector research project
Fiona (research participant) 100, 119, 140, 143, 144
Florin (research participant) 78–9, 118
Fokkema, T. 125
Foner, Nancy 128
France, highly skilled migrants in the financial sector research project 156–68
  research participants
    Adele 54
    Celine 86
    Chantal 2, 10, 68, 115, 118, 132, 142–3, 163
    Charles 114
    Colette 76–7, 86–7, 90, 108, 114, 132, 136, 145, 147, 157
    Damien 73–4, 108, 114, 132, 162
    Florin 78–9, 118
    Irène 53, 85–6, 106–8, *107*, 114, 116, 121, 123, 132–3, 159, 163, 164
    Martine 78–9, 118
    Odile 114, 123, 134
friendship 2, 104–6, 126–7, 158–60
  beyond homophily 110–13
  and Brexit 163
  child-based sociality 120–4
  ethnic diversity in 110–11
  life course perspective 106, 120–4, 124–6
  local neighbourhood relationships 117–20, 159
  with 'native' British people 107, 113–17, 160
  role in migration decision 61, 62, 64, 66

G

Gabi (research participant) 71–2, 113, 136
Gamper, M. 14, 19
Garapich, Michal 6
Gardner, Katy 47–8
gender norms 28, 33, 99
global financial crisis, 2008 6, 7
Goffman, E. 31, 53, 154
Goulbourne, H. 24
Grabowska, Izabela 6
Grainne (research participant) 93–4, 116
Granovetter, Mark 3, 24–5, 82, 84, 87
Grund, T. 105

Grzymała-Kazłowska, Aleksandra 6
Guyana, migrants from, research participants
  Howard 60–1, 116–17, 133, 141, 157
  Lalima 95, 133, 139
  Lohendra 119–20, 125, 147

H

Hannah (research participant) 92, 119, 144–5, 148, 158
Hartung, A. 22
Harvard University 20
Healy, K. 31–2
Heath, S. 30
Heering, L. 134
Hersberger, J. 52
Hickman, Mary 5
hobby groups, and friendships 115
holiday visits 142–4
Hollstein, Bettina 50, 51
homemaking 28
homophily 105, 110–13, 159
horizontal weak ties 3, 25, 77, 82, 88, 102, 157
Howard (research participant) 60–1, 116–17, 133, 141, 157
husbands, importance of support to working women 100–1

I

ICT (information and communication technology) organisations 78–9
immigration regimes 62–3, 145, 162
India, migrants from, research participants
  Jennah 67, 118–19, 149–50
Instagram 139
'institutional networking,' in the financial sector 86
internet
  social networking sites 31–2
  see also Facebook; Instagram; Skype; social media; social networking sites
interpersonal relationships *see* family life stages; friendship
intersectional perspective 23, 45, 58, 105, 111, 156, 164
intersubjectivity 31, 35
interviewing
  co-construction in 31, 45, 53
  ethical issues 49
  repeat interviewing over time 48–50, 57
  research questions on social ties 46–8
  self-presentation of participants 53–4, 86, 108, 138
  and sociograms 50–3, 58
  via email 49–50
'invisible ties' 47
IRA 116
Iran, migrants from, research participants
  Parisa 69–70, 160

Ireland, migrants from
  co-ethnic exploitation 96–7
  highly qualified migrants in Britain, post-economic recession research project 168
  nurses in Britain in the post-war era research project 166
  racism and anti-Irish hostility towards 92, 93, 94, 116, 119
  research participants
    Aisling 123, 124, 134
    Aoife 110, 112, 133
    Barry 96–7, 124–5, 140–1
    Bernadette 61–2, 99–100, 110
    Blaithin 77, 112, 132, 145
    Catriona 9, 88, 110
    Ciara 131
    Clodagh 135, 137
    Daragh 67, 83–4, 96, 158
    Deirdre 64, 116, 118, 138, 139, 145
    Desmond 72, 131
    Dymphna 66–7, 77
    Eileen 140, 146, 147–8
    Eithne 101, 109–10
    Emer 65, 148–9, 153, 161
    Fidelma 134
    Fiona 100, 119, 140, 143, 144
    Grainne 93–4, 116
    Kathleen 10–12, 64, 94, 156–7
    Laoise 109
    Liadan 112, 135, 137
    Mairead 140, 144, 161
    Maura 139
    Niamh 146, 147
    Noreen 144
    Owen 137, 138
    Roisin 148
    Rory 112, 117
    Seamus 74
    Sile 121, 131, 138
    Siobhan 92
    Sorcha 112, 131, 138
    Tricia 92
    Una 101, 110, 148
  scholarship on 7
Irène (research participant) 53, 85–6, 106–8, 107, 114, 116, 121, 123, 132–3, 159, 163, 164
Islamophobia 42, 149–50
Izabela (research participant) 75, 76, 79, 121, 132, 135, 139

J
Janta, H. 73
Jennah (research participant) 67, 118–19, 149–50
jobs *see* employment
Justyna (research participant) 73, 113, 145

K
Kaczmarczyk, Pawel 6
Karina (research participant) 53, 134–5

Kathleen (research participant) 10–12, 64, 94, 156–7
Kelly, P. 24
Keskiner, Elif 8
Kilkey, Majella 7
Klaudia (research participant) 136, 162
Kloc-Nowak, Weronika 6
Kofman, Eleonore 5
Krackhardt, D. 51

L
Ladkin, A. 73
Lalima (research participant) 95, 133, 139
Lancee, B. 22
Landolt, P. 97
language, and friendships 115
Laoise (research participant) 109
Latour, B. 21
Lavenu, D. 27–8, 121
Lazarsfeld, P. F. 105
Lazer, D. 109
Leszczensky, L. 110
letter-writing 139–40
Liadan (research participant) 112, 135, 137
life course framework 3, 13, 16, 27–8, 29, 35, 42, 48, 57, 82, 106, 115, 137, 156
likeability 90
Lilian (research participant) 125–6, 142, 147
Lin, Nan 24, 82
'linked lives' 29, 38
LinkedIn 32, 74
local relationships 117–20
Lohendra (research participant) 119–20, 125, 147
London Borough of Barnet, Muslim women research project 167
London Metropolitan University 8, 164
loneliness, and older migrants 125–6
Lopez, Maria 164
Lopez Rodriguez, M. L. 37
Lőrinc, Magdolna 7
Lubbers, M. J. 14, 19, 27
Lusis, T. 24

M
Magda (research participant) 108, 121–2
Mairead (research participant) 140, 144, 161
Marek (research participant) 76, 77, 88
Marika (research participant) 62, 109
marital breakdown 123–4, 134
marriage migrations 67–70, 71, 98–9
Martine (research participant) 78–9, 118
Martyna (research participant) 67, 122–3, 133, 148, 163
Maryam (research participant) 16–18, 21, 22, 24, 26, 32, 34, 78, 95–6, 120, 142, 156, 159
Mason, J. 32
Massey, D. S. 14

INDEX

Mateusz (research participant) 63, 89, 108, 157, 163
Maura (research participant) 139
McLeod, J. 49
Mehra, A. 30
memory 38, 47–8, 51
Merluzzi, J. 51
Merton, R. K. 105, 124
metaphorical use of networks 2, 15, 16, 18–19, 35, 59, 153
methodology 37–8, 57–8
  Adrianna's story 38, 53–4, 54–6, 57, 86, 108, 138
  large qualitative data sets 39–40, 58, 155–6
  reflexivity 9, 38, 43–5, 58, 156
  repeat interviewing over time 48–50, 57
  research questions on social ties 46–8
  self-presentation of participants 53–4, 86, 108, 138
  sociograms and interviews 38, 50–3, 58
  thick descriptions 38, 40–3, 58
Middlesex University 5
migrant exceptionalism 28, 34, 152, 165
migrant networks
  definition of 14
  metaphorical use of 2, 15, 16, 18–19, 35, 59, 153
migration
  and disease 11
  and spatial transformation 29
Miller, Tina 49
Mische, Ann 31, 32
mixed-ethnicity relationships 117
Moreno, J. L. 19, 50
Morosanu, Laura 135
Mulholland, Jon 5, 6, 51–2
Muneri, C. 43, 44
Muslim women in the London Borough of Barnet research 167

N

narratives 38
  narrative analysis 4, 32–3
  see also 'telling network stories'
'native' population
  friendships with 107, 113–17, 160
  strong and weak ties 23, 26, 81, 87
negative ties 46–7, 70–2, 154, 155
  and employment 92, 96–7
neighbour relationships 117–20, 159
network closure 85, 105, 160
  friendship with 'native' British people 107, 113–17, 160
network elasticity 109, 159
networks
  exclusionary power of 85
  importance of 1
  metaphorical use of 2, 15, 16, 18–19, 35, 59, 153

and resources 22–6
  tensions and difficulties in relationships 21
  see also migrant networks; SNA (social network analysis)
new ties, obstacles to formation of 28
NHS (National Health Service), recruitment of student nurses from Ireland 11
Niamh (research participant) 146, 147
non-human actors 21
Noreen (research participant) 144
North America, migrants' relatives in 133, 147
Northway, Mary 50, 51
nursing
  employment and family life stages 99–101
  experiences of racism in 91–2
  friendships in 111–12
  Irish nurses in Britain in the post-war era research project 166
  see also Ireland, migrants from

O

Odile (research participant) 114, 123, 134
Ó'Direáin, Máirtín 9
old boys networks 85
older migrants 96–7, 106, 124–6, 161
  London research project 169
Oliver, C. 124
Oliwia (research participant) 63–4, 108, 133, 136
organisational networks and ties 21
  ICT (information and communication technology) organisations 78–9
origin countries see return migration; transnational ties
Owen (research participant) 137, 138

P

Pakistan, migrants from, research participants
  Reema 67, 98, 116
Palmberger, M. 125
parents, care of ageing or sick 144–5
Parisa (research participant) 69–70, 160
Patryk (research participant) 77, 120–1
'performativity' of networks 32
personal reflections during research process 9, 10
Phillimore, J. 76
Phoenix, Ann 45
Phyllis (research participant) 65–6, 67, 73, 77, 91–2, 97, 115, 126, 145, 146–7, 157, 161
Pillow, W. 45
Plummer, Ken 33, 60, 61
Poland, migrants from
  post-accession Polish migration to London research project 166–7
  post-war period 7
  research participants

Adrianna 38, 54–6, *57*, 91, 108, 117, 138, 157, 158
Agnieszka 73, 129–31, *130*, 135, 136, 160
Angelika 115, 139
Darek 131–2
Dominik 115, 137, 147, 161
Ewa 53, 75, 89–90, 108, 113, 114, 122, 123, 143, 162–3, 163–4
Ewelina 108, 118, 139, 143–4
Gabi 71–2, 113, 136
Izabela 75, 76, 79, 121, 132, 135, 139
Justyna 73, 113, 145
Karina 53, 134–5
Klaudia 136, 162
Magda 108, 121–2
Marek 76, 77, 88
Marika 62, 109
Martyna 67, 122–3, 133, 148, 163
Mateusz 63, 89, 108, 157, 163
Oliwia 63–4, 108, 133, 136
Patryk 77, 120–1
Sonia 62, 114, 116, 117
Sylwia 124, 135, 147
Wiktoria 68–9, 98–9, 117
scholarship on 7–8
ten years since accession research project 168–9
Ponterotto, Joseph 40, 41
Portes, A. 97
positionality, of author/researchers 9
see also reflexivity
private sector, role of networks in recruitment 85
propinquity 10, 159
and local neighbourhood relationships 117–20
transnational care networks 142–5, 150–1
public sector employment, open recruitment in 82, 84, 85
'pull factors' in migration 64
Putnam, Robert D. 20, 22

Q

QLR (qualitative longitudinal research) 49
qualitative SNA 3–4, 12, 13, 15–16, 21–2, 30, 31, 34, 35, 38, 152, 164–5
quantitative SNA 16, 30–1, 35, 40

R

racism 42
and Caribbean migrants, post-war period 7, 116–17
and exclusion 105
and hostile working environments 91–6, 102, 158
in India 149–50
and local neighbourhood relationships 119–20

as obstacle to formation of new social ties 28, 116–17
and rented accommodation 95, 119
Razon, N. A. 45
recall 38, 47
Reema (research participant) 67, 98, 116
'reference groups' 124
reflexivity 9, 38, 43–5, 58, 156
relationality
patterns of 41–2
and SNA (social network analysis) 20–1
religious groups, as source of friendship and social support 116, 125
remittances 140–2
rented accommodation, and racism 95, 119
reputation, and employment 84
research career of author 4–8
research questions 39
resources, and networks 16, 22–6, 35
return migration 126, 129, 146–50
Reynolds, Tracey 147
Ripley Smith, L. 104
Ritivoi, A. 48
Roisin (research participant) 148
romantic relationships
and friendships 116
romance migrations 67–70, 88
Rory (research participant) 112, 117
Ross, K. 45
Rukhsana (research participant) 71, 111, 141, 149
rural life, as factor in migration decisions 63–4
Russia, invasion of Ukraine 162

S

Sales, Rosemary 5
Seamus (research participant) 74
self-presentation of participants 53–4, 86, 108, 138
Sile (research participant) 121, 131, 138
Simmel, G. 21
Siobhan (research participant) 92
Skype 138, 139, 142
Smith, Sandra Susan 24, 84
SNA (social network analysis) 1, 3, 14, 15, 20–1, 27
in migration research 19, 20
negative relationships 46–7
origins of 19
qualitative 3–4, 12, 13, 15–16, 21–2, 30, 31, 34, 35, 38, 152, 164–5
quantitative 16, 30–1, 35, 40
and relationality 20–1
Snijders, T, A. 27
social anthropology 19
social capital 75–6, 154, 155
barriers to transfer of 17, 24
bonding social capital 16, 22, 35, 154

bridging social capital 16, 22, 35, 56, 154
dark side of 46–7, 96–7
Maryam's story 16–18, 21, 22, 24, 26, 32, 34, 78, 95–6, 120, 142, 156, 159
social exclusion, as obstacle to formation of new social ties 28, 105, 115
social media 7, 137, 138–9
social mobility, downward 24, 55, 81, 91, 123–4, 160
social network analysis (SNA) *see* SNA (social network analysis)
social networking sites 31–2
social networks *see* migrant networks; networks; SNA (social network analysis)
Social Policy Research Centre, Middlesex University 5
sociograms 4, 6, 38, 50–3, 58, 90, *130*, 130–1
ethical issues 53–4
sociohistorical times and contexts 29, 33–4
sociometry 19
Somalia, migrants from, research participants
Maryam 16–18, 21, 22, 24, 26, 32, 34, 78, 95–6, 120, 142, 156, 159
Somers, Margaret 32–3
Sonia (research participant) 62, 114, 116, 117
Sorcha (research participants) 112, 131, 138
Souto-Manning, M. 29, 33–4
Spalter, T. 125
spatial transformation, and migration 29
stigmatisation, as obstacle to formation of new social ties 28
Stoite (Ó'Direáin) 9
storytelling 45
see also 'telling network stories'
strong ties 3, 23, 24–5, 56, 155, 156–7
arrival stories 60, 61–5
student friendships 106, 108–10
'Sustainable Care' research project 7
Sylwia (research participant) 124, 135, 147

T
Tawodzera, Obert 7
teaching
friendships in 112
graduate teacher training 99
non-transferability of qualifications 88
open recruitment in 84, 85
technology 7
and transnational ties 137, 138–9
see also Facebook; Instagram; internet; Skype; social media
'telling network stories' 4, 16, 32, 34–5, 38, 39, 47, 57, 59, 152
contribution of 153–5
temporal dynamics 16, 26–30, 33–4, 35–6, 37, 42, 48, 60, 154
and employment 82, 97, 98–101

repeat interviewing over time 48–50, 57, 156
themes, in research 39–40
thick descriptions 10, 12
ethical issues 43
methodology 38, 40–3, 58
Thomas, W. I. 140
Thomson, Rachel 41, 43, 48
Tilki, Mary 5
time, changes over *see* temporal dynamics
'transconnectivity' 128–9
transnational ties 128–9, 150–1, 160–1
Agnieszka's story 73, 129–31, *130*, 135, 136, 160
care networks and propinquity 142–5, 150–1
communication over time 138–40
family ties 131–5
friendship ties 106, 135–7
remittances 140–2
return migration 129, 146–50
Trevena, P. 37
Tricia (research participant) 92

U
Ukraine, Russian invasion of 162
Una (research participant) 101, 110, 148
University of North London 5
University of Sheffield 7
university students, and friendships 106, 108–10
US, migrants' relatives in 133

V
vertical weak ties 3, 25, 26, 56, 66, 77, 82, 83, 87, 89, 90, 93, 102, 157
visualisation techniques 6, 34, 50
ethical issues 53–4
see also sociograms
volunteering 55–6

W
weak ties 3, 16, 23, 24–5, 56, 77, 82, 83, 85, 87, 102, 155, 156–7
arrival stories 60, 65–7
and cultural capital 24, 81, 82, 88–91
horizontal weak ties 3, 25, 77, 82, 88, 102, 157
vertical weak ties 3, 25, 26, 56, 66, 77, 82, 83, 87, 89, 90, 93, 102, 157
Webster, Wendy 8
Wellman, Barry 1–2, 19, 20, 22, 23, 28, 51, 52, 59, 68, 114, 117, 143, 159, 161
Wessendorf, S. 76
White, Anne 6
White, Harrison 20, 31, 32
Wiktoria (research participant) 68–9, 98–9, 117
Wimmer, Andreas 44

Windrush scandal 162
  see also Caribbean, migrants from
women
  career adjustments to accommodate family migration 69, 98–100
  emotional labour of family migration 78–9
  and gender norms 28, 33, 99
  impact of care relationships on careers 144

work *see* employment
Wortley, S. 1, 20, 28, 114, 143, 161
writing letters home 139–40

Y
Yeandle, Sue 7

Z
Znaniecki, F. 140